CHOU EN-LAI: China's Gray Eminence

CHOU EN-LAI:
CHINA'S GRAY EMINENCE

by Kai-yu Hsu

DOUBLEDAY & COMPANY, INC.

GARDEN CITY, NEW YORK

1968

Endpapers and maps drawn by Jerry Kuhl.

Calligraphy by P. T. Hsu.

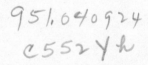

This book is also for Jeanne, Jean-Pierre, and Roland

Say nothing definite about him
Whose coffin is yet to be nailed.

—proverb derived from
The Biography of Liu Yi
in the *History of the Chin Dynasty* (265–420)

IN PREPARING THIS VOLUME, I owe much to many people who, for various reasons, will remain unnamed.

Since 1955 when I began to work on this book, I have had three friends working together with me for different periods of time. To the first friend I owe the initial encouragement and help, but soon his field of interest shifted, and I was left alone with a drawerful of notes. The second friend was to obtain interviews in Hong Kong with retired political leaders who had been associated with Chou En-lai, but this friend also soon lost interest in the subject. The credit for whatever merit this book may have, should go to the third friend who worked longest in securing relevant information. But because I alone am responsible for the final writing, treatment, and analysis of the data, I have deferred to his wish for anonymity.

Among other friends who have earned my deep gratitude and whose names can be mentioned here are L. Cline, A. Freedgood, H. Hart, J. Levaco, L. McCord, and the staff of the East Asian Collection, Hoover Institution, Stanford University, headed by E. Wu and now J. Ma.

Kai-yu Hsu

San Francisco State College
April 1967

CONTENTS

INTRODUCTION

THE WORLD RARELY WITNESSES such a phenomenon as the rise of Chinese communism from a police-hunted, whispering handful of political dreamers who gathered in a girls' school in Shanghai in 1921 to launch a Chinese Communist Party, to the towering Peking regime that controls the fate of the largest nation on earth—all within thirty years.

No single historical factor alone can explain this phenomenon, although it is relatively easy to name dozens that together paved the Communist road to triumph. One of the keystones was the existence of that very group of dreamers, who not only dreamed but worked with total dedication to translate their dream into reality. There were not too many of them—perhaps no more than twenty—whose words and deeds at the critical moments in the early history of Chinese communism really made a difference and shaped the course of events. Most of these people were executed; some left the Communist Party. And among the few survivors, the only person who has remained in the forefront of the Chinese Communist movement, from the beginning until today, is Chou En-lai, the premier of the Peking regime.

Today, as the tumultuous Great Proletarian Cultural Revolution engulfs nearly all the prominent leaders in Peking, Chou again escapes the Red Guard mobs. With each passing day he looks that much more like the person to save the Chinese Communist Party once again from disintegration and collapse, as he has done many times in the past.

Most of the Red Guards in the current upheaval are high school students answering a call to save the revolution by creating another revolution. This is precisely what Chou did some forty years ago as a student demonstration leader in Tientsin. He took his talent of leading and working with starry-eyed youth to France, and there he recruited and organized the first group of Chinese Communist elite at about the same time as the Party came into being back in Shanghai. And today after eight of the fifteen vice-premiers of the Peking government have been disgraced by the Red Guards, it is still the nucleus cultivated by Chou in France that continues to control the State Council under his personal guidance.

Chou built the Party elite for Chinese communism long before Mao Tse-tung emerged as the number one leader of the movement; then he built the Red Army elite by cultivating, ironically, the best cadets in the military academy founded and commanded by Chiang Kai-shek. Mao's current rival and heir-apparent, Defense Minister Lin Piao, was one of Chou's protégés. It was Chou who, as head of the political department in the Whampoa Military Academy and later as chief political commissar in Chiang Kai-shek's crack divisions, converted many of the most promising young officers and best trained troops to communism, making them into the first cadres of the Communist army. All of the key systems that the Communist Party set up, from the terrorist network in Shanghai in the 1920s to the mammoth national government machinery today, Chou organized and made work.

From crisis to crisis, all along the route of the Chinese Communist rise to power Chou never failed to come to the rescue of the Party. In 1925, when Chiang Kai-shek first felt the threat of communism within his own Kuomintang ranks and decided to purge it, Chou's dextrous peacemaking mollified the generalissimo and kept communism growing among those who later proved its bitterest enemy. When the bloodbath of 1927 nearly wiped out all of his key comrades, Chou

with his secret agents not only managed to save enough of
the Communist Party's Central Committee members to continue their clandestine work, but also led the CCP into a
new phase of its history by organizing a series of armed insurrections from Shanghai to Nanchang. It was the revolt he directed in Nanchang in 1927 that marked the formal beginning
of a Chinese Red Army, and since then the date August 1
has been honored as Red Army Day in Mainland China.

During all those years Chou served on the Party's Central
Committee and was in charge of the military affairs department, sometimes doubling as chief of the organization department, while Mao Tse-tung worked only on a local level,
cultivating his peasant followers in the field. Mao had to bow
to Chou when their politico-military strategies differed, which
more than once resulted in a severe reprimand for Mao.

The first serious contest of power between Mao and the
CCP's Central Committee reached a showdown in the
Kiangsi Soviet, a base developed by Mao where the Central
Committee found refuge after being driven out of Shanghai.
It was Chou who maintained an uneasy truce for more than
three years, upholding the party authority and making Mao
back down from time to time, until Chiang Kai-shek mounted
five crushing attacks on the Red base, which forced Chou and
Mao to start the 6000-mile Long March to Yenan. The
historic retreat would not have been possible if Chou had
not exercised his proverbial talent to mobilize 112,000 Chinese Communist Youth Guards in 1934 to swell the ranks of
the Long Marchers.

Chou shared with Mao the top command of the Long
March, charting a road of survival for and keeping together
the dwindling comrades. Chou's support enabled Mao to
overpower his arch-rival in 1936, a Trotskyite leader with
an army bigger than the Long Marchers.

The Chinese Communist Party was again saved, held together under Mao in the mountain caves of Yanan, until the
Kuomintang troops in North China caught up with it. With-

out Chou to persuade the Northeastern and Northwestern
Kuomintang troops to let up their pressure, without Chou
to win national and international sympathy for the CCP,
he and Mao would have long been Chiang Kai-shek's prisoners before, during, or even after World War II. The last time
he and Mao escaped the pursuing Kuomintang troops, only
seven miles behind them, was in 1947.

As the builder of one of the largest government machin-
eries on earth, Chou started from scratch in February 1949;
by September of the same year he had set up the Peking administration and started running it. Within five years he completed the development of a National People's Congress with
grass-roots support to back up the Peking administration. And
to function side by side with and serve as a check on the
People's Congress, he maintained and expanded the People's
Political Consultative Conference under his personal supervision. As chief architect of Peking's foreign policy, he wooed
and won for Red China the recognition of twenty-six countries within six months after the regime was established, and
achieved for himself the envied position of the most popular
leader of the rising African and Asian nations. At the Geneva
Conference of 1953 and the Bandung Conference of 1955, he
spoke as the revered champion of the world's underdeveloped
countries. After his visit, the largest Cambodian plywood
complex renamed itself after him. Only the hardening of the
Maoist ideological line spoiled his work, turning an ugly face
of Red China to belie Chou's winsome smiles.

But all is not yet over. At sixty-nine Chou still holds a pivotal position in Peking and may very well once again be the
person to salvage the situation for the CCP. As much havoc
as the Red Guards may be causing today, they represent only
one of the three main forces that move Red China—the fire
and dynamism of youth, which Chou released in Tientsin in
1919 as Lenin had done in Russia some twenty years before.
The other two forces are the army and the Party.

Having a bourgeois intellectual background himself, Chou

is the only one on the CCP top echelon who can understand and lead China's youth and intelligentsia. That is why, in spite of his neat appearance and constant urging that intellectuals be respected by and even better paid than manual labor, he has been spared by the Red Guards. He never directly commanded any regular troops, but the majority of Red Army leaders in the nation were his political pupils. They continue to look up to him. His successful record and rich experience as the chief political commissar in the Red Army, from its inception until 1949, still have a spellbinding magic for the military. As to his leadership within the party apparatus, he has said enough to prove that his interpretation of Marxism as applied to the political reality of any given moment in twentieth-century China was nearly always correct, but not enough to identify himself with any rigid position that could easily be branded heresy when the doctrinal winds veered in different directions. He is not likely to share the fate that befell the putschist Li Li-san in 1931 and the revisionist Liu Shao-chi in early 1967. The moment the Maoist hard line begins to be a strain on Peking and endangers Red China's continued build-up, the CCP will again turn to Chou to effect the kind of compromise for which he has already become famous. Toward the end of February 1967, signs were already emerging that indicate such a development.

Of even greater significance to the future of China and the world is what this compromise may mean when Chou again succeeds in knocking together the anti-Mao and pro-Mao heads. Now that the Comintern has passed into oblivion and Moscow no longer pontificates over a visionary Communist world empire, a man like Chou is more than likely to revise, however subtlely, Marxist doctrine according to the mood of the majority of his comrades. The older generation whose mixed concepts and values are open to a retrogression to the old order of Chinese society with all its pre-revolution evils will soon be replaced by the generation born after 1949. As soon as that happens, Chou and the majority of his comrades will feel that the fruit of their revolution is secure enough for them to shift to a more mellow party line. They know that such words as "revisionism" and "rightist tendency" are relative labels, which they can manipulate. They know that Mao has revised Marxism while continuing to honor the memory of Marx; they, too, if need be, can revise Maoism without having to remove his name from the Chinese Communist hall of fame.

A study of Chou En-lai, the unique revolutionary in whom the past meets the future, the politico-military strategist who is most likely to salvage Chinese communism, will reveal what has happened and why, as well as the shape of things to come in China. Through his life and experience we can learn enough to help us place in a proper perspective the unrest in China today and its contagious influence in the world.

CHAPTER 1

TWO MOTHERS AND SIX UNCLES

WATCHING the clear, fine-featured face at the banquet table on a sultry October evening in 1945 in Chungking, the wartime capital of China, one wondered if this could really be the man responsible for so many political and military feats in modern Chinese history that he had already assumed a legendary stature. He ate very little, barely touched his wine cup, and talked casually to the diners on his left and right in a soft voice. If it had not been for the sense of apprehension in the air, one would have been tempted to say that this was one of those traditional Chinese dinners where people of much education and little pressing business gather together to spend an unhurried evening. Actually, however, the head of the Chinese Communist Party (CCP) and the Chief of the Nationalists (Kuomintang, KMT) had just concluded the last of a series of truce talks brought about through the effort of American mediators. The banquet in the Victory Hall of the Military Commission was the last dinner before Mao Tsetung was to return to Sian, without a firm rapprochement between the two rival political and military forces in China. The struggle was by no means resolved, in spite of Mao's pledge to accept Chiang Kai-shek as the national leader, which set off thunderous rounds of applause interspersed with loud toasts.[1] Yet throughout the meal, Chou En-lai was the picture of serenity. His undisturbed composure led everyone present to speculate on his early background and discipline.

There have been many speculations, but in 1958, when he was reminiscing about the 1927 Shanghai Revolts he had led, Chou himself said, "I was responsible for leading the armed revolts, but I lacked experience and was weak in understanding political dynamics. I am an intellectual with a feudalistic family background. I had had little contact with the peasant-worker masses because I had taken no part in the economic process of production. My revolutionary career started abroad, with very limited knowledge about it obtained from books only."[2]

It was not quite true that he had had nothing to do with revolution until he went abroad, but what he said of his family background was revealing. Among the Chinese Communist leaders, he is the only one who, contrary to the popular impression of Communist ethics, time and again acknowledges his indebtedness to his past and family.

His feudalistic family background was an old-fashioned clan whose dimension and complexity suggests the extended family in the famous eighteenth-century Chinese novel, *Dream of the Red Chamber*. By the time of Chou's birth in 1898, such a family was already a dying institution in the changing society of China. But its vestiges and influence cannot be overemphasized, for they were the principal causes of the change that shook China to the roots toward the end of the nineteenth century. The year 1898, only three summers after Sun Yat-sen had failed in his first open revolt against the Manchus, saw the "One Hundred Day Reform," a valiant but fruitless attempt to salvage the crumbling empire. Led by K'ang Yu-wei and Liang Ch'i-ch'ao, two brilliant young scholars who were to influence Chou En-lai profoundly, the Reform was another desperate response to the cultural, economic, and political chaos that beset the country. Before it there had been the Taiping Rebellion of 1850–64; immediately following it there was the strange fiasco of the Boxer Rebellion of 1900. Intellectual leaders like K'ang Yu-wei and Liang Ch'i-ch'ao bombarded the Manchu emperor with memorials, and the populace with newspaper and magazine articles to urge adoption of Western ideas and institutions. They pointed out that the West had proved to be superior to China during the series of humiliating contacts since the Opium War of 1842, and suggested that China would soon be reduced to less than a colony unless there was a drastic change. Reform and, when that was too slow, revolution, became the order of the day. It was in such an atmosphere that Chou En-lai was born.

In a village called Pao-yu-ch'iao near the eastern Chinese city of Shao-hsing, in Chekiang Province, less than a hundred miles southwest of Shanghai, the Chou clan had its respected prestige symbol, an old family compound called Hundred-year Hall, so named because the family had at one time housed five generations simultaneously under the same roof, a record of family achievement very much to be envied in traditional China.

Chou En-lai's grandfather, Yün-men[3], married a girl of the Tseng family, which had attained prominence in the city of Huai-an in Kiangsu Province, thus beginning a long and involved relationship linking together these two old cities. Seven sons and one daughter were born of this union. At a fairly ripe age, the grandmother died, and the grandfather announced his intention of marrying again. The Tseng family objected on the ground that the children would suffer from a stepmother no matter who she was. When the grandfather insisted, an agreement was reached whereby the seven boys went to live in Huai-an with their mother's family, which also maintained an extensive household with large landholdings.

It was in the city of Huai-an that Chou En-lai's father and six uncles grew up. Although not quite so beautiful as Hang-chow near the West Lake about two hundred miles to the south, Huai-an had for centuries shared the affluence of the rice-rich Yangtze River delta region where families of means renewed their fortune generation after generation by educating their sons in Chinese classics and seeing them through

the imperial examinations to win government posts. Three of
the elder Chou brothers passed the second examination (at
the provincial level), and a fourth one passed the first examination (at the county level), but the times were already
changing, and the degrees earned through the examinations
no longer guaranteed fame and fortune by government ap-
pointments. Only one of the brothers, who later adopted
Chou En-lai, won a term of governorship. The rest had to
seek jobs where they could. One of them went into business,
something a gentry family would not normally condescend to
do. Another took training in police administration, also a
drastic departure from tradition. A third simply stayed home,
drinking wine and writing poetry. Chou En-lai's father, the
seventh and youngest, finished his schooling after the useful-
ness of the traditional education had been seriously ques-
tioned and the traditional avenues of social advancement
were no longer open. Tension and anxiety haunted the Chou
clan, whose problems were microcosmic reflections of those
troubling the whole country. Both the successful and unsuc-
cessful brothers lived in regret over a vanishing past and un-
certainty over the emerging future, unable to help their
children—Chou En-lai's generation—prepare for a changing
world that they themselves could not understand.

Chou En-lai was born in Huai-an, but old habit persisted
and all the members of his generation continued to claim
Shao-hsing as their home.[4] Each year they revisited it to pay
their respect to the Hundred-year Hall. Chou En-lai himself
faithfully carried on the tradition. In March 1939, during
the Second World War, when he went from Yenan to Anhwei
to settle the problems of the New Fourth Army, he took
time off on the twenty-eighth day of the month to call at the
Hundred-year Hall. He went by sampan, stopping at several
villages along the way to look over the Chou clan burial
grounds. Greeting him at different places and accompanying
him part of the way were six or seven cousins of his own
generation. Carefully remembering the customary practice,

Chou En-lai bowed three times (he did not go all the way in following the ancient tradition of kowtowing) to the clan head, an old man of about sixty. On the same trip he read and checked the family register and inquired about the life of the Chou clansmen in each area, but the unstable war front prevented him from revisiting Huai-an. In the evening of March 29, 1939, he and three of his brothers had a family-reunion dinner at the house of the manager of the Bank of China in Shao-hsing, and after dinner the four young people indulged in a game of composing epigrams dedicated to each other, a favorite pastime of the educated class throughout the history of China.[5]

Chou En-lai's mother was one of the four Wan daughters who married into the Chou family, but all four had distinctly different temperaments. The Wans were as prominent in Huai-an as the Chous and the Tsengs. The other three girls married Chou En-lai's second, third, and fifth uncles respectively, but Chou En-lai's second aunt was not born in the Wan family; she was adopted from a fourth prominent Huai-an family named Ch'en. She was the most strong-willed of all the women in the Chou family, and was to have much to do with Chou En-lai's childhood.

Chou's mother was perhaps the most talented and kindest of the Wan sisters. She was well versed in classical Chinese literature, had a disciplined hand for calligraphy and painting and a fine taste for the traditional Chinese arts. Unfortunately, she died early.[6] Chou's father, Mou-ch'en, a good match for his short-lived wife in disposition and interests, had a gentle nature but was overshadowed by his socially more successful brothers. Aside from serving a short term as a junior staff member in the telegraph bureau of the Department of Finance, Shantung Provincial Government, he was unemployed most of the time. Since he was not strong enough to defend his lack of political ambition before his brothers, he developed a resigned and retiring personality, contenting himself with any small sinecure that could supply him with a

daily ration of the celebrated Shao-hsing rice wine but spare
him the pressures of life. The way of life he chose and his
good classical Chinese literary training made him one of the
typical *shih-yehs* (bureaucratic clerks) for whom his native
town of Shao-hsing had always been famous. If Chou En-lai
had grown up under his father's direct influence, he might
not have been the En-lai of today. But Chinese tradition provided ways to relieve ineffective parents of their charges. It
was agreed within the Chou clan that En-lai was to be raised
by his second uncle, T'iao-chih, a prominent citizen in Shanghai, who had no son of his own at the time.

From that moment on Chou En-lai saw very little of his
own father who married again, had two more sons, and continued to hop from one sinecure to another until World War
II found En-lai an important man in Chungking. Penniless
and jobless, Mou-ch'en went to Chungking to see his son
and plead for his support. When En-lai failed to get him a job
immediately, he complained to one of En-lai's childhood
schoolmates that the monthly allowance, thirty Chinese dollars, he said he received from En-lai, was not enough even for
his daily wine.[7] Chou En-lai could easily have intervened on
behalf of his father to get him a lucrative job, but he never
did. And yet, when Mou-ch'en died in Chungking on July 10,
1942, Chou En-lai observed the traditional custom to the full,
including running typical obituary notices in the official CCP
organ, the *New China Daily News*, phrased exactly in accordance with old protocol, which was something the Communist
revolutionaries had long renounced.[8]

Chou En-lai did not, however, spend all his early childhood
in his foster father's home. At ten he was taken by his fourth
uncle, the police commissioner, to Mukden, Manchuria, to
attend elementary school there. Thus for several years he
lived in a different Chou family and regarded his fourth uncle
as his father. Such snarled family relationships, complicated
by cross-adoptions and by the custom that obliged a successful brother to help raise the children of his less fortunate

brothers regardless of who actually adopted them, although not uncommon in China, were developed to an extreme degree in the Chou clan.

Yet, strangely, Chou En-lai seems to have developed a genuine affection for his foster mother, who, in many respects, was not an easy person to love. She was illiterate, not because her foster family, the Wan family, had not wished or could not afford to give her an education—all the other Wan sisters read and wrote very well—but because her temper was so peppery that when she refused to study, nobody could bend her will. The only things she learned well were the practical management of a household, cooking, and embroidery. After her marriage, she immediately asserted her authority and began to run the household with an iron hand. Some time after the adoption of Chou En-lai, she bore a son herself whom she named En-chu. Showing her unusually independent mind, she insisted over the criticism and objection of most of her in-laws on inviting some Western missionaries to teach her children "the new knowledge," including the English language, an unheard-of act at the time.

In spite of her tyrannical manner in running the household, she was a kind mother to both En-lai and En-chu. In fact in most cases she showed a preference for En-lai, who proved himself to be the best-behaved and most intelligent member of the family. Household discipline was rigid. When the matriarch stood, nobody, including En-lai, dared to sit down. When she was angry, nobody dared to say a word, except En-lai who, undisturbed by her temper and always with a discreet smile on his face, would offer a suggestion or two to pacify her without explicitly taking any side. Chou En-lai's art of dealing with people in the most trying circumstances, for which he is now famous, was apparently learned early. He was able to please not only the old lady; later in the 1930s when he lived for over a year in Shanghai, he was well liked and respected by everyone in that complicated household. He was attentive to his foster mother and thoughtful toward the other members of the family. He would stop in the middle of any conversation to inquire if a younger member of the family had enough to wear. He showed a genuine interest in household affairs, tidying up his own room himself when he could easily have ordered one of the many servants to do it for him. He never raised his voice under any circumstances, while En-chu on occasion lost his temper.

Chou En-lai's attachment to his family, especially his foster mother, manifested itself repeatedly in later years. After he had already become spokesman for a powerful political and military force in China, he surprised his audience on many occasions by making references to his family. On a spring afternoon in 1941, he addressed an assembly of students and reporters in Chungking on the destruction of the Communist New Fourth Army by the Nationalists. After urging the audience to forget the fratricidal past and look to the future of a genuine united front against Japan, he said, with his handsome head bent as though in pain, "As for me, the grave of my mother to whom I owe everything that I am and hope to be, is in Japanese-occupied Chekiang. How I wish I could just go back there once to clear the weeds on her grave —the least a prodigal son who has given his life to revolution and to his country could do for his mother . . ." Five years later, on April 28, 1946, the cultural circles in Chungking arranged a farewell party for him on the eve of one of his trips back to Yenan. In his formal remarks he again mentioned his mother and foster mother, and then in an emotion-choked voice, something not commonly expected of a seasoned Communist leader, he added, "It has been thirty-eight years since I last saw my old home. The poplars in front of my mother's grave must have grown very tall by now."[9]

In 1908, after he had moved to Manchuria with his uncle, Chou En-lai attended the Sheng-ching Elementary School, a missionary-sponsored institution located just inside the Great Eastern Gate of Mukden. In those days the missionary schools' eagerness to spread Western ideas and knowledge of the world often took precedence over the Christian gospel. In each of these schools there were a few earnest teachers who kept themselves abreast of the current developments. Chou En-lai had two such teachers,[10] who encouraged him to read Chang T'ai-yen's *Kuo-ts'ui* (*National Essence*) *Journal* for its critical analysis of China's cultural tradition, and to study the political essays of K'ang Yu-wei and Liang Ch'i-ch'ao for their penetrating commentary on current events and lucid prose style. To learn about nationalism, the teachers gave Chou the works of Wang Fu-chih and Ku Yen-wu, two philosopher-scholars who fought against the Manchu invaders toward the end of the Ming Dynasty in the seventeenth century. Mainly through Liang, Chou En-lai became vaguely aware of Darwin, Mill, and Rousseau, and of human rights that could be constitutionally guaranteed. From K'ang, he learned of a visionary utopia, which was a conglomeration of Robert Southey's Pantisocracy and Nathaniel Hawthorne's Brook Farm built on the foundation of an ideal society described in a Confucian classic, *The Book of Rites*. With its theory of free love and common property, K'ang's utopia was idealistic communism carried to the extreme. Ordinarily politics is something a fifth- or sixth-grader couldn't care for less, but formal Chinese literature (novels and drama were excluded) had always been inseparable from government and politics, and Chou En-lai went through the essays with relish and fervor. Thus half-digesting and half-parroting Western ideas, Chou spent several years in the Manchurian elementary school, writing compositions that expressed his youthful patriotism.

There was no question about what he should do after elementary school. Many of his classmates had to go home to help their family, or start learning a trade as apprentices, but the Chou family, no matter how difficult it had become for them, insisted that he continue his schooling. The only question was which school. The 1911 revolution had overthrown the monarchy and plunged the nation into confusion. The

old-fashioned schools that specialized in the recitation of
Chinese classics were now discredited, yet the modern ones
patterned after the British or American system were still very
few. Chou and his classmates who were bound for middle
school were all anxious to try what appeared to them the
golden opportunity of going to study in America.

The opportunity was offered by the Tsing Hua School,
predecessor of the Tsing Hua University, organized jointly by
the United States and China with the Boxer Indemnity funds,
to train selected youth for a period before sending them to
American colleges. In order to achieve a fair distribution of
benefit, the criteria for selection included some consideration
of the geographical origin of the candidates. Partly because
of the larger number of candidates from the Yangtze River
delta region, Chou En-lai failed the entrance examination.[11]
The blow to him was more severe than the disappointment to
his family, who considered the examination a parallel to the
old imperial examination, which many of Chou's elders had
failed before. But when Chou persisted and successfully
passed the examination for the Nankai School of Tientsin, he
turned his family against him.

His uncles did not approve of the Nankai School, which,
although still very new, had already acquired an anti-tradition
and nonconformist reputation. Rumors were rife that these
modern schools were breeding grounds of rebels. Nevertheless Chou En-lai enrolled at Nankai, defying his family's open
objection, particularly his prominent sixth uncle's.

CHAPTER 2

FROM SCHOOL TO PRISON

THE NANKAI MIDDLE SCHOOL in Tientsin was a boarding school. In its dormitory students followed the old tradition of the candidates staying in Peking for the imperial examination in the Manchu days—they fell into small groups by their native towns. The group from northeastern China (Manchuria) made itself most noticeable because the boys were taller, noisier, and more fun-loving than the rest, and the oldest among them, Han, who was also a wrestling champion, was the leader.

Chou En-lai passed the entrance examination for the Fifth Class, but because of his superior background, the school allowed him to skip a year and join the Fourth Class. On a spring morning in 1913, he walked into the Fourth Class to find that all the seats had been taken except one next to Han. Chou walked over and sat down to share a desk with Han. He felt the eyes of the whole class fixed on him, and, blushing slightly, he bent down to his books.

When the class was over, he rose and introduced himself to his deskmate who stood almost a full head above him, and they walked out of the classroom together. From behind them one of the Manchurian boys called, "Hey, Han, where did you find such a nice-looking boy?" Another voice remarked, "And pretty fancy socks too." Han pretended that he didn't hear them, but he did notice the red-and-blue patterned socks on his new classmate—something the Manchurian boys dis-

dained. He showed Chou En-lai around the school and helped
him get settled in the dormitory.

For several days, each time Chou passed the room of the
Manchurian boys on his way to class, he would hear one of
them make some teasing remarks about his neat shirt and
colorful socks. He said nothing in return, but neither did he
change his way of dressing. Finally one day when Han again
walked with Chou to class and overheard the teasing remark,
he turned back and spoke sternly to his fellows. After that
nobody joked any more about Chou's socks or his blushing.

Some weeks later Chou began to feel at home at Nankai
and to enjoy his newly made friends. Even those who had
made fun of his fine features at the beginning began to ap-
preciate his gentle manner and his facile command of language. The school principal, Chang Po-ling, also discovered
his talent after watching him time and again finish a two-
hour composition assignment in less than an hour. Having
enrolled in the school against his family's wishes, Chou resolved to support himself. Principal Chang gave him a job as
his student assistant to do occasional clerical work, which was
an opportunity available at very few Chinese schools at that
time. Chang, a former naval officer whose experience in a
Japanese prison had decided him to turn educator, believed
in encouraging each student to develop himself according to
his own propensity, and Chou's weakness in natural science,
which was amply compensated for by his progress in social
studies and language, did not keep him from being admired.

Chang's educational philosophy of cultivating a balance
between initiative and self-government encouraged Chou to
take the lead in organizing a student association called Ching-
yeh lo-ch'ün ("respect work enjoy group-life"), which published a journal. In it Chou's articles frequently appeared
under the pen name Fei Fei.[1] Busy holding meetings and
running the journal, Chou began his four happy, exciting and
purposeful years at Nankai. His knack for political and social
commentary nurtured in elementary school was now put to

good use, and there was no lack of grist for his mill. Sun Yat-sen had just won a republic, but all he inherited was chaos. Without military support he had to surrender control of the country to the old political tycoons and warlords within three months. The warlords continued to run their own private kingdoms with absolute autonomy, while the political ty-coons, including many survivors of the defunct Manchu im-perial court, manipulated the so-called national parliament, disbanded and reassembled it at will, and even staged a brief tragi-comic restoration of the monarchy under Yüan Shih-k'ai in Peking. Every day the nominal central government re-shuffled its cabinet, and every day some prominent political leader was assassinated. In 1913 alone, there were seven major political murders, thirty-two changes in cabinet posts, six large-scale bloody mutinies and riots, and eleven revolts of military leaders who marched their troops on Peking. Mon-golia and Tibet agitated for secession; their troops frequently clashed with the Chinese. The continued disorder and po-litical vacuum invited aggression from abroad. Japan, wax-ing energetic after its own political and industrial reform, had designs on Manchuria, which the Peking politicians were in no position to resist, since they had to beg for loans from not only Japan but Britain, France, Germany, and Russia as well.

Chou responded to these issues with gusto. In the per-suasive style of his intellectual mentor Liang Ch'i-ch'ao, he discoursed in the Nankai student publication on China's need for industrialization and unification. He speculated on the impending war with Japan and argued the importance of pre-paring China's new youth in both the library and the gym-nasium. He talked about patriotism without savagery and economic progress without losing sight of the nation's moral conscience. Not infrequently he championed free marriage. There was nothing strikingly original in all this, but for a fifteen-year-old schoolboy his student following was phe-nomenal.

Being a popular student leader in those days also had its lighter side. The school was planning a program to celebrate its anniversary, including a play entitled *One Dollar* which required a heroine to portray the victim of the evil of money. Nankai was a boys' school, and although there was a girls' school nearby, mixed casts on stage had never been presented before. Because of his good looks and out of his enthusiasm to serve a cause, Chou donned a female costume and saved the program. To his elders at home, it was a degradation, stooping as low as the profession of female impersonators in the Peking opera, but to his thunderously applauding schoolmates it was a great feat. His teachers also cheered, and Principal Chang shook hands with him to congratulate him.

The memory of his talents lingered long. In 1945 when Chou was the chief delegate of the CCP negotiating with Chiang Kai-shek in Chungking, Principal Chang, now also a senior statesman, was frequently with him. One evening, they went to see a play presented by a group of college students. When the mixed cast appeared on the stage, Chou whispered to Chang, "Teacher (he has never changed his way of addressing his former teachers), the times have really changed. Now boy and girl students can freely join the same cast in a play. I remember how we had to stage shows without girls at Nankai." Chang turned to stare at his former pupil on whose shoulders now rested the war and peace of the country, squinted his eyes a moment, and said, "You know, you still can put on make-up and get up there to do it. I bet you'd be better than that girl on the stage."[2]

Those were indeed Chou's happy and formative years. With the protective indulgence of teachers like Chang and the enthusiastic admiration of fellow schoolmates like Han and another able student leader, Ma Chün, the vision of being a leader of China began to assume realistic proportions in his adolescent mind. Ma Chün, two classes behind him, was from Manchuria, one of the boys who at first teased Chou and later became his ardent admirers. Before his execution by the

KMT, Ma was to have much to do with Chou's early revolutionary career.

Chou's sentimental attachment to Nankai remained undiminished in his mature life. In the late 1940s he often repeated his wish that after his retirement he could write a biography of each of his Nankai friends. Even in 1927–30, the darkest days in the CCP's history when arrest and execution constantly threatened him, each time he traveled incognito to Tientsin he telephoned Principal Chang to give him his greetings. And whenever he was in Manchuria, he always talked, at least on the telephone, to an old Nankai friend, a railroad station master who had no interest in politics. Chou repeatedly risked these mysterious calls to his old friends with total confidence that they would not betray him to Chiang Kai-shek's police. In 1936, in the wake of the Sian Incident when the nation was up in arms over the kidnaping of Chiang Kai-shek, Chou went to Nanking to approach the KMT for a united front against Japan. He again risked death to call on a former Nankai teacher whom he had liked. The first thing he asked was, "Teacher, are you still willing to take me back as a student?"

The bond of friendship between Chou and his former school principal, Chang Po-ling, was firm and deep, and the younger man sought every opportunity to reinforce it. When Edgar Snow visited Chou in the Yenan caves in 1936, Chou gave him an English message for Chang who, on his part, retained an unshakable faith in his former pupil as a warm-hearted, reasonable human being, even after he had proven himself to be a shrewd negotiator in dealing with the KMT in the late 1940s. In private Chang told his close associates that he was certain he could persuade Chou to sever his Communist affiliation.

After the end of World War II, the Nankai School was reopened in Chungking. Chou prefaced each of his official visits to Chungking with a personal call at Chang's residence and participated in every Nankai alumni reunion, of which there were at least two every year, one on the anniversary of the school, and the other on Principal Chang's birthday. On such occasions wine-loving Chou invariably appeared informal and gay, drinking heartily with his fellow celebrants. He would present his former schoolmates to his wife, Teng Ying-ch'ao, by saying, "This is so-and-so about whom I have talked so much. We were like brothers when we studied at Nankai together."

Always a welcome visitor, Chou's frequent appearance at Chang's house in Chungking continued until an incident occurred on the fortieth anniversary of the founding of the Nankai University (which came into being a few years after the Nankai Middle School), on October 17, 1944. The Chinese had just repelled an all-out Japanese attack on several fronts in Hunan, Kwangsi, and Kweichow. The newspapers were all cheering the victory with banner headlines. Only the CCP paper, the *New China Daily News*, treated the event casually. Chang confronted Chou and demanded, "Is the *New China Daily News* a Russian paper? Why does it purposely ignore such reports of our victory?" Nobody heard what Chou said in answer.[3]

The last service Chou rendered Chang was in November 1949 after the Chinese Red Army had occupied Chungking. The CCP wanted the support of Chang because of his stature and influence, and Communist emissaries proceeded to besiege him with polite visits. Much irritated, Chang sent a message to Chou who intervened and freed the old man of the harrassment.[4]

Upon his graduation from the Nankai Middle School in 1917, Chou felt ready to travel and see the world. Beyond the China Sea, despite the ominous international tension in the air, Japan with its bustling activities focused on modernization and westernization beckoned. Following the footsteps of several of his good friends, Chou embarked for Tokyo at the age of nineteen.

He was met at the Tokyo dock by his Nankai friend Han

and his wife, both studying there under a Chinese govern-ment stipend. Knowing that Chou was without any financial support, Han promptly got together with four other sti-pended Chinese students and they each pledged ten Chinese dollars a month for Chou's keep.[5] With his room and board amply taken care of, he settled down to prepare for the en-trance examination to the Tokyo Teacher's College, a school known for its strict standards and solid curriculum.

But Tokyo in 1917 was far from being a place for cloistered academic pursuit, especially for the Chinese students there. In their fatherland wave after wave of revolts continued, even after the Yüan Shih-k'ai regime in Peking had collapsed and Sun Yat-sen re-emerged as leader of the national revolution to try to effect a unification. Irresponsible government spokes-men had concluded many treaties and agreements with foreign powers to borrow money for railroads, ammunition, and simply to keep the regime in operation, as exemplified by the humiliating Sino-Japanese Treaty of Twenty-One De-mands signed in 1915. The series of agreements reached during the ensuing two years further surrendered China's in-terests and sovereignty, particularly to France, Germany, Japan, and Russia. Foreign troops and police moved in, with the French in the Tientsin area, the Germans in Shantung, and the Japanese and Russians in Manchuria and on the southeastern Chinese coast. During the last five months of 1916, there were five major clashes with Japanese troops in Manchuria alone.

Some of the Chinese students in Japan hoped to acquire an education and status in order to return to high govern-ment posts later, just as their elders had done with their imperial examinations in Peking. Others were after new knowledge with which they hoped to help their country rise. But none of them could escape the daily reminders of the chaos at home and the Japanese insults to which China was being subjected. Even in their daily life as students in Tokyo, their Japanese hosts all too frequently made them aware of

their inferior status. Many of them, including Chou En-lai's
four financial supporters, gave up under this pressure and returned to China without finishing their study. Those who
managed to stay on in Japan banded together in separate student groups with one kind of political leaning or another. Of
these the leading one was the New China Society (Hsin
Chung-kuo hsüeh-hui).

Left with only Han to turn to for financial help, Chou had
to modify his schooling plans. He lived frugally on a meatless
diet, gave up trying to enroll as a regular student in any
school, and divided his time between avid reading on his own
and participation in Chinese student-group activities. For
about a year he stayed in Tokyo, reading everything he could
lay his hands on and debating with his fellow students about
what they should do for China.

Winter came. The bitter cold of Tokyo made Chou nostal-
gic for his Nankai days. He wrote to Han who was enrolled in
the social science department at Kyoto University. Han
promptly replied, "Please come right away. We have more
than enough room for you. You stay with us, and we will take
our time talking about your going to Kyoto University. The
social science faculty at Kyoto, as you well know, is very
strong, and you just may like it there . . . I have asked you
several times already, but each time you said you did not want
to live off a friend. However, even if you don't consider our
Nankai friendship, we are all foreigners in a strange country
now. Shouldn't we help each other?" The last sentence, Chou
said later, made up his mind, and when he walked into the
open arms of Han at the Kyoto station, he had tears in his
eyes.

With an able and considerate wife and two government
stipends, Han lived quite comfortably for a student in a small
rented house. The addition of Chou to his household livened
their daily routine. In the morning Chou not only cleared
away his bedding from the tatamied floor but always volunteered to help Mrs. Han with her other household chores.

When the two Hans had late classes, they frequently found a meal already prepared for them upon their return. They all sat down, with Han producing a bottle of wine he had picked up on his way home, and enjoyed Chou's culinary art, which never failed to bring back their memories of Tientsin. Han reported on his social science classes, purposely giving details of interest in an attempt to convince his friend that Kyoto University was a good school. Chou offered the ideas he had gleaned from that day's reading. The conversation almost always became more and more animated as Chou argued with Han on the best approach to save China; and as he became more excited, he seized the wine bottle and kept filling his own cup again and again, quite oblivious of manners. Han would glower at Chou while the hostess looked on, smiling helplessly.

On one occasion Chou was quite carried away by his own eloquence, "You cannot salvage the situation with strong leadership alone. You have to have strong followers to support the leadership. You have to start with a thorough reeducation of the younger generation—and the older generation, if that's possible—of the students, the workers, and even the peasants. You have to have them all with you before you can push a revolution to successful conclusion. And without a revolution China cannot be saved!"

Han leaned over, snatched the bottle from Chou, and dashed it to the floor, saying, "You are not going to save China if you hang on to that stuff!" Suddenly jarred out of his delirious mood, Chou smiled in embarrassment and quickly turned to the corner of the room to look for the broom, while the hostess tried to make peace by remarking, "En-lai, you must take care of yourself and not drink too much. Before you reached here Han had been very worried about your staying alone in Tokyo. He said that even at Nankai you were already too fond of wine . . ."

No peace was lost over wine between the two friends after that incident, but a rift gradually developed between their

political ideas. Both were disturbed by Japan's aggressive designs, but Han wanted to see a strong leadership emerge in
China to take drastic steps to repel foreign encroachments,
as Bismarck did in Germany. Chou, on the other hand,
stressed the importance of the ideological remolding of
China's mind and was opposed to the Bismarck approach.
Often upon reaching an impasse in their argument, they
would interrupt their meal, turn to the books and journals
at hand to review a statement or a theory, and then resume
their dinner and carry on the debate. Chou fell under the spell
of a socialist scholar at Kyoto University, Professor Hajimi
Kawakami. *The Social Studies Journal*, a bi-monthly edited
by Kawakami, became Chou's daily reading. Through its
pages Kawakami's interpretation of Marxism, the first authoritative writing on this subject in Japan, was permanently
imprinted on his mind. Chou even tried to cajole Han into
introducing him to Kawakami, but Han, sensing the widening
ideological gap between them, refused. Otherwise the year
in Kyoto passed quite pleasantly in reading and arguing.
Somehow the dates of the school terms at the university were
never right for Chou to enroll.

This was 1919, the year of the famous May 4 Movement in
China. Ma Chün, who had watched Chou's departure for Japan with envy and had just now graduated from the Nankai
Middle School, promptly became involved in student demonstrations.[6] China had officially taken part in World War I and
nominally had emerged one of the victors along with the
Allies, but curiously, at the Paris Peace Conference, Germany's pre-war rights and privileges in the Chinese province
of Shantung were not returned to China. Instead, they were
to be transferred to Japan, which by that time had virtually
occupied most of Manchuria already. The students in Peking,
over three thousand strong, marched on the house of the
Minister of Communications, burned it, and turned to beat
up the Minister to Japan, who was home on leave. To the stu-

dents, these were traitors who had sold their country to the enemy.

News reached Tokyo where the Chinese students immediately headed for the legations of Britain, the United States, France, Russia, and Italy to protest. One column of students reached the Chinese legation to demand an open conference to discuss the issue. As the Chinese chargé d'affaires hesitated, Japanese police arrived on the scene and arrested most of the demonstrators. Over twenty of them were wounded in the fracas.

At this juncture, a letter from Ma Chün reached Chou. It contained a brief message, "If even our country is about to disappear, what is the use of studying?"

That night, lights burned late at the Han house in Kyoto. Han, still free of financial pressure, decided to stay on but to speed up his education; Chou determined to return to China immediately. Packing for him was simple. Next morning, Mrs. Han went to town to sell an expensive ring to raise travel money for him, and in the same afternoon she put him on a train to Tokyo.

The moment Chou arrived back in Tientsin, Ma Chün briefed him on the extent of student involvement in that area and the program of action. One student strike had already been called in sympathy with a fellow student killed in the Peking demonstration. Another general student strike was underway, coordinated by two associations, the Tientsin Student League and its female counterpart, the Tientsin Women's Patriotic Association. Ma was in charge of the League, while Teng Ying-ch'ao, later Chou's wife, was an active member of the girls' group.

Ma needed a hand to run the League's daily newspaper, which gave all the signals for the demonstrations.[7] Reflecting the character of its predecessor, which had been the Nankai Middle School student paper edited by Chou En-lai, it carried an English slogan under its masthead: "Democracy: of the

people, for the people, and by the people." The first thing Ma
did was to take Chou to the editorial board meeting where
Chou argued for a change from classical Chinese to modern
vernacular in the paper. At the end of the meeting, the board
elected Chou editor-in-chief.

The next person Chou called on was Chang Po-ling, now
a university president. Chang gave him a job as his part-time
secretary and sent him to register at the Nankai University,
which had just started operation. Under Chang, the educational philosophy of the new university was an extension of
the spirit that permeated the Nankai Middle School.

With more strikes to organize but few classes to attend,
Chou devoted most of his attention to editorial work. Every
morning he started his day early with a bowl of soybean milk
and some cheap refreshment, which he bought from one of
the roadside food stalls. Then he stopped at the public la-
trine for a few minutes where he began planning the day's
editorial. By the time he arrived at the office of the paper, he
already had an idea or a lead for his column. During the
morning he completed a draft of his article so that it could
be discussed at the staff meeting early in the afternoon. If it
encountered serious objections, he would argue persuasively
with his fellow editors, modifying his statements where he
had to, until agreement was reached. Beyond the editorial
office, student strikes raged and spread from Tientsin to
Shanghai, to Hankow, to Chengtu, and to nearly all the major
cities of China. But within the office where Chou presided,
his calm influence and gentle manner prevailed, and he was
as well liked as during his Nankai Middle School days. Only
once did he allow himself to show the strain of his work. It
was almost four o'clock in the afternoon, and the printer
still had not delivered the next morning's issue, which contained an announcement altering the route of a student march
scheduled for that very morning. When for the last time that
afternoon Chou paused in his floor-pacing to inquire if the
printed copies had arrived, and the messenger still had not

returned, he frowned and slammed a book down on the desk.
A teacup fell off and broke. He picked up a chip, examined
the glaze on it, and said with a wry smile, "Oh, look! I've
just ruined the hours of patient labor of one of our poor
compatriots. What a shame!"

This preoccupation with the suffering laborers of China was
characteristic of his thinking at the time. Besides excoriating
the incompetence of the disorganized government, a popular
subject among the student strikers, Chou's editorials also
took up a wide range of China's political and social problems.
He urged all-out efforts to improve the life of the laborers
through compulsory education and labor-management co-
operation and profit-sharing, with government intervention
only when voluntary negotiation failed. He called for the cultivation of the dynamism of China's youth, more or less
through the kind of liberal education available at Nankai, and
the "engagement" of this dynamic force in sweeping China
clean of her old evils—warlordism, economic stagnation, and
popular ignorance. He occasionally wrote on free marriage,
but his condemnation of the old family system was mild in
comparison to his denunciation of the exploitation of cheap
Chinese labor by foreign capital, to which he never failed to
return in summing up the plagues of his country. The Japanese
cotton mills and British textile factories in Shanghai were a
favorite butt of his criticism.

Basically his political orientation at the time was in tune
with Leo Tolstoy's humane idealism. A little starry-eyed in
his outlook and perhaps overbold in simplifying the facts, he
nevertheless managed to couch his arguments in such effective rhetoric that he overshadowed most of his fellow student
leaders who had more radical views to express.

But Marxism, supported by the recent Lenin experiment in
Russia, had already started knocking on China's door. While
Chou was still reading Kawakami in Kyoto, two professors,
Li Ta-chao (executed by a warlord in 1927) and Ch'en Tu-
hsiu (regarded as founder of Chinese communism and the

first secretary-general of the CCP) had started a serious
Marxist study group in Peking and Shanghai. Articles on
Marxism had begun to appear in some of the new journals.
Using the pseudonym Lenin II, a Peking University student
wrote an article, "A World-shaking Event," in which he
praised the Russian Communist revolution of 1917. Many of
Chou's associates greeted the article with enthusiasm, but
Chou's reaction was cool; he expressed doubt that China
would have to go through a similar series of violent and
bloody revolts before a new order could be established.

Before long his work brought him into closer contact with
the sources of socialist thought and revolution. The Russian
example could not be ignored, and one afternoon he took
several student delegates with him to the French Concession
in Tientsin to call on Sergei A. Polevoy, a Russian teacher at
Peking University who served at the same time as the cultural
liaison for the Comintern.[8] And thus Chou En-lai's direct involvement with the radical left began.

Through the pages of the Tientsin Student League paper
he continued to lend support to the agitating students. In
September 1919, he advocated calling an all-China student
conference to stage nationwide protests. Police raided the
paper's office. Chou had a narrow escape, but Ma Chün was
caught and put in jail. For days Chou went around Tientsin
and Peking until he had mobilized enough people of influence to intervene and obtain Ma's release.

From that day on his writings began to reveal a smoldering
fire of anger. Incensed by the treatment his friends received
from the police, he talked less and less about peaceful education and persuasion, more and more about the need to rid
China of the local police forces and garrisons that he called
the "claws and fangs" of bandit chieftains. The repercussions
contributed to the suspension of the league's paper in November 1919. On January 23, 1920, he led a group of students
to the governor's office to present a petition demanding the
dismissal of Police Chief Yang Yi-teh for his part in man-

handling the student demonstrators. He never got within sight of the governor. Instead, he and sixteen other students, together with the secretary to the local chamber of commerce, a teacher from the Nankai School, all landed in jail.

The police stockade where the group was held for days without trial was cold and damp and virtually windowless. Ma Chün and the managing publisher of the Student League paper, another radical leftist student, tried without success to reach their incarcerated friends. A week passed and then a mysterious note appeared simultaneously in all the cells, calling a hunger strike. The prisoners responded. Immediately, the Student League publicized the strike, which renewed the vigor of the mass petitions for the prisoners' release. Partly because of these pressures and partly because of fear of greater violence, the police transferred the prisoners to the regular city jail. While awaiting trial, Chou organized his fellow prisoners and held classes in social studies and arithmetic,[9] for which Ma Chün and his friends regularly delivered reading materials and notebooks. At the same time they brought back from Chou notes and ideas on how to keep up the coordination of the student movement in different parts of the country.

The Tientsin Student League took the lead in planning every activity, and the Tientsin Women's Patriotic Association supported the action. During the first few weeks after Chou's return from Japan, he renewed his acquaintance with a girl who during his Nankai Middle School days had been among the most active students and had been quite fond of him. But soon her wealthy family sent her abroad and, since she was a bold champion of free marriage and love, she became involved in a rather sensational way with a fellow passenger. Years later when someone mentioned the episode to Chou En-lai and asked him what he thought of it, Chou laughed heartily. The next girl with whom Chou struck up an acquaintance in the May 4 Movement was Teng Ying-ch'ao, a lively high school student whose well educated widowed mother was sympathetic toward what the students were doing.[10] More than once when police pressure made it impossible to hold their meetings, Chou and the key members of the Tientsin Student League went to the Teng house in the French Concession, where they were able to discuss strike strategy without interruption. Teng marched with the demonstrators a number of times, but, like all the girls, she stayed in the middle of the column protected by the boys, and it was always the boys who fell into the hands of the police.

Chou remained in jail until the middle of May 1920. When he came out, the Tientsin Student League had already been forced to cease its activities, but similar student organizations had sprung up in many other cities to carry on the work Chou and his friends had initiated in North China. The May 4 Movement had catapulted students to the forefront of Chinese society, which was ripe for political action and change. Heretofore, the government and the traditional forces controlling society had paid little attention to the youthful segment of the population. Now it became clear that youth, particularly such young people as Chou En-lai and his fellow student leaders, could no longer be ignored.

Yen Fan-sun, one of the founders of the Nankai School, was so impressed by Chou's ability to act and lead that he approached him through friends, offering his daughter in marriage. A prominent attorney of Tientsin, Liu Ch'ung-yu, who defended the jailed students, made a similar approach. Even after Chou turned down their matrimonial offers, they maintained great interest in the young man, to the extent of giving him $500 each to finance him to study in France.

CHAPTER 3

FRANCE: THE BEGINNING OF A COMMUNIST CAREER

TOWARD THE END of the summer of 1920, the *S. S. Borthos* sailing under a French flag returned to her home port. Among her passengers was Chou En-lai. He entered a high school (Collège de Château Thierry) to concentrate on the French language, and at the same time continued to write reports for the daily newspaper in Tientsin, *I-shih-pao*,[1] to earn his room and board. When he was unable to arrange everything to his liking immediately in France, he went to England, hoping he might do better there. Failing again to make the right kind of contact in England, he promptly returned to France. By this time his original desire to pursue academic study in a regular school had cooled off. Instead of the classroom and library, he was drawn to the group of Chinese students in Paris who were actively planning a Chinese Communist Youth Corps abroad.[2]

The climate in France was favorable for such a development. Two groups of Chinese had already assembled there. The first consisted of the laborers who went to France during the First World War and stayed. The second included the batches of students who arrived from 1910 on, attracted by the prospect of being able to secure part-time employment to finance their schooling.

The movement to enroll students to study in France under this arrangement, known as the Work-and-Study (literally,

diligent-work and thrift-study) Program, was spearheaded
by two well-known statesmen[3] in 1903. The leaders of the
movement were, however, so excited by the prospect of such
a short cut to obtaining educated manpower for China that
they exercised little care in selecting the students to go
abroad. Anyone with two hundred Chinese dollars could apply
and was accepted almost without exception. On the receiving
end in France, problems mounted.[4] The Chinese Legation
in Paris, without any special financial support, tried to do
its share to take care of the onrush of students. It mobilized
some sympathetic educators, including a schoolmaster named
Chabot, to lend their school facilities as a temporary shelter
for the Chinese students, and Madame Chabot volunteered
to serve as their house mother. A kind-hearted woman, she
took pains to counsel the students, heretofore accustomed
only to chopsticks and padded quilts, on how to live in a
French house. She had to explain to them that the night pot
was not provided for storing midnight snacks, and that in
France one slipped between two sheets when going to bed.
She had to order extra loaves of bread because many of her
charges dug out the soft middle, leaving the delicious crust
(it looked burned to them) of the French *baguettes* un-
touched in the basket. When a few of the Chinese students
secured part-time work in French factories, they were confronted with the language barrier. One of them, frustrated
by the all-day non-communication with his French fellow
workers, once halted in the middle of his job and burst into an
aria from a Chinese opera. His astonished colleagues rushed
him to a mental hospital for emergency observation. The
mechanics of the Work-and-Study Program in France were
not working out at all, and the accumulated frustration encouraged political agitation among the students stranded
there.

In another attempt to help the students, the Chinese Legation in Paris established a Chinese student center on the rue
St. Sulpice, complete with bedrooms, cooking and recrea-

tional facilities. It was a choice spot for the students and was soon monopolized by a small group of early arrivals. Later comers eyed it with envy and found fault with it, accusing the entrenched old-timers of misusing the building for gambling and prostitution. Thus in the early 1920s the center had already become a source of friction and tension among the many factions of Chinese students in Paris.

The two hundred Chinese dollars each student brought with him usually vanished soon after arrival. Delegates returned to their home districts to plead for relief funds, but only those from Kwangtung Province brought back enough money to help their fellow Kwangtung students—consequently few of this group were pressured into accepting political subsidy. In this way students able to secure and hold down employment and those with a continuing source of funds in China were able to carry on, but the rest had to turn to other means. It was a time when the political and intellectual atmosphere in Paris was extremely volatile. The Communist Party and the Socialist Party had been functioning in France for some time. Within the French National Assembly the Socialists filled over one hundred seats. One of the most active leftist writers was Henri Barbusse, author of *Le Feu*, and leader of the Le Clarté group. Barbusse approached the Chinese students and arranged weekly meetings for them to discuss current affairs. Glib-tongued, attractive French co-eds appeared to lead the discussion while senior Chinese students, some of whom had studied in Russia, served as interpreters. Through this kind of contact students with leftist leanings were persuaded to accept help from the Comintern in Paris. Each of them received about three hundred francs monthly to spend time reading *L'Humanité* and other socialist publications.

Lines emerged among the Chinese student factions in France. Between the Comitern-fostered extreme leftists and the extreme Nationalists, there were anarchists, reformists, international democrats and others, altogether over forty

clusters, each with its own organization and program of action.
The first Communist-front organization was called the Work-
Study Society, led by Ts'ai Ho-sen (or Tsai Ho-shen, key
member of CCP Central Committee in the 1920s who disappeared in 1931), Li Fu-ch'un (now vice premier in Peking),
and Ts'ai Ch'ang (later the wife of Li Fu-ch'un and in CCP
Central Committee from the 1920s until today).

Chou's reputation as student strike leader and inflammatory editorial writer had preceded him, and he was immediately welcomed into the Communist group. They needed his
organizational experience and diplomatic suavity, his facility
to dash out a declaration at a moment's notice, and his impressive appearance. Since working with students was a familiar milieu to him, he quickly felt at home in Paris with its
many Chinese student hangouts already well established in
cafés (one near the Panthéon, and the Wan-hwa or Pascal
Restaurant on the rue de l'Ecole de Médicine whose pro-
prietor regarded it as his patriotic duty to help the Chinese
students) and in the flats of some wealthy fellow students.
As soon as he settled in a small room in the Billancourt section, he put on his best student jacket, which buttoned neatly
up to the collar, groomed his hair, and went out to have his
photograph taken and printed on personal postcards. The
photographer touched up his picture with colors, which he
did not order. But when he saw the result, he was pleased
and immediately sent one to his old friend Han still in
Kyoto.[5]

"Paris beautiful!" Chou wrote on the card. "Many friends,
many sights. Would you like to come?"

He continued to send postcards to his friends, who spread
halfway across the world, but soon he was to realize that it
was not a good idea to put his photograph into so many
hands.

In the spring of 1921, the Chinese government began negotiating with France for a huge loan. The May 4 Movement

had sensitized Chinese students to their country's inferior position in the world, and they were at once highly suspicious of any arrangements that would make China still more dependent upon foreign powers. When word spread that the government in Peking had dispatched its Finance Minister[6] to Paris, they interpreted his mission as the conclusion of the loan negotiation and started a demonstration in Paris, marching on the Legation building. The helpless Chinese Minister[7] tried to appease the demonstrators by promising them room-and-board subsidy during their stay in Paris. Then, just as the situation was becoming unbearable for him, another development occurred.

In an effort to improve the Work-and-Study Program in France, the sponsors raised enough funds from their influential friends in China to build a new university at Lyon. The French government supported the move by agreeing to have the Chinese authorities divert the French share of the Boxer Indemnity money for this purpose. At the same time, the sponsors began to recruit better qualified and disciplined students to replace those already in France. As news of these preparations reached Paris, the Chinese students there were incensed. They elected over a hundred delegates, including Ts'ai Ho-sen, Li Li-san (CCP secretary-general in 1929), Li Wei-han (CCP Central Committee member since the 1920s), and Ch'en Yi (now Foreign Minister), from all parts of France to go to Lyon to demand that the new university be open to all of the students already in France. The Chinese Minister in Paris seized this opportunity to encourage the protesting students in Paris to march on Lyon, even providing them with transportation. On September 21, 1921, Lyon became the scene of the largest Chinese student concentration abroad since the beginning of history.

Chou En-lai, now wearing a pair of old overalls that blended in well with the Renault automobile workers in the Billancourt neighborhood, was elected leader of the student delegation. Assisting him in organizing the Lyon march were

Li Li-san and Chao Shih-yen, later head of the CCP's labor department and executed by the KMT in 1927. Although many other non-Communist student leaders were equally active in preparing the demonstration, leadership was rapidly gravitating toward the leftists. Chou and his close associates stayed in Paris, mapping out strategy until the very last moment. As Chou was bending over a small desk in a hotel room writing a declaration, one of his friends remarked, "You are really getting to look like an automobile worker, except for that fat briefcase. Nobody at the Renault plant would carry a thing like that around."[8] Chou looked up without stopping his pen, which was in the middle of finishing the last sentence. "Here, take this," Chou said, handing the briefcase to his friend with his left hand. "We may all need this to while our time away when we get to Lyon."

And they did. The thick stack of books and pamphlets Chou had in his briefcase proved extremely useful when they were all locked up by the police the next day.

The troubled French authorities in Lyon made inquiries to the Chinese Legation and were told that the students were mainly radical leftist agitators. Acting upon this information, the Lyon police arrested the students and kept them in custody at the Mont Luc Barracks.

At Mont Luc the students went on a hunger strike. Several Chinese statesmen[9] personally went to visit them in an attempt to halt their demonstration. A deadlock lasted until the French government decided to deport the students en bloc. After about three weeks' incarceration at Mont Luc, during which time some of them had escaped, the group of over a hundred Chinese students was rounded up and put on trucks, which carried them to a whistle-stop in the countryside to board a special train for Marseilles. Marseilles police took their residence permits and placed the students on a ship bound for China via the Suez Canal. En route a few more jumped ship, but among those who returned to China was Li Li-san, later a member of the CCP's Politburo and leader in 1929–31. Chou En-lai was one of those who escaped deportation.

With Chou En-lai and several of his close associates still active in Western Europe using Paris as their center of activities, the Chinese Legation in Paris had yet to see the end of its woes. The students continued to agitate various groups to petition the government to modernize China and improve her international position. Chou was behind all the demonstrations. One such demonstration, led by a girl student named Hsiang Ching-yü (later Ts'ai Ho-sen's wife), stormed the Legation on February 8, 1922. According to Ts'ai Ch'ang, an active leader of Communist women in China today, that demonstration was planned by Chou En-lai, Wang Jo-fei (CCP's representative in Chungking killed in an airplane crash, 1946), and her brother, Ts'ai Ho-sen.[10]

The Chinese student population in Berlin was not quite as large as that in Paris but equally active. Political groups of different colors vigorously competed in recruiting new members, and their leaders traveled from one center to another. From the end of 1921 to late summer of 1922, Chou En-lai was frequently on the train between Paris and Berlin. While in Berlin, he stayed in a house on Wilhelmstrasse, a relatively high-class residential area, paying a monthly rent of forty-eight marks, which amounted to about twelve American dollars.[11] His French experience and record had made him more cautious. Early in 1922, a former Nankai friend called on him. The first thing he noticed was Chou's wardrobe and the interior of the house, which was luxurious for a student. He remarked, "En-lai, I see you are doing all right."[12]

"So long as I keep receiving something from home and something from the publishers, I guess I will manage," said Chou. But his friend, who had been a leftist student before and knew about the Comintern's aid to the leftist movement in Europe, did not take Chou's explanation seriously. They reminisced about their high school days and compared impressions of different places in Europe. Chou carefully skirted political subjects. Just before the visitor left, he asked Chou, "Have you made any new discoveries lately?"

"You mean . . . girls? No."

"I don't believe it, not with a handsome young man like you and your set up here."

"I don't think I want to get involved. It's better to stay single. You get more done that way."

"How about Teng Ying-ch'ao? Haven't you been writing her every other week?"

"How did you know?"

"She told me. You know, once in a long while I also receive a note from her." And the friend left.

By the fall of 1922 Chou had succeeded in setting up a small Chinese Communist Youth Corps in Germany. Chu Teh, the old CCP soldier whose name later became inseparably linked to Mao Tse-tung until 1967, was among them. As representative of the Youth Corps in Germany, Chou returned to Paris early in the winter of the same year to participate in the founding of a similar organization in France.

At the meeting to inaugurate the Chinese Communist Youth Corps in France, there were over a dozen participants. Leading the assembly gathered informally on the lawn of a Paris park was Chao Shih-yen, already a full-fledged member of the Chinese Communist Party. It was he who insisted that the Chinese student organization in France must not be called a branch of the Communist Party because party membership should be more carefully screened. He proposed, with the CCP's secretary-general in Moscow, Ch'en Tu-hsiu, supporting him, that the group be called Chinese Communist Youth Corps in France to serve as a training ground for potential party members. Full-fledged CCP members could function in the Corps, but not vice versa. As head of the Corps, Chou was responsible for its ideological indoctrination.[13]

An actual branch of the CCP was also set up in France

under the leadership of Chao Shih-yen, who functioned as corresponding secretary. The office was located in a small hotel at 17 rue Godefroy near place d'Italie in Paris.[14] Soon Chao Shih-yen went to Moscow, and his secretaryship was handed to Yin K'uan. The executive committee of this party branch included Chou En-lai, Chao Shih-yen, Ch'en Yen-nien (Ch'en Tu-hsiu's son, executed in 1927), Wang Jo-fei, and several others.

The Chinese Communist organ in France appeared first as *Shao-nien* (*The Youth*), with Chao Shih-yen and Yin K'uan (who was ousted from the CCP in 1929 as an eliminationist) responsible for its publication. Teng Hsiao-p'ing, considered Mao's likely successor for years until the Red Guard revolt of 1966, was in charge of the mimeographing. Because of this assignment and the excellent work he did, he earned the title of "Ph.D. in mimeographing" from his associates. When Chou En-lai took over the editorship upon Chao Shih-yen's departure for Russia, the publication was renamed *Ch'ih-kuang* (*The Red Light*). Chou's articles appeared in it under the pen name Wu Hao.

Again, among the first to receive Chou's publications was his old friend Han in Kyoto. Toward the end of 1922 Han received a tightly rolled sheaf of onionskin paper which contained the complete proceedings of the inauguration of the Chinese Communist Youth Corps in France. Each character was only about the size of a sesame seed, but each stroke was finely drawn and clearly printed—a remarkable piece of calligraphy and mimeographing much to the credit of Teng Hsiao-p'ing. Han read it and committed it to the fire. Two postcards later, another roll of mimeographed document reached Han who again read and immediately burned it. Then came another postcard from Chou, this time without his colored photograph on the back, asking, "Twice sent you publications. Did they reach you? Reply please. —Your younger brother, En-lai."

Han reciprocated with a letter, "Twice received your docu-

ments. Our ideas were never compatible. Let us each develop
his thinking in his own way but remain friends forever. —Your
elder brother, Han."

There followed a fourteen-year silence between them.

In *The Red Light* Chou wrote mostly commentaries on
current affairs, condemning the warlords in China and blaming the ineffective government in Peking for the continued
chaos. The emotional refrain in his rhetoric, which was his
specialty, touched students, dishwashers, and laundrymen
alike, regardless of their political leanings. In spite of his responsibility to indoctrinate his fellow corpsmen with communism, the actual work of interpreting and spreading Marxist
ideology was left to another committee member, Yeh,[15]
who later was arrested by the KMT in China, tortured, and
shot, but miraculously dragged out of the execution ground
at night and nursed back to health by his comrades. Yeh was
strong in theory but weak in its presentation. He and Chou
together formed a powerful team, which made *The Red
Light* an influential circular much dreaded by its opponents.

With the CCP branch in France now well underway, Chao
Shih-yen and Ch'en Yen-nien made arrangements to study
at the Eastern University in Moscow, an institution formed
to train a communist elite from East Asian countries. Chou
accompanied the two to Berlin and assisted them in preparing for the trip. When he returned to Paris, the party leadership was in his hands alone.

Disputes among the various Chinese factions in France
were gaining intensity. Two other major groups contended
with Chou and his followers. One was the Nationalist Party
(KMT), which in the fall of 1923 followed the Communist
example and set up a branch in France with official govern-
mental support. Since this was before the KMT closed the
door to the Communists, Chou and Li Fu-ch'un joined the
KMT and worked closely with the head of its local branch.[16]
With the latter's help and confidence, both Chou and Li

were given membership on the KMT committee in France and both appeared in public as though they were spokesmen for the KMT.

The other major political group was led by Tseng Ch'i and Li Huang, two students from Szechwan Province who later became the mainstay of the third force in China's politics. Even before they formally organized the Ch'ing-nien-tang (Young China Party) on December 2, 1923, they had started to advocate a "total revolution" in China to do away with all the old forces and political parties and start with a clean slate. They criticized the CCP for its submission to Russia, the KMT for its loss of revolutionary spirit. In return the Communists attacked the Young China group as chauvinistic and impractical, and the KMT saw it as just another expression of youthful impatience. The Young China group had their organ, a journal named *The Herald* (*Hsien Sheng*), which was renamed *National Salvation* after the party was formally launched. The KMT soon began to distribute its own fortnightly called *The Nationalist*.[17] Among these journals and the CCP's *Red Light*, heated polemics raged.

Centering around the issue of opposing the warlord-controlled Peking government to prevent further loss of China's interests and sovereignty, but more immediately around the issue of what to do with the students in France who had neither guidance nor money, the various Chinese groups got together and set up a Joint Conference of All Chinese in France, which became the arena where Chou, the KMT, and the Young China group fought for leadership.

For the Joint Conference the most urgent task, and in reality the only one that could be undertaken, was propaganda—petitions and more petitions. Before Chou arrived on the scene, Tseng Ch'i took the lead in drafting these petitions and declarations, but Chou's eloquence in *The Red Light* showed that he could not be ignored. Back in China, a gang of bandits at Lin-ch'eng in Shantung Province kidnaped a whole trainload of passengers, including many Westerners, on May 5, 1923. The Western powers in China moved to set up a joint Allied commission equipped with armed guards to control Chinese railroads. Word about the incident reached Paris, and Chou and Tseng planned a general meeting of the Joint Conference of All Chinese in France to protest the Western encroachment upon Chinese sovereignty. On July 3, the meeting was held in the headquarters of the Overseas Chinese Association. Tseng, Chou, and Hsu T'e-li (whom Mao Tse-tung has often referred to as his teacher) were chosen to draft a declaration in the name of all the Chinese in France, addressed to their compatriots in China and throughout the world.

Two days later the three-man drafting committee met again in the Overseas Chinese Association office where Chou presented his draft.

"Excellent, excellent!" said Tseng after reading the draft. "The only thing that disturbs me is that you have presented no concrete program of action for our compatriots to follow."[18]

"Are they ready to consider any specific program of action? Don't you think we should arouse them first and then talk about specific steps?" said Chou, running his fingers through his smoothly combed hair.

"But they have had enough of this arousing. They are tired of it." So saying, Tseng proceeded to outline his program of calling popular meetings to elect representatives from the county level up to the national level, using general strikes to coerce the government and the warlords to unite and reform in the national interest, and revamping the education system and economy of the country. He was so agitated as he spoke that he paced the floor from one end of the room to the other, at times with his back to Chou and Hsu, and constantly took off and put back on his heavy eyeglasses.

Chou listened quietly, occasionally exchanging a calm smile with his companion Hsu on the other side of the table. When Tseng finished his discourse, Chou immediately agreed to

revise his draft. Four days later Chou alone met with Tseng
for several hours to go over the revised document and other
drafted telegrams to the government leaders in Peking and
the Chinese diplomats abroad. On July 10, the three drafters
met with the full committee of over ten representatives of
the major Chinese groups in France in the Café de la République to review the finished drafts and plan the general meeting scheduled for July 15, 1923. From seven until eleven
o'clock the committee argued, with Tseng insisting on sending petitions separately to Sun Yat-sen, the warlord Wu
P'ei-fu who controlled the Peking government at the time,
and other leaders. Hsu T'e-li disagreed, feeling that a severe
condemnation should go to warlord Wu only. Others preferred an appeal to Sun Yat-sen alone, urging him to take a
stronger stand. Finally Chou En-lai noted the lateness of the
hour and terminated the debate with a plea that the committee listen to the majority's wish in the general meeting
five days later.

Over four hundred attended the general meeting, which
began at 4 P.M. in the auditorium of the Musée de Cluny.
Before the preliminaries were over, a noisy debate had started.
The chairman,[19] a KMT member, had to pound the table
vigorously to regain control and turn the floor over to Tseng
Ch'i. Tseng offered four courses of action, which he believed
should be simultaneously pursued but by different people,
each according to his preparation and interest, and these
courses were: propaganda through mass media, strikes, and
demonstrations; revolts co-ordinated for a total revolution;
and terrorist movements. Another long session of confused
argument ensued, with many people talking at the same time.
When Chou En-lai managed to obtain the attention of the
audience, he said, "Now that you have heard just about all
the possible kinds of action to be taken, it must be quite
clear to you that the only thing we can do immediately is
the mobilization of mass media to arouse world opinion to
sympathize with our cause. Let us first consider the drafted

declaration and petitions to reach a decision, otherwise . . ."

While Chou talked, several small clusters of Chinese workers held their caucuses in the back of the room. One of them
raised his voice and was hissed by a student nearby. The
man felt insulted and proceeded to curse aloud. The dispute
developed into a fist fight involving dozens of participants.
When calm returned to the assembly half an hour later, two
students had to be taken to a hospital for treatment, and a
number of broken chairs lay around. With the help of Chou
and Tseng, the chairman managed to get a show of hands
approving the drafted documents.

As each of the three major groups strove to consolidate its
position and competed for a following, the ideological lines
between them were drawn tauter. Hotheaded students and
workers picked fights more and more often at the joint meetings whenever the drift of the discussion was not to their liking. Even the co-leader of the Young China group, Li Huang,
acquired a pistol for self-protection. The joint meetings became increasingly explosive and hazardous. Because of his
patient work among the most frustrated students and workers, cultivating both the educated and the uneducated, which
was something the Young China leaders neglected to do,
Chou stepped between the most belligerent disputants, and
they listened to him.

The Young China's *Herald* accused the CCP's *Red Light*
of being a Russian echo, while the *Red Light* criticized the
Herald for spreading Napoleonic whims under the guise
of patriotism. In these two journals, particularly, invectives
mounted, while the KMT's *Nationalist* was bland in comparison because it published a wider range of articles, including
both the left and the right. On December 2, 1923, the Young
China group under Tseng Ch'i met at No. 2 rue de la République in Fontenay-aux-Roses south of Paris to inaugurate
the Young China Party and proceeded to firm up their stand
in opposition to the CCP and Russia. The mutual incrimina-
tion became increasingly personal, especially between Tseng

and the CCP theorist, Yeh. When the journals were not printed frequently enough to keep up with the brisk pace of exchange of accusations, they resorted to personal letters.

All through the winter of 1923 Chou tried to explain away the basic difference between the Young China Party and the CCP.[20] He told Tseng that there was no fundamental difference between what the two parties wanted, that Tseng's total revolution had to have a national basis, and that the ultimate goal of revolution was to make a better world for all nations, hence the ultimate international nature of the revolution advocated by both parties.

Tseng agreed with the general thesis, but disagreed on the CCP's policy, which was also the KMT's policy in those years, of alliance with Russia and acceptance of aid from the Comintern. Chou maintained that the world situation made it necessary for the Chinese revolutionaries to unite with their Russian comrades. Each of their written or oral exchanges inevitably reached an impasse over this last issue, and it was the same impasse that ended their longest face-to-face discussion on April 28, 1924, at 2 rue de la République, which lasted from early afternoon until 8:30 in the evening.

Despite the violent disagreements among these groups, which pulled them apart in all directions, all of them realized that joint action was imperative, and each time a joint meeting was to be called all of them turned to Chou. Only he could bring the quarreling factions at least to sit down and talk together, even though such talks did not always reach any concensus or end peacefully. He did this when another Peking government emissary[21] was scheduled to be in Paris in May. Chou brought the heads of the factions together and worked out a strategy to approach the emissary, but their work proved to be superfluous because the emissary was beaten up by Chinese students in Berlin before he had a chance to face the Paris assembly.

The factional strife came to a head in the summer of 1924, threatening to break the already over-strained fiber of the

Joint Conference of All Chinese in France. Chou proposed
another meeting of the heads of the groups to develop a new
modus operandi. This took place on June 7, with Chou representing the CCP, Li Fu-ch'un speaking for the KMT, and
Tseng as head of the Young China Party. They spelled out a
ten-article agreement defining the terms of co-operation, and
then called a general joint meeting to review the agreement.
On July 20, representatives of over thirty-eight Chinese
groups assembled in Paris with Tseng presiding. Chou spoke
for twenty minutes, urging a revision of the theme of the
Joint Conference from "Remove the traitors and resist foreign
aggressors" to "Down with the warlords and overthrow international capitalist imperialism." The disorderly quarrel
that followed prevented the motion from being voted on,
and, as the left-wing and right-wing groups appeared to be
equal in strength and neither side agreed to let the chairman
cast the deciding vote in case of a tie, the long meeting ended
with nothing decided. The meeting did, however, end all
hopes of co-operation among the Paris factions.

Away from the Joint Conference, Chou, wearing two hats
at the same time, worked to cement the CCP-KMT alliance
against the Young China Party. Once at a KMT meeting he
accused a KMT member, a worker, of leaking party secrets to
the Young China group. The accused denied it and counter-
charged Chou with defamation of character. Chou stood up
and, pointing at the soiled overalls he wore, launched an
impassioned plea for the workers to close ranks behind the
KMT, which, he said, unlike the ivory-tower dreamers of the
petit-bourgeois Young China gentlemen, really had the interest of the working people at heart. Then with moistened
eyes he added, "They (the Young China group) talk and talk
about petitions and strikes, but when there is a demonstration, who march at the head of the column to face the guns
and clubs of the police, get beat up, arrested, jailed, and even
butchered? It is we, the KMT cadres, not they! They talk
about assassination and terrorism, but it is the KMT com-

rades' blood that is shed, not theirs."[22] The assembly was
visibly touched, and the audience left the meeting without
thinking about whether or not the accused was really guilty.
Instead, they remembered Chou En-lai's greatness, for they
agreed that Chou knew what he was talking about, since they
frequently saw him in those soiled overalls, meeting and
working with the laborers in the Billancourt section, day and
night.

Among the laborers of Billancourt and Colombes, the students of Fontenay-aux-Roses, and the laundrymen and restaurant workers scattered throughout Paris, Chou cultivated
leftist cells by meeting with them regularly to discuss political tracts and current affairs. After these regular sessions
and the frequent meetings to fight the opposition, he still
found time to write love letters to Teng Ying-ch'ao and spend
an occasional casual evening with his wealthier fellow students who lived in the Sceaux section. On these evenings he
would shed his overalls and put on his neat student jacket. If
he arrived a little early, he would go to the kitchen and volunteer to prepare a dish of *chiao-tzu*, a northern Chinese favorite, which he made very expertly. He would appear completely
relaxed, drinking and joking with abandon; but at the end of
the party he would always be the one to see everybody to
his proper Métro stop, never showing any excessive effect of
the wine.

The "Beautiful Paris" Chou had exclaimed about in his
postcard message to his friend Han assumes a prophetic meaning when one realizes that it was there that Chou first rubbed
shoulders with the more sophisticated factions to perfect his
art of political compromise. The united front he tried to
achieve in Paris was not a complete success, but his approach
became a respected hallmark of his later statesmanship. In a
heterogeneous assembly his tact and quick thinking never
failed to set him above the rest. Always the master of the
situation, particularly a confused and violent situation, he

chose the line for the crowd to follow. At times he did not
hesitate to launch sharp attacks on his opponents, but immediately after the attack he always softened his voice to
explain away the point of dispute, emerging in triumph as a
resourceful peacemaker.

The "many friends" he had forecast in his postcard later
turned out to be his admirers and devoted comrades in the
CCP hierarchy. The only member of the CCP branch in Paris
senior to him was Chao Shih-yen, who was arrested and executed by the KMT in 1927. Others whose seniority in the
party could rival his, such as Yin K'uan, Ts'ao Ho-sen, Ch'en
Yen-nien, and Ch'en Ch'iao-nien, all died or left the CCP
soon after their return to China. The noted survivors, including Ch'en Yi (now Foreign Minister), Li Fu-ch'un (now
Vice-Premier), Li Wei-han (eclipsed after December 1964),
Nieh Jung-chen (another Vice-Premier), Teng Hsiao-p'ing
(CCP secretary-general since 1956), and Ts'ai Ch'ang (the
most senior woman comrade, always a member of Central
Committee), have remained his supporters even today.[23]
And the French component of the CCP remains the most
effective and influential among all the CCP groups, even after
the Red Guard upheaval of 1966.

CHAPTER 4

INFILTRATION, INTRIGUE, AND INSURRECTION

RECRUITING AND TRAINING revolutionaries in Paris was a rewarding assignment, but after three years the call for more direct action and involvement at home had become too insistent to be ignored. A number of Chinese student leaders in Europe were planning to return, and Chou also started packing.

At the farewell party arranged for him by his KMT and CCP associates in Paris on a sunny afternoon in late 1924, he and his well-wishers reviewed the developments in their fatherland and looked forward to Chou's imminent contribution to national revolution the moment he joined forces with the revolutionary military government of the KMT headed by Sun Yat-sen in Canton. Although the warlords in the various parts of China were still fighting one another in confusion and the Canton military government could rely upon the loyalty of only very few troops, Sun Yat-sen had declared war on the discredited Northern Government in Peking, had convened the First KMT National Congress, and had assigned Chiang Kai-shek to start building an elite KMT army at the Whampoa Academy outside Canton in April of the same year. Chou agreed with his friends that in Canton a spark of hope had finally been kindled that promised to spread, and that he would make his organizational talents available to Chiang Kai-shek immediately upon his arrival. After making sure that Chou had a proper introduction to the key KMT people in Canton, his friends at the farewell party drank a toast to his future and the new China, had a souvenir group photograph taken, and waved him good-by.[1]

Through the CCP apparatus Chou knew that joining the KMT in Canton was also the wish of the Party. The Comintern, the only source of inspiration and concrete support for the fledgling CCP, had adopted a resolution on China during an emergency session on January 12, 1923, suggesting that the CCP "while taking care not to lose its own revolutionary identity, work through the KMT to overthrow the warlords before concentrating on a proletarian movement toward socialism."[2] This was precisely what Chou had been doing in Europe. To facilitate further Chou's return the KMT's First Congress, which contained a left wing and a right wing of about equal strength, resolved on January 20, 1924, to accept CCP members on an individual basis.

Sun Yat-sen needed every bit of support he could find wherever it might be. Although he had been named Supreme Commander by the refugee National Congress in Canton in September 1917, his command was but an empty title. He had to wait three years before he obtained the support of two Cantonese armies. Only a month after his two armies started their northern march to fight the warlords, the garrison troops in Canton turned against him and almost caught and executed him. He had to call his men back to save him and recapture his headquarters. The same thing happened five times,[3] the last time being in January 1925, only two months before his death. The Yunnan and Kweichow troops supported him for a while, and with their help he managed to keep alive the hope of a northern expedition, but they too rebelled soon after his death.[4]

With the need to train his troops becoming more urgent every day, Sun Yat-sen appointed Chiang Kai-shek to organize the Whampoa Academy (China's West Point) in January 1924. Chiang, having just returned from a three-month visit as Sun's personal envoy to Moscow to learn from the experience of the Russian revolution, encountered enough opposition to make him hesitate for over three months before he finally returned to Canton on April 26, 1924, to receive the first batch of Whampoa cadets as their commandant. First he tried to concentrate on the military, leaving politics to other KMT leaders who had already started squabbling over the appointment of the Russian Communist Mikhail Borodin as Sun Yat-sen's adviser and the reports of the CCP's ultimate design to replace the KMT.[5] Rumors became so disturbing that Sun himself had to issue a statement declaring that the KMT was not being Sovietized.[6] Next Chiang had to deal with the entrenched local political forces in Canton, including the governor appointed by the warlord-controlled government in Peking, whom he replaced with a KMT man.[7] Just as his military training program got under way, the private guards of the Canton merchants, backed by British interests in Hong Kong, revolted, and Chiang had to order his cadets, who had had only five months' training, into action.[8]

All these conditions made it necessary for Chiang to do what Sun Yat-sen had done and accept within his ranks all those willing to work with him. Chou En-lai's ability and experience soon earned him a trusted position among Chiang's political officers at Whampoa.

Upon his arrival in Canton,[9] Chou assumed the secretaryship of the military committee in the CCP's local branch.[10] The KMT promptly teamed him up with another Communist,[11] one of the thirteen at the first CCP Congress (July 1921, Shanghai and Chiahsing), to take charge of the Training Department of the National Military Commission set up by Sun Yat-sen. When the Whampoa Academy was established, Chou became Deputy Director of the Political Department and head of the Court Martial in the Academy.[12] The Director of the Department, a senior KMT man[13] soon let Chou take all the initiative and run the whole department, which he staffed with some of the best brains of the CCP.[14]

Whatever disagreement there might have been between
Chiang Kai-shek and Borodin, they agreed wholeheartedly on
the importance of political training and control of the army.
A political commissar system was set up whereby every unit
of troops, including those still under training in the Academy,
had a KMT party representative who had to countersign
every order before it could become official. This made the
Commandant of the Academy (Chiang Kai-shek himself!)
and the commander of the army merely instruments to carry
out such orders. And Chou saw to it that CCP members and
secret Communist agents became constantly more numerous
among the KMT army commissars.

In January 1925, one warlord[15] finally forced a coup d'état
in Peking, driving out the discredited President and taking in
another old statesman[16] to function as temporary head of the
state. Sun Yat-sen, still holding the empty title of Supreme
Commander of Revolutionary Forces, thought that time had
come for a thorough reorganization of the government, but
he was disillusioned upon his arrival in Peking. In Canton,
Chiang Kai-shek, after repelling the fifth local rebellion
against the KMT, decided to take his Whampoa cadets into
the East River area to mop up the remaining opposition
forces. Thus the first real Eastern Expedition of the KMT
began. Chou headed the commissar system in the First Division. The first showing of the politically motivated Whampoa graduates in action, largely inspired by Chou En-lai, was a
resounding success. They overran many cities in eastern
Kwangtung Province and were about to push their victory
farther north when the supporting Yunnan and Kweichow
troops revolted against the KMT, necessitating Chiang's return to Canton to put down the sixth rebellion.

Before the second Eastern Expedition in October of the
same year, Chiang Kai-shek regrouped his forces into the
First National Army under his personal command, and kept
Chou as his chief commissar. Below Chou, eight of the nine
commissars at the regimental level were Communists. When

the troops marched out, Chou was given an additional assignment, as Special Commissioner in charge of the East River
District. Now wearing a smart KMT army uniform complete
with a well-polished Sam Browne belt, Chou, at twenty-
seven, was the political head of Chiang's armed forces and
chief administrator of the largest area that had come under
KMT control. As the guards at the entrances to the leading
hotels in Canton and in Swatow saluted him,[17] everyone in
that southern revolutionary bastion was whispering his name,
half in admiration, half in awe.

And above the din of political confusion throughout the
country, Chou's authoritative voice was heard. He exhorted
the KMT and the nation to follow Sun Yat-sen's policy, which
was clearly a leftist policy, to carry out the revolution. "The
lawless bandit chieftains who jumped on the revolutionary
bandwagon,"[18] he said, referring to several army commanders
whom Sun Yat-sen had to involve in his setup because no one
else was available, "are undoing what our comrades have
given their lives to accomplish!" He urged the "progressive"
elements in the KMT to close ranks to chase those "bandits"
out; and he proved to be right, for one after another the warlords later turned against Sun Yat-sen.

The moment Sun Yat-sen left Canton for Peking toward the
end of 1924, Chou spoke up against those who followed Sun
northward. They were deserting the revolution, Chou said,
and going where there might be political spoils to share. Turning to those who stayed in Canton, Chou did not hesitate to
name names and charge them with engaging in unprincipled
political intrigues.[19] And again he was proved right, in that
Chiang Kai-shek had to fight them as late as in June 1925.

Chou's position of influence in the KMT army was hard-
earned. Before he reached there he had had to prove time and
again his pivotal value of keeping the left-wing and right-wing
Whampoa cadets together while cultivating their revolutionary zeal. The latter was the assignment Chiang Kai-shek had

specifically given him; the former was his voluntary contribution, which Chiang appreciated until the Chung-shan Gunboat Incident of March 20, 1926 precipitated a break between
the CCP and the KMT.

Even more urgent for Chou was the task of strengthening
the CCP's structure. Under the aura of the popular revolutionary leader Sun Yat-sen, the KMT continued to grow in
spite of all the difficulties posed by the warlords and the
Northern Government in Peking. Since Chou En-lai insisted
that the CCP and the KMT were carrying out the same national revolution, the temptation to join the winner was too
great for many Communist comrades to resist. As senior
member of the Executive Committee of the CCP's Kwangtung Branch, Chou had to try everything to prevent his comrades from switching over to Sun Yat-sen's side.

One evening in the winter of 1924, when Chou had barely
gotten settled in his rented house in Canton, a messenger
brought him a sealed message. He quickly read it and stuck it
into his pocket while going about entertaining his visitor, a
KMT official, as usual. It was close to midnight when the
visitor finally left, and, glancing at the message once again,
Chou carefully burned it before walking out into the darkness.

In a side alley he found the address he wanted. The man
opening the door for him looked vaguely familiar. Before he
finished returning the greeting, it dawned on him that he
was facing Chou Fo-hai, one of the thirteen at the CCP's
First Congress in 1921.

"Comrade Pao[20] said that you'd like to see me," Chou
said.

"Oh?" Chou Fo-hai said, slightly surprised. "I've just
spoken to him this afternoon, and I've just finished the letter
he told me to write. It's all in here." He handed an envelope
to Chou En-lai.

"I hope you don't mind," said Chou En-lai, and he tore
the letter up without reading it. "Comrade Pao has told me

what you wanted to do, but I don't think it is necessary at all. May I sit down with you for a moment?"

Chou Fo-hai had wanted to resign from the CCP without having to explain to anybody, but Chou En-lai had already sat down, and the reluctant host had to listen to his hour-long argument about why he thought Chou Fo-hai was making a mistake. Chou Fo-hai responded by saying that he had found Sun Yat-sen's doctrine completely adequate to fulfill the aspirations of the Chinese people; therefore he saw no need to borrow Russia's communism. Chou En-lai maintained that the KMT had inherited too many problems from the old society of China, and the revolution needed a more thoroughgoing approach. When Chou Fo-hai disagreed, Chou En-lai finally said that two political parties would in any case be superior to a one-party system in the new China. At the end of the long conversation, Chou Fo-hai was growing weary while his visitor retained his composure, his eager eyes under broad, dark eyebrows fixed with unwavering intensity on his host.

"Why don't you think it over some more tonight, and we'll talk about it again tomorrow?" Chou En-lai said, glancing at his watch.

"I have thought it over. I may think some more, but I don't believe I will change my mind."

Chou En-lai's persuasion failed this time, but during the next two years he was to repeat this kind of nocturnal performance frequently, not only to keep his comrades from leaving the CCP, but also to win new converts and settle violent disputes between the two political extremes, particularly those within the Whampoa Academy, which led to the Chung-shan Gunboat Incident.

As soon as Chiang assembled his first group of Whampoa cadets in 1924, he hand-picked some thirty or so of the most promising young men and instructed Chou to groom them as models for later Whampoa students. These selected elite were promptly inducted by Chou into a Communist-front organization called the Young Soldiers Association. One day the leader[21] of the association misplaced a CCP circular addressed to all the Communists at Whampoa severely criticizing the KMT, which fell into the hands of a right-wing member of the KMT. Disclosure of the circular and the list of distribution prompted the rightists at the academy to propose the formation of a counter-group, which, upon Chiang Kai-shek's formal approval, was to be named the Sun Yat-sen Society. At the end of its preliminary membership drive, however, the Sun Yat-sen Society organizers discovered that nearly all the signers were on the distribution list of the CCP circular. This discovery, plus the First Eastern Expedition of February 1925, compelled the KMT to shelve the formal inauguration of the Society.

Knowing that the right wing would not abandon its plans to check the growth of the Young Soldiers Association, Chou, as chief commissar of the division, called one night during a lull in combat on the sponsor[22] of the Sun Yat-sen Society, a Whampoa graduate who was serving as the commissar of a battalion. Chou knew the young officer well, and their conversation started informally with the combat situation, gradually broaching the subject of the society. Chou tried to convince his former student that basically there was no difference between the KMT and the CCP, and that Sun Yat-sen's doctrine of "People's Livelihood" was socialism. He said that the cause of revolution would be better served if factional struggle within the army could be eliminated and if the junior officer would join the Young Soldiers Association instead of setting up a rival organization. He spoke softly, but with determination. Two hours passed and the oil in the lamp was getting low while the grain storage cubicle the troops had borrowed was getting stuffy. Chou unbuttoned the collar of his uniform.

"You've just returned from Russia yourself," Chou said. "You've talked with the revolutionary leaders in Russia and you know that they are our friends. Who among all the powers gave us guns and ammunition? Only the Russians, and by the shipload too! You were there last year on October 7 when the Russian supplies were unloaded at Whampoa. The British sent arms to the Cantonese merchants to fight us. The French, the Germans, and the Americans continued to extort our money, rights and interests through the Northern warlords . . . You of all people should know that the international situation requires us to collaborate with Russia. Otherwise our revolution would be doomed."

The young officer listened, and when Chou paused for a moment, he countered with a question about the Russian ambassador Karakhan's reversal about restoring to China the ownership of the Eastern Railroad in Manchuria and about the Russian agreement with the warlord[23] in Manchuria, which was not in China's best interest. Chou said that those were before the delivery of Russian arms to Canton, and that he was sure the Russians would abrogate all the agreements concluded with the Northern government and the warlords as soon as the Chinese revolution was completed. The flame on the lamp flickered, threatening to go out. It was already the small hours of the morning. Chou waited for the young officer's final reply.

"But the Commandant has approved it, and, even if I said nothing from now on, there will be enough Whampoa schoolmates who will insist on setting up the Society," the officer said at last.

Chou sighed and, standing up to leave, offered his hand to the young officer. "For the unity of the revolution camp, the one thing you and I and all the true revolutionaries will keep fighting to preserve, I hope that nothing too bad will happen."

The organizers of the Sun Yat-sen Society, now alerted to the CCP's all-out effort to block them, called a meeting to approve their charter when the Eastern Expedition troops were pausing in Mei-hsien to regroup themselves. In order to forestall any disturbance by the radical left, about twenty right

wingers started the meeting two hours ahead of the schedule
with a senior KMT officer presiding.[24] But Li Chih-lung,[25]
the CCP commissar who was soon to be involved in the
Chung-shan Gunboat Incident, got word of it and stormed
into the meeting room. He gathered up a handful of the
mimeographed documents, statements and the charter,
waved them at the assembly, and shouted at the chairman,
"This organization runs counter to the policy of alliance with
Russia and acceptance of Communist Party members." He
demanded that the meeting be dismissed immediately, otherwise those present would be charged with violating party
discipline and insubordination. Someone in the audience
shouted him down. Li protested, "If you don't let me talk, I
will resign! What sort of democracy is this?" More shouting
followed.

Just as the chairman was wringing his hands without knowing what to do, Chou En-lai walked in. The chairman immediately asked Chou to take disciplinary action against Li for
improper conduct in front of a party superior. Chou pleaded
for calmness, promised that he would look into the whole
matter, and allowed Li to leave the room quietly. He also
persuaded the assembly to postpone the meeting.

The determination of the Sun Yat-sen Society organizers to
challenge the CCP was by no means placated by Chou En-
lai's order to transfer Li back to Canton, and they watched for
the first opportunity for revenge. It came when they inter-
cepted a message addressed to the South China Bureau of the
CCP by Chou En-lai's secretary,[26] reporting on the progress
of Communist influence on the division commander. Several
right wingers brought Chou's secretary, tied in ropes, before
Chiang Kai-shek, requesting that the man be punished for his
anti-revolutionary activity. Chou rushed to Chiang's office,
where he spent over an hour vouching for the loyalty of his
secretary and explaining that the CCP might have appeared
overzealous, but its first and last wish was the success of the

[1] After 1925, Chou was never again seen in public in a western suit like this. (The Bettmann Archive Inc.)

[2] Building from which Chou directed the August 1, 1927 Nachang Uprising.

[3] First All-China Congress of the Soviets at Juichin, Kiangsi, on November 5, 1931. Chou made it just in time to share the speaker's platform, after days of travel under disguise as a long-bearded missionary in a western clergyman's robe.

毛澤東同志在瑞金茅家屋住過的房子

朱德總司令在瑞金時的辦公室舊址

[4] The Command Headquarters of the Chinese Red Army where Chou spent most of his days, 1931-34, in Juichin, Kiangsi.

revolution. Above all, Chou pleaded, every effort must be made to avoid schism within the revolutionary ranks at a time when revolt was brewing in the Kwangtung, Kwangsi, and Yunnan troops, and the navy threatened to mutiny. He further suggested that he would rather see the Young Soldiers Association disbanded than have its opposition constantly find fault with it. Chiang gave his consent for Chou to transfer his secretary to another division, and the next time Chiang addressed his officers he told the Young Soldiers Association members and the organizers of the Sun Yat-sen Society to stand up, salute each other like good comrades, and forget their enmity. Chou En-lai on that occasion persuaded a senior KMT statesman[27] to respond to Chiang's admonition by assuring the Sun Yat-sen Society supporters that they need not be concerned about the Communists in their midst. "Once I was a Communist Party member myself," he said, "but there was neither any committee meeting for me to attend nor any party dues to pay. And I am still here. The Communist Party did not liquidate me." The assembled officers laughed. Because of the speaker's stature, the tension was temporarily relieved.

In addition to ideological disagreement, personal rivalry played a large part in the continuing left-right dispute among the Whampoa officers. Even troop commanders with no particular political prejudice became resentful of the CCP commissars and Russian advisers because of their constant interference. In December 1925, rightist agitators obtained authorization and financial support from Wang Ching-wei, Chairman of the KMT government, to inaugurate the Sun Yat-sen Society. Chou En-lai enlisted the help of the chief Russian adviser, Borodin, who threatened Wang with the withdrawal of all Russian aid if the organizers of the society could not be stopped. Wang had to lead a delegation[28] personally to plead with Borodin, who reluctantly yielded but warned Wang to be aware of the consequences.

Three months after Borodin's warning, the Chung-shan Gunboat Incident[29] occurred.

The KMT's navy, consisting of a number of gunboats, had been riddled with personnel problems. In May 1923 Sun Yat-sen had to replace all the captains to avert a mutiny; even so a series of rebellions followed, and Chiang Kai-shek was forced to assign trusted Whampoa officers to keep the boats under surveillance.[30] Early in 1926, the chief of the navy department, a Russian adviser, went on leave of absence, and Li Chih-lung, Chou En-lai's subordinate who had confronted the Sun Yat-sen Society organizers the year before, was appointed acting chief. Li's enemy in the society mobilized four persons[31] from the navy department, each with a personal grudge against Li, to deliver a forged order from Chiang Kai-shek to Li on March 18, 1926. Simultaneously the same four persons reported to Chiang Kai-shek, warning him of a sinister plot to kidnap him and take him to Russia.

Following the order supposedly from Chiang Kai-shek, Li dispatched two combat-ready gunboats, the Chung-shan and the Pao-pi, from Canton to Whampoa to await further instruction. The next day he received another message from the chief of naval operations advising him to have the Chung-shan, the largest vessel in the entire navy, ready in Canton for Russian advisers to inspect. Li telephoned Chiang Kai-shek directly for permission to recall the ship.

At first Chiang was somewhat skeptical about the secret report of a kidnap plot. Then, on the morning of March 19, 1926, he received three phone calls in succession from someone (whom he refused to identify) inquiring if he was going to Whampoa that day. His suspicions aroused, Chiang purposely stated over the phone that his plans for the day were still uncertain. About an hour later, Li Chih-lung's voice came on the other end of the phone. Only then did Chiang learn of the presence of the ships and the extra combat-ready troops on board. This seemed to confirm his suspicions, and he moved swiftly. He ordered the gunboat Chung-shan held for investigation, Li Chih-lung and over forty of his men put in jail, and the Russian advisers and CCP commissars removed from the army at once.

Surprised by the sudden arrest, Li could only repeat that he had acted under orders and explained that the extra soldiers on the boat had been assigned there by none other than the chairman of the KMT government, Wang Ching-wei, to prevent a recurrence of earlier mutinies.

The situation became grave. The quarters of the Russian advisers in Canton were besieged and their guards disarmed. The Russians protested to Chiang; Chiang apologized but insisted that they go home. On April 2, 1926, Teng Yen-ta, a left-wing KMT leader and Dean of Instruction at Whampoa (jailed and murdered in 1931), criticized Chiang's action and had a heated verbal exchange with him. The next day Chou En-lai and several Russian advisers called on Chiang to ask for an explanation. Chiang declared that under the circumstances he had to act resolutely and he alone would be responsible for the consequences. The same afternoon he proposed to the Central Committee that all Communists be purged from the KMT.

On April 11, 1926, Chiang fired Chou En-lai from the post of director of the First Army's political department. The next month Chou lost his second political post, special commissioner for the East River District.

Before Chou had time to attempt to pacify Chiang, he had to settle a dispute within the CCP stemming from the Chung-shan Gunboat Incident. Stepanoff, representing the Comintern, reprimanded the CCP members working within the KMT for their overbearing attitude and admonished them to make peace with Chiang.[32] Ch'en Tu-hsiu, secretary-general of the CCP, and the majority of the Central Committee in Shanghai supported Stepanoff. However, the Communist leaders in Kwangtung, except for Chou En-lai, favored a tough policy and drastic action against the KMT, and they had Borodin's backing. Chou expressed no personal preference for either policy. Instead he had lengthy talks with Borodin and his more impulsive comrades, urging them to be patient with Chiang because the CCP had as yet no troops under its direct control and a tough-line policy could very well lose the sympathy of the KMT left wing. The radical left finally accepted Chou's advice and offered the resignation of one of them[33] from the KMT army to placate Chiang.

Chou En-lai said nothing to Chiang about his dismissal, but his feverish work in Kwangtung to salvage the strained CCP-KMT relationship did not go unnoticed. Chiang realized that, short of ordering his troops to turn their guns on the Communists, the only hope of holding the CCP in check was through Chou En-lai. With enough trouble on hand already, Chiang simply could not afford an intraparty (the CCP was still considered part of the KMT at the time) vendetta. Therefore as a gesture of compromise on his part, he established an advanced training center for the CCP members and commissars withdrawn from the army and put Chou in charge.[34] Furthermore, he offered both the KMT and the CCP an equal opportunity to nominate candidates for the critical post of chief commissar of all the troops readied in July 1926, for the long-awaited Northern Expedition to fight the warlords. The CCP put up Chou and another senior Communist to compete with the KMT candidates.[35] A deadlock ensued, which Chou broke by drafting Teng Yen-ta, the leftist KMT leader, for the assignment. Because of Teng's complete confidence in Chou, he relied upon Chou to recommend men for his staff, and as a result the commissar system in the Northern Expeditionary army was once again dominated by Communists,[36] including Li Fu-ch'un, Chou's closest associate in Paris and now Vice-Premier in Peking.

For the CCP, the Chung-shan Gunboat Incident was a lesson, pointing up the weakness of the Party without military support. Just as Sun Yat-sen's fruitless struggle for sixteen years since 1911 had led him to accept Russian aid and found the Whampoa Military Academy, the CCP now learned to heed Stalin's advice "to overthrow the armed anti-revolutionary forces by arming the revolutionary forces."[37] But Chou En-lai's job to win direct control of the troops was difficult because Chiang made only his trusted students field commanders. Without an official post in Chiang's army and faced with continuing left-right clashes among the Whampoa graduates,[38] Chou had to depend upon his personal contact with the leftist commissars in the Northern Expeditionary troops to retain Communist influence over his former students at Whampoa and win new converts. For the success of his delicate politico-military work in Canton through the end of 1926, the CCP officially acknowledges its debt to him as the man who accomplished the most in laying a foundation for the future Chinese Red Army,[39] and consequently has reserved for him a permanent post on the Party's Military Committee.

During the most trying days in Canton, Chou was ably assisted by his wife, Teng Ying-ch'ao, whom he married in 1925. Their marriage has been an exemplary one among Chinese Communist couples.

Having come to share Chou's political ideas first during the May 4 Movement in Tientsin, then through correspondence with him while he was in Europe, Teng was encouraged to embrace the Communist cause by another CCP leader in Peking.[40] When she arrived in Canton to join Chou, she already was a member of both the CCP and the KMT. The latter assigned her to head up the women's department of Kwangtung Province, in which position she developed lasting friendships with the top KMT women leaders.[41]

A rather small, round-faced, energetic woman, she was a delightful match for her husband in making and keeping friends. Their house in Canton, furnished not lavishly but in good taste, became a favorite gathering place for both the

senior political leaders and junior Whampoa cadets. In spite
of her own heavy schedule, she never appeared too busy to
receive a visitor and make him feel at home. And after the
visitor had found out from her servant that the window curtain was Teng's choice and the dinner was prepared under
her own supervision, he walked away marveling at her ability
to maintain her own political life and be a good housewife
at the same time.

When Chou went with Chiang's troops on the expedi-
tions, Teng concentrated on the New Student Society, a
Communist-front organization she sponsored in Canton, rallying impressionable youth to support her husband's work.[42]
She was already a veteran in working with the students.
When Chou was still in Japan, Teng and her friends[43] in the
Girls Normal School of Tientsin had organized a Society
of Awakening (Chüeh-wu-she) which later supported the
demonstrations under Chou's leadership. When the Tientsin Student League needed operational funds, Teng was one
of Chou's most enthusiastic representatives to go around the
city collecting contributions.

Though impressively eloquent—at times outshining even
her husband—she never expressed any extreme views to
shock her KMT associates who elected her an alternate member of the Central Control Committee during the Second
KMT Congress in 1926. From that time on she remained
at her husband's side. Together they formed a team of able
organizers among the top-flight Communists, and a team of
talented diplomats whenever the CCP and the KMT were
on speaking terms.

Chiang Kai-shek's Northern Expeditionary army, starting
from Canton in July 1926, made good progress and by the
end of the year, it had become clear that the tide was turning
in Chiang's favor. A race began between the KMT and the
CCP to capture such political and economic centers as Han-

kow and Shanghai. The KMT pushed its army, while the CCP accelerated its political insurrection.

At first opposed to the Northern Expedition on the ground that the revolutionary forces in China were still too weak to be pitched in frontal attacks against the warlords,[44] the CCP quickly switched its position to go along with Chiang's troops. Thus when the Western Route army of the Northern Expedition reached Hankow, the Communists also reached there and promptly infiltrated the Hankow Government set up by the KMT under Wang Ching-wei.

The Eastern Route army of the Expedition drove through the provinces of Fukien and Chekiang, heading for Shanghai. Anticipating the imminent arrival of Chiang's troops, Ch'en Tu-hsiu, the CCP's secretary-general, called a meeting of the Communist leaders in Chekiang and Kiangsu Provinces to map insurrections in the various cities. His blueprint called for mass meetings to create people's assemblies that would replace the local governments. "If peaceful mass meetings are impossible, then spring an armed revolt!"

In Shanghai, the largest industrial center in China, both CCP and KMT agents[45] started organizing the laborers, the former for seizure of the local government, the latter to facilitate the entry of the Expeditionary army. Since both were aiming at undermining warlord and local control in Shanghai, the agents of the two parties at first worked quite closely together. On October 23, 1926, a premature revolt was touched off involving several thousand striking workers, only a small portion of whom were armed. Inadequate coordination caused the revolt to fizzle, with the loss of two automobile workers.

Shortly after the failure of the first revolt, Chou En-lai arrived in Shanghai. In his apartment at 29 rue Lafayette, he worked with Ch'en Yen-nien and Chao Shih-yen, both his comrades in Europe, to strengthen the indoctrination of the political workers in labor unions and smuggle arms for the strikers. In February 1927, the troops of the warlord occupy-

ing the Shanghai area retreated[46] in the north. As panic
spread in Shanghai, Chou ordered a general strike on February 20, to overthrow the warlord and greet the Northern
Expeditionary army. Over 500,000 workers responded. The
warlord summoned reinforcements from his fresh troops outside the city and, with the help of the International Concession police, destroyed the armed squads of strikers. About
a hundred were killed in the skirmishes, several hundred more
were jailed. Two days later, a large number of the demoralized
strikers went back to work, and the Shanghai Federation of
Labor was forced to call off the strike.

The disastrous result of the second revolt alarmed Chou
and his lieutenants. They were rapidly losing the race to the
KMT because the Northern Expeditionary army was moving
closer and closer to the suburb of Shanghai. Without waiting
any longer for the downfall of the warlord and a mass meeting, Chou proceeded to set up an underground city council
for Shanghai and a provincial council for Kiangsu[47] ready
to assume control at a moment's notice. At the same time
he pressed for a third revolt.

The KMT agents were also alarmed as they watched the
progress of the second revolt. They realized that the Communists were bent on setting up a Soviet-type government
in Shanghai, and, if a general strike delivered the city to the
Communists, the entry of the Expeditionary army would be
challenged. The KMT agents began to work on the city garrison commander[48] and before long succeeded in reaching
an agreement with him whereby he would surrender the city
to the advancing KMT troops. Word of the agreement
reached the Expeditionary army, and the KMT was about
to celebrate its strifeless victory in Shanghai when Chou
issued the strike order in the city.

In the evening of March 20, 1927, Chou personally led 300
armed labor-union guards who stormed the Post Office building and moved on to occupy Police Headquarters and the
Ordnance Depot. Altogether seven rebel columns went into

action. One column advanced toward the railroad station, seized it, and halted all rail transportation. Without the use of the railroad, Chiang Kai-shek's Expeditionary army was temporarily blocked from entering the city.

For three weeks the fate of Shanghai hung in suspense. In town Chou En-lai and his comrades installed the city council, but scattered clashes continued. Outside the city the bulk of Chiang Kai-shek's troops[49] took up their positions and waited for clarification. It came on April 12, and the bloodbath began.

The entering KMT troops had orders to shoot every armed man at sight and establish control over the city. Chou En-lai's labor-union squads resisted, and street fighting flared up. In the confusion many guards organized by the KMT agents also fell by mistake. The CCP leaders scattered. Ch'en Tu-hsiu, the secretary-general, found shelter in the house of a merchant friend who managed to smuggle him out of the city. Chou En-lai hid in the building of the Commercial Press for some time and escaped only minutes before the KMT search party reached his hideout. Under torture a number of arrested Communists betrayed their underground comrades who were rounded up and shot after dark in the Lunghua suburb. For months the rumble of KMT military trucks on the road to Lung-hua nightly spelled death to Chou's followers. On June 29, Ch'en Yen-nien was arrested and executed. Four days later he was joined by Chao Shih-yen. Over twenty of the Red-sponsored Shanghai municipal council also shared the same fate.

Dodging the KMT police who had posted his photograph at railroad stations, Chou En-lai made his escape to Hankow, where he joined Ch'en Tu-hsiu and the few Central Committee members who had survived the Shanghai purge to plan the Fifth Party Congress, scheduled for May 1, 1927. The left-wing KMT government at Hankow had not gone along with Chiang Kai-shek in his purge of the Communists, and Chou, staying in the house of the chief of political de-

partment of the KMT government there, found himself surrounded by old friends and former subordinates, including
Ch'en Yi.[50]

The question of just what had gone wrong in Shanghai
took up most of the meeting time during the Fifth CCP
Congress. Ch'en Tu-hsiu reappraised the situation and reiterated that he had been right in advocating a political erosion
of the KMT because the premature armed revolts in Shanghai proved catastrophic. Chou En-lai, however, held that in
view of the successful Communist infiltration of the Hankow
government, which was the only legitimate KMT government, there seemed to be no need to stress political infiltration any further. On the other hand, the decision by Chiang
Kai-shek, the military chief, on April 12, 1927, had nearly
brought an abrupt end to the entire Chinese Communist
movement. Therefore, he argued, the CCP should henceforth
concentrate on winning over the military.[51]

In the re-election of party officials Chou En-lai became
secretary-general, while Ch'en Tu-hsiu, Chang Kuo-tao (one
of the original thirteen at the first CCP Congress), and Li
Wei-han (of Chou's Paris group) made up the Central Committee's Executive Committee. Soon Chou handed the number one party post to Ts'ai Ho-sen,[52] another of his Paris
group, in order to concentrate on his job as head of the
Party's military department, which had become his specialty.

The CCP suffered a severe defeat in the Shanghai revolts,
but Chou, the chief strategist, emerged from them trium-
phant. He was elevated to the Central Committee and there
he has remained within the top three of the party hierarchy
until today.

CHAPTER 5

BAPTISM IN BLOOD

ON APRIL 4, 1927, when skirmishes between the strikers, war-lord troops and KMT advanced units were in progress in the streets, Chou En-lai was seen walking alone toward the customs building in Shanghai where Wang Ching-wei, the KMT left-wing leader and chairman of the KMT government, was lodged after his recent return from Europe. Chou identified himself to an aid who took him into a room adjacent to Wang's bedroom and immediately closed the door. As Wang came out to shake hands with Chou and offered him a seat, the aid observed how youthful both of them looked. Though sixteen years Chou's senior, Wang, the one-time would-be assassin of the Manchu Imperial Regent, looked as boyish as his visitor, both clean-shaven, with clear, lustrous eyes and heavy black eyebrows, Wang's drooping a little at the corners. Chou produced a folded paper from his pocket and handed it to Wang, then leaned back to watch the latter read.[1]

"Comrade Ch'en Tu-hsiu drafted the statement himself," Chou said, after Wang had finished reading it. "If you sign it now, I can have it distributed tonight."

"It seems to cover all we agreed to say yesterday, but . . ." Wang paused to reach for the telephone. He checked with Chou to make certain where he could reach Ch'en and had a fairly long conversation with him on the phone, rereading aloud some parts of the statement. Chou sat still and listened. When Wang finished his phone call, he walked back

to his room and a few minutes later returned with the signed
statement for Chou.

That night right-wing KMT leaders pored over the statement, which Chou had just released. It was a joint declaration
by the CCP and the KMT stressing the need to cement
their alliance and dispel the rumor that "the CCP is preparing
to form a worker's government to overthrow the KMT . . .
while the KMT intends to make war on the Communists,
suppress the labor unions and dissolve their self-defense
squads . . ."

Although Chiang Kai-shek himself had declared the day
before that Wang Ching-wei was to take back the reins of
the KMT government the moment he returned to China, his
right-wing extremist colleagues had started preparing for the
coup to purge the Communists in Shanghai. The municipal
council, clearly dominated by the CCP, was their target, and
to remove the council they had to destroy all the Communist-
controlled armed strikers first. Wang Ching-wei sensed the
imminent outbreak of violence and, while still urging a high-
level meeting in Nanking to unify the parties and factions,
secretly left Shanghai for Hankow where the left-wing KMT
government under his leadership promptly denounced Chiang
Kai-shek for ordering the April 12 purge in Shanghai and
ousted him from the Nationalist Party. The next day (April
18, 1927) Chiang set up his KMT government in Nanking,
renounced the Wang regime in Hankow, and reiterated his
determination to complete the nationwide anti-Communist
purge.

The refuge Chou En-lai and his surviving comrades found
under Wang's regime in Hankow turned out to be only temporary. Less than three months later, the left-wing KMT in
Hankow, while not yet reconciled with Chiang Kai-shek, also
found it necessary to part company with the Communists.

In the Hunan-Hupeh area of which Hankow was the
center, Communist agents under Mao Tse-tung had succeeded in organizing some two million peasants into peasant

OUTER
MONGOLIA

Harbin

Changchun

Ssupingchieh

Mukden

Chi-ning

Kuei-sui

Changchiakou

Peking

GREAT WALL

Wangchiawan

Yenan

Yellow River

Huai-an

Kao-yu

Shanghai

Sian

Nanking

Shao-hsing

Hankow

Yangtze River

Nanchang

Chungking

Changsha

Taipei

Canton

Hong Kong

Nanchang Uprising directed by Chou En-lai August 1, 1927.

associations to seize land and form their own government. Mao, who attended the first CCP Congress in Shanghai in 1921 as a delegate from the Hunan area and who worked for KMT-CCP co-operation until the summer of 1925, had gone to Canton where his talent as a specialist in the peasant movement was not particularly appreciated in spite of his position on the Central Executive Committee of the KMT and his acquaintance with such KMT leaders as Tai Ch'uan-hsien (first chief of the political department at Whampoa Academy) and Wang Ching-wei (first KMT government head after Sun Yat-sen). Mao's writings were excluded from the official publications of the CCP's Central Committee, which most frequently featured articles by Chou En-lai and Ch'en Tu-hsiu. During his few months in Canton, Mao had little direct contact with Chou, who enjoyed greater popularity among the KMT leaders and therefore functioned as a more trusted liaison between the two parties. Soon after the Chung-shan Gunboat Incident, Mao went back to Hunan to resume his organization work among the peasants.

By April 1, 1927, the peasant associations promoted by Mao in the Hunan-Hupeh area had set up "people's courts" to try the landlords and local bosses who refused to surrender their property. In the cities, militant labor unions were organized after the Shanghai fashion to prepare for insurrections. These developments posed a threat to many military leaders who supported the Hankow government but were not necessarily enthusiastic about communism. On May 19, when an army commander's[2] father was harassed by some labor unionists in the city of Changsha, he protested to the Hankow government, and two days later his subordinate, a regimental commander,[3] ordered his men to open fire on the strikers, killing over a hundred Communists and arresting many more.

The commissar of the army responsible for the clash, a CCP member named Liu Ning, launched a propaganda campaign to denounce the regimental commander as a butcher of revolutionary comrades. Chou En-lai saw the posters in Hankow and, as head of the CCP's Military Department, he reprimanded Liu for further aggravating the already strained relations with the left-wing KMT.

"What do you mean?" Liu protested. "Are we somebody's concubine? Are we to accept their spitting and beating without any right to speak up in protest?"[4]

"Comrade Liu," Chou said, "we must be patient. For the sake of our revolution we must be very patient. For the sake of our revolution we can play the role of a concubine, even of a prostitute, if need be . . ."

Still unconvinced, Liu went to see Ch'en Tu-hsiu, the CCP's secretary-general. Ch'en told him that all comrades must support the Party's policy, which was alliance with the KMT left wing to win over the middle-of-the-roaders and destroy the right wing. Ch'en himself had some reservations about the feasibility of preserving such an alliance, but he said that Chou was acting strictly in accordance with the Party's directive.

The CCP, still without military backing or an established base of operation, had to follow faithfully its only ideological and material supporter, the Comintern. As Stalin triumphed over Trotsky in the Comintern, the directives from Moscow repeatedly exhorted the CCP to stay with the left-wing KMT. Just as Chou En-lai was making every effort to prevent further deterioration of the situation after the May 21 outbreak, another directive from Stalin reached Hankow on June 1, 1927, urging the Chinese comrades to seize political leadership of the KMT and infiltrate the KMT army with 70,000 trained Communists. In order to destroy the right-wing KMT, Stalin advised, the CCP must maneuver to have only left-wingers in charge of all the legal courts to deal with the anti-revolutionaries, military or civilian. At the same time Stalin also asked to have the peasant movement of land confiscation accelerated.[5]

Stalin was in effect asking the CCP to do the impossible —to stay within the left-wing KMT and simultaneously to develop local Soviets in the various parts of China to replace the KMT government. Wang Ching-wei was not ready to surrender to the CCP, and, even if he were, his military backing was no match for Chiang Kai-shek's. To make matters worse, M. N. Roy, the Comintern envoy who was a Trotsky sympathizer and disagreed with Borodin, after some hesitation showed the secret directive to Wang Ching-wei.[6] The left-wing KMT leaders were shocked and immediately prepared to expel the Communists from their midst.

To attempt the impossible ordered by Stalin and, more immediately, to deal with the tense situation in Hankow, Ch'en Tu-hsiu called an emergency conference of his Central Committee. "The Hankow government has already surrendered to Chiang Kai-shek," he said. "If we don't adjust our policy, we will also be selling out to Chiang." An awkward silence followed, then Chou summed up the dilemma by saying, "If we got out of the KMT, it would be more convenient to push our worker-peasant movement, but our military activities would suffer." After a series of such meetings, Chou finally, with great reluctance, supported Ch'en Tu-hsiu on two resolutions in the Central Committee on June 20 and July 3, which, if carried out to the full, could change the alliance into a complete surrender because they directed all the comrades to lay down their arms and take orders only from the KMT government.[7]

In accordance with these resolutions, Chou went to the residence of Borodin, whose wife had just been arrested by the soldiers of a northern warlord,[8] to discuss conciliatory gestures toward the left-wing KMT. The army commander, whose father had been harassed by Red workers in Changsha in May, had started an anti-Communist purge within his army, and the purge threatened to spread into the divisions under General Chang Fa-k'uei, the real strength behind the Hankow KMT government. Borodin and several other CCP leaders at the conference were uncertain about General Chang's political stand, but Chou, speaking for the CCP's military department, insisted on appeasing Chang by having the Communist-controlled labor-union guards surrender their arms to and join General Chang's army. "This way," Chou said, "we would demonstrate our good will to Chang and through him to the Hankow government, while strengthening our infiltration in his army."[9]

But before much could be done to relax the tension, the Hankow government acted. On July 20, 1927, a ruthless purge began, and Chou had to repeat his Shanghai experience of three months before, keeping just a few steps ahead of the Hankow police.

Roy left China. His replacement, Besso Lominadze, a peppery Georgian the same age as Chou En-lai, and Stalin's confidant, arrived to make sure that the CCP conformed to Comintern instructions. He felt, together with some CCP leaders, that the revolutionary high tide for insurrections had arrived. Thus the CCP's Central Committee, while continuing to claim that they had not walked out on the progressive left-wing KMT, accelerated preparations for armed revolts to establish Soviet-type regimes in various areas. Plans were completed to instigate peasant uprisings in Hunan, Honan, Kiangsi and Kwangtung Provinces where Communist infiltration of the peasantry had met with greater success than elsewhere. The time for action was set for the harvest season of that year, and the place selected to ignite the first spark in the string of explosions was the city of Nanchang, the economic and political center of Kiangsi Province.[10]

To prepare for the uprising, Chou reached Nanchang on July 25, 1927 to join Chu Teh, senior officer from Yunnan who had returned from Germany and was serving as commander of the instructors' corps for three armies and chief of Nanchang security forces. A day later, Li Li-san, Hsü T'e-li, and Nieh Jung-chen, all Chou's associates in his Paris days, also arrived. They were followed by Generals Ho Lung and Yeh T'ing who brought their troops close to Nanchang, setting up temporary command posts in the Kiangsi Hotel in town. On July 27, Chou held a meeting with the CCP leaders on the scene who elected him to head up a Frontline Committee in charge of the operation, with headquarters located adjacent to General Yeh T'ing's in the same hotel. Chou set the zero hour at 4 A.M. on August 1, 1927, and went to inform Ho Lung himself.

A professional soldier from Hunan known for his reticence, Ho had not expected action so soon. But his immediate response was, "I accept the Chinese Communist Party's orders and I shall carry them out."[11]

A junior officer in Ho's army betrayed the Communist plot to the Hankow KMT faction.[12] On July 29, Wang Ching-wei and several political and military leaders[13] of the Hankow government rushed to Lushan near Nanchang and ordered Ho and Yeh to lead their troops back to Kiukiang, about sixty miles north of Nanchang. A house-to-house search was started in Kiukiang to round up the Communists.

Chou ordered a counter-measure in Nanchang to arrest all the right-wing KMT agents and seize the city bank. Ho Lung and Yeh T'ing, ignoring the KMT order, summoned their subordinates for emergency conferences in the afternoon of July 29 to pledge support to the Communist cause. Another day passed in tense expectation. Chou sized up the rapidly changing situation and decided to advance the zero hour. The signal was given at midnight, July 31. Thirty thousand troops under Chu Teh, Ho Lung, and Yeh T'ing raised the banner of revolt. Fighting continued in Nanchang for five hours before the Communists gained control of the city.[14]

The mass rally on August 2 before the Pao-tien Gate in Nanchang listened to Chou announce the establishment of a new regime, called the [Kuomintang] Central Revolutionary Committee, with several left-wing KMT leaders heading the list.[15] Below the committee, there were five departments in the new administration. Military affairs were handled by a staff corps under Chou's personal supervision. The old KMT designations of the armies were preserved but regrouped under a unified command with Ho Lung in charge.

Chou further announced to the people of Nanchang that the new regime would promptly implement land reform, establish rural self-governments, and consolidate the revolutionary forces.

Back in the hotel room used as the revolutionary headquarters, Chou was busy receiving Communist leaders who, upon hearing of the new regime, had rushed to Nanchang. Among them was Liu Ning, the commissar who had quarreled with Chou about the "concubine" role of the CCP in Changsha. Chou put him in charge of the propaganda department and told him to draft a manifesto on the August 1 Uprising. Liu prepared to take notes as Chou dictated an outline to him.

The Kuomintang under the leadership of Sun Yat-sen, Chou said, was indisputably the proper vehicle for China's national revolution. After Sun's death, party leadership was properly assumed by Liao Chung-k'ai. With the assassination of Liao, the Kuomintang had lost its revolutionary spirit. The Central Revolutionary Committee was established in Nanchang to carry on from where the KMT had left off.

Liu interrupted Chou to ask, "Since all of us are Communists, how can you say that the Central Revolutionary Committee is pushing forward to accomplish the KMT's unfinished mission?"

After a moment's reflection, Chou said, "Aren't we all at the same time also members of the Nationalist Party?" And he gave Liu a second assignment to draft a policy statement on land reform, calling for confiscation of land holdings in excess of 200 mu (about 32 acres).[16]

General Chang Fa-k'uei, Yeh T'ing's superior, who had been approached by the CCP but had chosen to stick to Wang Ching-wei, was now ordered by Wang to cordon off

Nanchang with his troops. The Communist rule in Nanchang, under the name of left-wing KMT, lasted only two
days. On August 4 Chou En-lai ordered a withdrawal, heading south toward Kwangtung Province. The insurrectionist
troops were split up into three groups, all of which ran into
KMT armies and fought pitched battles along the retreat
routes. Chu Teh[17] led the 35th Division to guard the San-
ho-pa line and later fled eastward into Fukien Province.
Thence they wound their way from Hsün-wu to Pei-chiang,
joining Mao Tse-tung at Chingkangshan in Kiangsi Province the next year to found the Kiangsi Soviet, the first CCP
base of real strength. Two other divisions[18] under Chu Teh
struck out in a different direction, were ambushed by superior
KMT forces at Ma-shih, and surrendered. Chou En-lai, Ho
Lung, and Yeh T'ing went toward Swatow with the Central
Revolutionary Committee and the rest of the CCP troops.
On September 23 and 24, 1927, Chou and his men paused
in the Swatow area where they encountered a sustained KMT
attack. Although he was ill with a fever of 104 degrees, Chou
stayed on the front line to direct the troops under punishing
enemy fire.[19]

Outnumbered and overpowered, Chou ordered his men to
fall back toward the southeastern coastal cities of Hai-feng
and Lu-feng (known as the Hai-lu-feng area). The VIPs of the
Central Revolutionary Committee were covered by the
newly reinforced Security Guard Regiment under Kung Ch'u
(who later defected during the Long March of 1935). Kung
dispatched one battalion to escort them via sampan to
P'u-ning about ten miles further inland on the Nan-ch'i
River. From P'u-ning Chou and the other top CCP leaders
walked on foot to the nearby village, Liu-sha, where they
held an emergency strategy conference in a small Catholic
church. It was decided that Ho Lung and Yeh T'ing would
lead the beleaguered troops to the Hai-lu-feng area, while
the rest of the leaders would escape to Hong Kong in whatever way they could to await further instructions.

The KMT troops[20] closed in, blocking Chou's retreat route. In the ensuing battle, Chou and his comrades lost everything they had with them, including several dozen baskets full of silver dollars, the only treasury reserve for the Central Revolutionary Committee. The ailing Chou had been riding on a stretcher, but in the confusion the carriers fled, leaving him to negotiate his own way on foot. Two orderlies half-carried and half-dragged him to escape by way of a dry ditch at night. Autumn chill assailed him and aggravated his fever; he groaned with every step he took.

The painful overnight trudge ended the next morning at the coastal town of Chia-tzu, where Chou waved his comrades on their way to Hong Kong in separate sampans. He himself decided to stay with the troops and go to Hai-lu-feng, which was only a few miles to the west. But even a few miles proved to be too much for his condition, and he was forced to stop for the night in another little village. There he yielded to persuasion that he get immediate medical attention in Hong Kong. When he was being carried on board a hired sampan, he told Kung Ch'u[21] to lead what was left of the Central Revolutionary Committee, about a hundred cadres and key staff members together with some twenty or so guards, to the Chin-hsiang-chen village in Lu-feng where they were to turn their arms and equipment over to the local CCP-directed peasant association, and then proceed individually to Hong Kong to join him. Sick, penniless, and in tatters, Chou entrusted his fate to the coastal winds and tides off the Kwangtung shore. He managed to reach Hong Kong, but for quite a few days before he established his contact there, he and his most unimpressive entourage had to share the meager fare of the ricksha pullers at roadside food stalls.[22]

The CCP chiefs thus temporarily parted their ways. Under Chou's order, Yeh T'ing led the remnants of the CCP troops to Hai-lu-feng where he joined another CCP leader,[23] who had been cultivating peasant associations there, to establish

the very first Chinese Soviet regime. Now that they had
dropped all pretense of being part of the left-wing KMT, they
renamed their reinforced troops the Worker-Peasant Revolutionary Army. Ho Lung went to the Hunan-Hupeh border
area to stake out a base of his own. Chu Teh hid under
the protection of a Kwangtung warlord[24] for a while, then
fought his way to Kiangsi to join Mao Tse-tung.[25]

Some Communist historians blame the failure of the Nanchang Uprising on its inadequate preparation, or on the "im-
pure" composition of the Central Revolutionary Committee,
or on the lack of co-ordination of peasant uprisings in South
China.[26] They criticize the leadership of the CCP of 1927,
but they do not criticize Chou En-lai, in spite of the fact
that he was the masterminder. The failure at Nanchang actually added a unique distinction to Chou's service record:
he was hailed as the person who led the CCP out of its
parasitic existence within the KMT to independence. At
Nanchang, the CCP came of age, and the date, August 1,
has been officially observed as the Chinese Red Army Day
ever since.

While Chou was fleeing Nanchang for his life, the few
Central Committee members of the CCP not involved in
the revolt were brought together by Lominadze for an urgent
conference in Hankow on August 7, 1927.[27] Ch'en Tu-hsiu
was accused, in absentia, of being a rightist opportunist who
attempted to surrender to the KMT, and was removed from
leadership. Chou En-lai, also in absentia, together with two
other veterans of his Paris group, was elected to team up
with a Moscow-trained new leader, Ch'ü Ch'iu-pai (executed
by the KMT in 1935).[28] After the day-long meeting, the
new CCP leadership hurried back to Shanghai to direct its
policy of more armed revolts,[29] with Chou still running for
his life between Nanchang and Swatow.

A series of violent insurrections followed. In Hunan, Mao
Tse-tung filled the second and third week of September 1927

with peasant uprisings. In Hupeh, Hsiang Ying, who was to compete with Mao Tse-tung for leadership in the Kiangsi Soviet, responded with a wave of revolts that he directed. The Hai-lu-feng Soviet on the coast waged a campaign of expansion toward the end of October, and in Kiangsu and Chekiang, the heartland of China's political life, the uprisings were organized by Chou En-lai.

His health recovered, Chou returned from Hong Kong to Shanghai in October 1927. As soon as he moved into a small Western-style house on the Wei-hai-wei Road, he sought out his underground comrades and plunged into feverish rounds of conferences to plan the revolts. Liu Ning, who had quarreled with Chou over the May 21 incident in Changsha, found Chou on October 28, 1927. For three hours Chou briefed Liu on the current situation, explaining that the CCP's Central Committee had divided the country into five regions for the purpose of planning insurrections, and that the Kiangsu-Chekiang area was his responsibility. Before parting, Chou put Liu on the CCP's Chekiang Province committee and told him to start planning a revolt in the beautiful West Lake area near Hangchow.

Armed with Chou's instructions, Liu went to Hangchow where he discovered much to his dismay that the local CCP membership consisted of only seven. He appealed to the provincial party branch chief who told him, "If everyone of your seven comrades each set fire to a house, there would be seven houses on fire, wouldn't there?" Disturbed and perplexed, Liu went back to see Chou. Chou was giving instruction to another comrade of the Chekiang province.[30] After listening to his worry, Chou assured him that there was sufficient support in the Hangchow area for a revolt.

"I have approached the commander of the Provincial Garrison.[31] He has about two companies of soldiers and with no more than five or six hundred silver dollars we can get them to start a mutiny for us. There are also around sixty

comrades among the 700 held in the KMT's military stockade. At our signal they can engineer a bastille to support
us . . ."

"But what about the masses?" asked Liu. "Without support of the masses we are going to have another Nanchang,
only in miniature."

"You are new here and you haven't done your homework
well enough," Chou said, exchanging a smile with the other
comrade in the room. "In the areas surrounding the West
Lake we have several dozen trustworthy comrades who command the confidence of over 10,000 farmers covering a broad
region."

At the conclusion of the conference, Chou gave Liu a
schedule of action: The soldiers, bribed to revolt, would
storm the stockade to release the prisoners. The mutineers
would form a Red Army to attack the provincial government.
If successful, the insurgents would establish a Soviet regime
in Hangchow. If anything went wrong, the men would retreat to the West Lake area to regroup for a second try. If
they failed again, they would move northward. Liu found
himself the head of a special revolutionary local committee
with its operational base in the O-no village. D-day was set
on the twenty-eighth day of the twelfth month according
to the old lunar calendar of the farmers.

"At the end of the year," Chou added after finishing his
instructions, "cold and hunger will put the peasants in the
right mood for revolt. Your assault on the richest and most
hated local landlord family will rally all the villagers behind
you."

"Shall I strike without waiting for the soldiers?" Liu asked.

"Yes, you go ahead first. The burning house of the local
tyrant will spark action," said Chou.

The hour arrived. The insurgents gathered around the target house. But word had reached the garrison troops and police in town, and they rushed to the rescue of the besieged

family. Liu fled, without the torch he had prepared for setting the house on fire. One Communist of the district[32] and about a dozen of his fellow peasants were arrested and executed.[33]

CHAPTER 6

INFALLIBLE BOLSHEVIK
AND IMPECCABLE FILIAL SON

EARLY IN SEPTEMBER 1928 Bukharin sat across the table from
Chou En-lai in a small conference room in Moscow, going
over some of the preparations for the imminent Sixth Congress of the CCP scheduled to take place as a rump session
to the Sixth World Congress of the Comintern. The weather
was still warm, but the slight flush on Chou's face—something rarely seen on him since his early Nankai Middle School
days—had little to do with the heat.

In a voice befitting his status (which he was soon to lose)
as Stalin's equal, Bukharin said with his eyes fixed on Chou,
"Comrade Chou En-lai, you have been in charge of military
affairs for the Chinese Communist Party. You should have
been able to estimate the strength of your men a little more
accurately. And if you had done so, there would not have
been such repeated disasters—plainly blind actions of armed
revolt."[1]

The slow process of oral translation by an interpreter
cushioned Bukharin's barb, and Chou did not immediately
respond to his Russian senior, who went on to berate Ch'ü
Ch'iu-pai, sitting next to Chou, for his faulty leadership of
the CCP, which verged on "playing with insurrections."

Chou and his fellow CCP leaders had been in Moscow
listening to the Comintern's agonizing reappraisal of the
Chinese situation for several weeks already. Six months be-

fore, Stalin and Bukharin had set up a special committee in the Comintern to investigate the failures of armed revolts in China, and had come up with a resolution, which, in the self-contradictory manner typical of Stalin, severely condemned the CCP's leadership for miscalculation of the Chinese revolutionary situation, while in the same breath it urged the CCP to work harder at building an effective Red Army and establishing local Soviets.

And the CCP Sixth Congress, which had to be held in Moscow because of increasing KMT pressure at home, carried on the reappraisal under the watchful eyes of Stalin and Bukharin, who told Chou En-lai and his Chinese comrades to go home to win the masses, build a Red Army, and establish more local Soviet regimes in anticipation of "an upsurge of the high tide of world revolution which is imminent!" Ch'ü Ch'iu-pai, the CCP leader fostered by the Comintern agent Lominadze during the August 7 (1927) Emergency Conference in Hankow, was now detained in Moscow to rethink his errors. Chou En-lai, Li Li-san, and Hsiang Chung-fa, formerly a boatman (executed by the KMT in 1931), were elected to steer the CCP.

Thus, mildly chafed but left in charge of the CCP's military department, Chou returned to China in the early fall of 1928 to rejuvenate, or rather revive, a Communist Party that had been all but wiped out by the KMT after the series of abortive armed revolts and the subsequent "reign of white terror."[2] Soon he was given the additional assignment of head of the organization department, which gave him the official responsibility of rebuilding the Party and starting a Red Army.

He saw his two jobs as one and inseparable. Every Communist comrade must be an effective propagandist and party worker in politics, as well as a combat soldier when ordered to the battlefield. In the urban centers, he instructed the militant labor unions to go underground to preserve their strength. While waiting for the "revolutionary high tide," the comrades were told to develop such publicly acceptable front

organizations as athletic clubs, study groups, and welfare organizations. In rural areas he sent his agents to continue
agitating for the organization of peasant associations, but, he
told them, "hide your arms and don't start any revolt until
the Central Committee specifically tells you."[3]

Through a clandestine mimeographed circular called *Central Military Communique*, which he edited, he co-ordinated
the development of a number of Communist army units of
varying sizes and types scattered throughout the country,
each occupying an area and carrying on guerrilla warfare with
Chiang Kai-shek's troops. The motley origin of the Red
troops, ranging from defected KMT soldiers to bandits and
hunger-stricken peasants, necessitated urgent political indoctrination, retraining, and re-outfitting. Above all, their leaders
held different views on Chinese revolution and looked up to
the guidance of the CCP's Central Committee with varying
degrees of enthusiasm. Chou En-lai's job was to knead these
scattered bands of dubious dedication and strength into a
mighty Red Army under one unified central command. The
progress was slow but, aided by the continuing civil war
among the warlords and the worsening life of the poor, Chou
was able by the beginning of 1930 to count fourteen Communist armies of which the two under Mao Tse-tung and
Chu Teh at Chingkangshan on the Hunan-Kiangsi border
were most redoubtable. Chou described the experience of
Mao Tse-tung and Chu Teh in building their two armies
and urged the other Red troop commanders to emulate them.
"Many valuable experiences can be found here," said Chou,
"and they are all unique in China, heretofore unseen and
unheard of . . . All the Party branches and Red Army units
throughout the country ought to learn from these experiences."[4]

The major difficulty confronting Chou En-lai was the lack
of a secure base of operation. He and his Central Committee comrades operated in hiding in Shanghai, while the
Communist units were scattered far and wide. Therefore, in

1930, he had to pull in the reins, contrary to Party chief Li Li-san's wish, and modify the demand to centralize the Red Army command while continuing to urge caution against un-calculated risks of scattered guerrilla warfare. He was severe in his criticism of the substandard quality of the combat-readiness of the Red troops, and he spoke out against the loose discipline among some of them, but, knowing that it was impractical, he opposed the Central Committee's wish that he give orders directly to the troops.[5] It has since become clear that Chou's modifying influence, as shown in his policy of 1928–30, saved the Party and the Red Army from total disintegration.

Disintegration remained a constant threat to the CCP during 1928–31. On the one hand, the Central Committee led by Li Li-san disagreed with Mao Tse-tung in the field; Chou En-lai had to try to reconcile the disagreement and uphold the theoretical supremacy of the former. Then Li Li-san disagreed with the Comintern; and Chou En-lai had to explain away the difference and uphold the latter. Before this period of intense intraparty strife was over, Chou was to reprimand Mao Tse-tung, apologize for Li Li-san, and witness the liquidation of hundreds of troops, their commanders, and some members of the Central Committee.

Li Li-san as secretary-general of the CCP had the main responsibility of interpreting Comintern directives, and he did not hesitate to assert himself. "Our revolution needs a Lenin," he said to Chou En-lai one day. "Our revolution needs a man like me," he said to Chou the next day.[6] Putting the two remarks together, Chou realized that he had a problem on his hands.

Fortunately, Hsiang Chung-fa, the boatman, was not an assertive personality, and at least within the triumvirate leadership of the CCP's Central Committee operating underground in Shanghai, Chou could knock heads together and manage to keep a unified voice that spoke for the Party's highest authority. When soft-spoken words failed, Chou had to crack the whip. "There is an historical tradition in the party that stresses the importance of intraparty peace," he said. "To allow this concept to prevail all the time would tend to becloud the correct party line, reduce the level of the comrades' political alertness, and consequently harm party unity and retard progress . . . Only through relentless struggle in behalf of the correct party line can true party unity be achieved . . ."[7]

Unity was not, however, easily achieved, especially when the CCP was caught between its need to side with Russia and a rising nationalism without which no revolution in China could be sustained. From the spring of 1927 to the summer of 1929, relations between China (first the warlords, then Chiang Kai-shek's Nanking government) and Russia became increasingly strained and finally broke altogether, as a result of the KMT's raids on the Russian embassy and consulates and its seizure of documents that spelled out a plot to Sovietize China, and of Russian troop movements in Manchuria. Li Li-san declared that the CCP would fight to defend Russia if war broke out; Ch'en Tu-hsiu, already disgraced at the Sixth Congress of the CCP in Moscow (September 1928), objected; in the summer of 1929 he and his faction of Communist leaders were charged with Trotskyism and expelled from the CCP. The CCP suffered a great loss.

The gathering strength of Mao Tse-tung at Chingkangshan rapidly developed into a challenge to the authority of the CCP's Central Committee. Twice in the spring of 1929 he defied Li Li-san's order, refusing to surrender his military command or even to go to Shanghai for conference. Li, the self-styled Lenin of China, believed that the revolutionary high tide was really coming, as the Comintern had repeatedly predicted, and asked the military forces in the countryside to march on the urban centers and seize national power. Mao Tse-tung preferred to stay in the mountain fastness of Hunan and Kiangsi to nurture his strength. Finally, Li won with a Central Committee resolution on June 11, 1930, calling for all the scattered Soviet bases to send their troops into action.

On July 30, Mao obeyed and attacked Changsha and Hankow. His army failed to seize either and, after occupying the small city of Chi-an briefly, was forced to retreat back to the mountain bastion. The failure vindicated Mao's policy, but was another serious loss for the CCP.

Hardly having had time to work out the difference between Mao and Li, Chou En-lai now found that the troops and field staff of the party offices, many of them appointed by himself and supposedly loyal to the Central Committee, were taking sides in the Mao-Li dispute. Skirmishes among the Communist troops increased as some of them began to doubt the wisdom of the Central Committee's policy of "fighting for Russia" and others wavered under the mounting pressure of Chiang Kai-shek's troops. In early December 1930, a number of these restless troop commanders in the southern Kiangsi village of Fu-t'ien passed secret messages calling for the liquidation of Mao Tse-tung. Mao moved first, arresting and killing close to 5000 of his enemies.[8]

Repercussions of the Fu-t'ien Incident rumbled on, and the ruthless manner in which Mao dealt with the dissidents drove more Communists to revolt. Chou rushed out a series of directives to check Mao Tse-tung and others who imitated him. Finally, on January 7, 1931, Chou circularized a resolution in the name of the Central Committee, condemning Mao Tse-tung because his action "has created fear and suspicion among the party ranks and reduced our comrades to living under abnormal strain . . . During a certain period . . . the local Political Security Bureau [Mao's set-up] placed itself above the party and its regular political authority."[9] And this, said Chou, must not be tolerated.

Mao Tse-tung and other recalcitrants who carried on fratricidal skirmishes in the field were not Chou En-lai's only worry. He was even more deeply concerned over the problematic interpretation of the Comintern's series of instructions, which at times seemed to be saying that a favorable condition for nationwide armed insurrection existed in China, and at other times cautioned the CCP to watch and wait. The confusion seriously impaired the Central Committee's ability to lead and directly contributed to the bloody intraparty strife.

Different interpretations of the Comintern's decrees and of China's syndrome of revolution and personality conflict gave rise to two powerful cliques, which competed with Li Li-san in the party's central apparatus in Shanghai; and Chou was promptly caught in the middle of this triangle. One clique was led by Ch'en Shao-yü, trained in the Sun Yat-sen University in Moscow by the Comintern agent Pavel Mif, who had been president of the university and later supported the Ch'en Shao-yü group of his pupils back in China. The other group belonged to Ho Meng-hsiung, a veteran Communist labor organizer in North and East China. Pavel Mif had hoped to form an alliance of the Ch'en and Ho cliques to overthrow Li Li-san, but the strong-willed Ho refused to bow to "those young students who had done nothing for the Chinese revolution and . . . were taking milk at their mothers' breasts when we were carrying out the revolution."[10]

From the beginning of 1930 on, Ho had made his opposition to Li Li-san clear by insisting, among other things, that, contrary to Li's view, the revolutionary high tide had not yet arrived in China. After Li adopted the June 11, 1930 resolution calling for nationwide insurrections, Ho personally confronted Li to discuss the resolution. Li, confident of his authority and impatient with any criticism, told Ho to "shut up."[11] As Li's policy went bankrupt in the Changsha debacle of July 30–August 2, Ho pressed his criticism, calling the Changsha attack "tribal insurrection" by a group of bandits. Whereupon Li ordered Ho relieved of all his party assignments.

Ch'en Shao-yü also incurred Li's ire with his criticism of the June 11 resolution. Because of his junior status, Ch'en was dealt with even more harshly; his party membership was suspended for six months, during which time he was to re-examine his errors of insubordination and make amends.

But these severe disciplinary actions failed to silence the opposition. Li drew increasing fire from all directions within the Party. Finally Chou En-lai had to turn to the Comintern for help.

With encouragement from the Comintern and the approval of the Central Committee, Chou went to Moscow in early summer of 1930 to seek clarification.[12] The moment he alighted from the train in the Russian capital, he found himself surrounded by Russian comrades, who not only turned to him for the latest information on the situation in China, but also looked up to him as the only really experienced Chinese Bolshevik leader. Among the Chinese Communists then in Moscow, Ch'ü Ch'iü-pai, retained there for more Bolshevik education because of the CCP's failures in 1927, was distrusted for over-intellectualism. His literary flair made Stalin wonder if he was not constantly writing dramatic fiction when he talked and planned revolution. Several other equally senior CCP leaders had been branded as rightist opportunists or Trotskyites. The rest—students enrolled in the Sun Yat-sen University set up especially for training a Chinese Communist elite—were too junior and inexperienced to be considered seriously.

Standing before the assembly of the Sixteenth Congress of the Russian Communist Party on July 5, 1930, Chou made an hour-long report, describing the development of the revolutionary situation in China as "uneven" and the urban labor and rural peasantry movements as "uncoordinated." He urged caution about a nationwide insurrection, but believed revolts to seize power in certain areas were possible. A central Chinese Soviet government, he said, could be organized only after the Chinese Red Army had become strong enough and at least one major industrial and economic center had been occupied.[13]

The Comintern promptly made use of Chou's report to formulate a new directive for the CCP, repeating everything Chou had said, except—and this was the root of all the trouble—an emphatic sentence which was added at the very beginning: "The new upsurge in the Chinese revolutionary movement has become an indisputable fact!"[14] Two weeks later (July 23, 1930), the new directive was dispatched to form a basis for another re-examination of CCP policy and practice to take place at the Third Plenum of the Central Committee. Ch'ü Ch'iü-pai returned to Shanghai first to prepare for the Third Plenum, but he did not dare to start the meeting without Chou, who alone enjoyed the confidence of both the Comintern and the majority of the Chinese Communists.

Meanwhile Li Li-san had pushed through his June 11, 1930 resolution and ordered Mao Tse-tung to attack Changsha and Hankow. And the disastrous failure, with the loss of 2000 Communists in the streets of Changsha alone, had set Li's enemies clamoring for his blood. Most of the CCP leaders expected to see a showdown against Li at the Third Plenum, but they were disappointed when the meeting opened on September 4, 1930 in Shanghai.

First, they were surprised to see Ch'ü Ch'iü-pai chairing the meeting instead of Chou En-lai, who, characteristically chose to take the second seat. Next, they were surprised to hear no condemnation from Chou or Ch'ü who delivered what amounted to two smooth apologies for Li Li-san. At last they realized that Chou En-lai was consistent in his analysis of the Chinese situation and his interpretation of the latest Comintern directive. And they found in him the much needed cohesive strength and dexterity to hold the Party together.

Chou made his now famous Shao-shan Report.[15] After analyzing the current situation and the Comintern directives, he concluded emphatically, "It is clear that there has been some difference between the Comintern and the Central Committee (of the CCP) in their evaluation of revolutionary readiness throughout the country. The Central Committee realized that the development was uneven, but did not take this into account . . . The Central Committee made exaggerated and incorrect estimates of the speed and degree of development of the revolution, planning action on the basis of a situation that was yet to come. Thus tactical mistakes were made. This is what the Comintern wants to correct."

He agreed with the Comintern that "the new upsurge in the Chinese revolutionary movement has become an indisputable fact!" But, more importantly, he underscored the second sentence in the Comintern directive, which stressed the "unevenness" of the situation. "The situation has not ripened sufficiently to warrant nationwide armed insurrections," he declared. "Do the errors of the Central Committee lie in a difference in line (basic approach) from the Comintern? Absolutely not! There is no difference in line."

As to the tactical mistakes of the Central Committee, Chou readily admitted that "I myself committed mistakes . . . We accept the criticism of the Comintern and point out that Comrade Li Li-san should shoulder more responsibilities in ideological interpretation, but we must not tolerate irritating remarks by other comrades such as those made by Comrade Ho Meng-hsiung, aimed personally and individually at Li Li-san . . . We should carry on self-criticism on a collective basis."

Then Chou went on for another thirty minutes, mainly to criticize Ho Meng-hsiung and Ch'en Shao-yü. "Among those who, due either to the activities of the Ho Meng-hsiung group, or to their own confused political concepts, or to their own hidden designs which are different from the Central Committee's official line, have already started clamoring about a nonexistent basic difference between the CCP line

and the Comintern line, were Comrades Ch'en Shao-yü and
Liu Chün-shan [Ho Meng-hsiung's man]. They have al-
ready demonstrated that they are ready to compromise the
CCP-Comintern line to suit theirs [Ho Meng-hsiung's]. The
CCP must fight these tendencies resolutely."[16]

The Third Plenum ended on the high note of party unity
sounded by Chou En-lai, and Li Li-san, though gently rapped
during the meeting, remained the head of the Party. As a
gesture of reconciliation with the Comintern, Chou persuaded Li to appoint Ch'en Shao-yü to succeed Li Wei-han
(one of Chou's Paris group and out of Comintern's favor at
the moment) as party chief of the Kiangsu Province, a critical
post since both Shanghai and Nanking are in that province.
This move further irritated Ho Meng-hsiung who had, not
without justification, considered Kiangsu his territory.[17]

Meanwhile the self-styled Lenin of China, far from being
subdued, continued to rave with righteous indignation about
the Comintern's arbitrary directives when "it does not understand the local situation in China." "The Moscow leaders,"
he charged, "do not comprehend the tendencies of the Chinese revolution, which is exceptional . . . To observe the
discipline of the Comintern is one thing, and to be loyal to
the Chinese revolution is another. The Comintern will talk
to us in a different voice when we have taken Hankow and
established our own Soviet government."

Reports of Li's rebellious attitude reached the Comintern
and produced an order to Pavel Mif to tighten the squeeze
on Li and remove him from the CCP leadership. For three
months Chou worked feverishly to modify the sharp intraparty accusations and to mollify the ruffled feelings of the
Ho, Ch'en, and Li factions, while he continued to defend Li
Li-san's policy in order to uphold party authority.[18] But he
had to sacrifice Li for party unity after the Comintern delivered an official condemnation of Li on November 16, 1930.
In the Central Committee and the Politburo, Chou made
Li Li-san back down and rescind the penalties meted out to

Ch'en and Ho five months before; but he also persuaded Pavel Mif not to reorganize the central authority of the CCP in the way recommended by Ho. Thus, instead of selecting only anti-Li leaders for an emergency conference—which would have been parallel to the August 7 (1927) Emergency Conference that had created the short-lived Ch'ü Ch'iü-pai leadership—Pavel Mif acted upon Comintern authority to call a Plenum (the Fourth) of the Central Committee which, Ho had charged, was packed by Li's friends and compromisers.[19]

The Ho faction leaders received notice of a meeting on January 8, 1931 only a few hours before the opening time. When they rushed to the place, they found the Ch'en Shao-yü faction had already deployed its delegates at the end of the table near chairman Mif. Ho and his men sat down at the other end of the table. Chou En-lai, symbolically, sat in the middle of the two groups. Li Li-san was conspicuously absent. Only then did the Ho faction realize that, contrary to their expectations, this was to be the Fourth Plenum of the Central Committee. The position of the Comintern's chief delegate to China was august, and his voice stern. Adding to the atmosphere of destiny were the armed Communist secret agents who lined the walls of the room. It was too late for the Ho faction delegates to walk out.[20]

Everybody who had said anything nice about the Li Li-san line was now to recant. Some of the most abject confessions[21] in the CCP's archives were presented at that meeting, which nailed the coffin of Li's leadership. Chou En-lai, however, merely redistributed his famous Shao-shan Report, originally released during the Third Plenum three months before, with a new preface: "I am releasing the original document without any revision. Even though the document, as a verbatim record of my report, is a bit too brief, it may serve as an example for those who attempted to compromise between the Li Li-san line and the Comintern line. I am releasing it so that our Party can identify and renounce my error. And I myself shall also criticize this persistent, serious error in our party organs."[22]

He never said a word more, and nobody asked him for any more recantation for his part in trying to defend Li and party unity. At the end of the Fourth Plenum, Li Li-san was out, but Chou stayed in to continue directing the Party's most important function—the military affairs,[23] in collaboration with the new secretary-general, Ch'en Shao-yü. The disgruntled Ho Meng-hsiung faction promptly declared a secessionist move on January 17, 1931. Less than twenty-four hours later, Ho and forty-eight of his top lieutenants were arrested and executed by the KMT in Shanghai. Some say the Ch'en Shao-yü faction betrayed them.[24]

This was the end of Chou's troubles as far as his key role in the Li Li-san dispute was concerned, and it set a pattern for his subsequent political triumph. He continued to enjoy prominence in the CCP, while others guilty of the same crime to a much less significant degree had to face wave after wave of self-criticism. In the buffeting surf of the intra-party power struggle, many a seasoned man of war was wrecked. Indeed, during the next two or three years, the current of Chinese Communist history was laden with the debris of a multitude of party stalwarts whose record and stamina could very well have enabled all of them to share the glory as founding fathers of the Communist regime now in Peking. Chou alone emerged from the purges unscathed and even unruffled, as though he had not been touched by so much as a drop of the flying spray of blood.[25]

Furthermore, his Shao-shan Report comprehensively covered all aspects of the Chinese Communist revolution and its future tasks. Much of what he said in that report has survived the many subsequent changes in leadership personnel and remained in substance the Party's ideological line. Chou emphasized that the Chinese revolution "must go through a great many preparatory stages . . . before transforming itself into a socialist revolution"; Mao Tse-tung instructed his victorious Party in June, 1949 to "go through the People's Democratic Dictatorship before reaching the classless socialist society."[26] Chou said, "The Chinese agrarian revolution is entirely under the leadership of the proletariat (workers) . . . and the peasants are the strong foundation of a worker-peasant alliance"; Mao echoed him by saying, "The foundation of the New Democracy (People's Democratic Dictatorship) is the worker-peasant alliance . . . which provides the main force to support the transition from the New Democracy to socialism." Chou wanted land reform to distribute land to the tillers, but not to deny even the rich peasants an equal share; so did Mao. Chou urged continuance of private property and free trade and free business; Mao warned against "undue haste to abolish private capital." Above all, Chou insisted on a united front including the intellectuals, the petite bourgeoisie, and even the nationalistic (patriotic) capitalists, so long as they loyally supported the Communist Party; Mao stressed the base of revolution as including not only a worker-peasant alliance, but also alliance with the petite bourgeoisie, and he even went further to warn against a "closed door" policy toward friendly non-Communist intellectuals.

The Shao-shan Report was perhaps not completely original, but it was the basis of the fateful July 23, 1930 Comintern directive to the CCP, and, as such, it demonstrates Chou's Olympian grasp of the Chinese Communist revolution and deserves its exalted position in the CCP archives.

Shanghai in the 1920s and 30s reached the peak of its phantasmagorical history as a sixty-square-mile arena of strange crimes and stranger punishments, and, even more often, of crime without punishment. The massacres of 1927, when the Chinese hammer-and-sickle banner was for the first time dyed in real Communist blood, were matched in the intensity of tension and fear if not in the number of heads that rolled, by the Grand Guignol of the early 1930s. And behind the scene directing the gory proceedings was the mild-mannered, soft-spoken, almost effeminate-looking Chou En-lai.

The major participants were the KMT occupation forces and the clandestine CCP and, always, the Yellow Gangs—the underworld thugs hired or inducted by both and by the moneyed businessmen. These, plus the foreign police, detectives, and troops and guards assigned to protect their interests inside and outside the International Concession, kept up with the murder-a-day pace of that "Pearl of the Orient," otherwise known as "The Paradise of Adventurers."

When Chou En-lai returned from Moscow after the 1928 CCP Congress, he brought with him not only the top CCP leader, Hsiang Chung-fa, the boatman, but also the latest of the Russia Cheka program (Lenin's secret police, first organized on December 20, 1917, later known as OGPU, then NKVD, then MVD) with which to protect his comrades during the bleak days ahead. Death tailed him and his comrades every step they moved. The first thing he did was to organize a Red Guard (ch'ih-wei-tui, not to be confused with the Red Guard, hung-wei-ping, of 1966), with himself in charge of strategy, assisted by Ku Shun-chang, a Shanghai mechanic trained by Russian secret service experts at a Vladivostok school and famous for his expertise in strangling his victims with bare hands, leaving no telltale marks.

One day in April 1931, a Red Guard named Wang[27] was apprehended by the KMT counter-intelligence. Hours of interrogation and torture failed to elicit any confession from him until he was confronted with Ku Shun-chang, who had been arrested earlier.[28] Jolted out of his pain-induced stupor as if by an apparition at the sight of his former boss, Wang exclaimed, "Please, oh, please don't blame me. Chou En-lai told me to do it. You know what the iron discipline of the Party means . . ."

Ku was led away. There was no need for him to listen to the rest of Wang's confession, which was simply the conclusion of one espionage episode Ku had already described himself, giving the details of how four of the five members of Ku's family were stripped, bound, and buried alive.

It had already come to light that Ku, in the early spring of the same year, had been ordered to check the secret Communist supply route along the Yangtze River, a life line of the CCP activities in Shanghai and other Red centers in East China as Comintern aid had dwindled and logistics from the Kiangsi Soviet base had become Chou En-lai's only means of support.[29] Disguised as a magician leading a small band of vaudeville artists, Ku stopped at every checkpoint to look over the Communist relay mechanism. One defected Red Guard recognized him and betrayed him to the KMT police in Hankow. An hour later, the confidential secretary to the chief of the KMT Bureau of Investigation in Nanking handed his boss a telegram, which he had just decoded: "Rush No. X to . . . at . . ." The place named in the telegram was in Hankow, but the chief got the message. A few hours later, the secretary disappeared.

Realizing the importance of his catch, the chief of the KMT Bureau of Investigation personally met the boat that transported Ku to Nanking and sped him, wedged between two KMT guards in a car with blinds drawn, to the Central Hotel in the city. As the car turned the last street corner, Ku caught sight of a familiar landmark. His face ashen, he muttered with a smothered cry of surprise, "Why do you take me here? This is my own headquarters!" His captors were equally surprised to discover that their own headquarters in the Central Hotel had been immediately adjacent to the lair of their deadly enemy.

Closeted in a room with Ch'en Li-fu, the KMT's political security chief, Ku completed his defection after a long conference by requesting protection for his family in Shanghai. As a token of faith to convince his family, Ku removed his shirt, hand-sewn by his wife, and entrusted it to the KMT messenger.

The messenger, a high-ranking KMT secret agent, rushed
to Ku's house on Wei-hai-wei Road in Shanghai. The house
looked deserted. Pushing the door open he noticed only a few
pigeons pecking away in the courtyard. He began to inquire
in the neighborhood. One neighbor said that the whole family
had left in a hurry to join Ku who was supposedly ill in Hankow. And there the clue faded out.

Meanwhile the KMT agents failed to lay hands on their
elusive enemy. The KMT intelligence chief's confidential secretary who had vanished after delivering the telegram was
ahead of them. As they descended on the hideouts of Chou
En-lai and other top CCP leaders, which Ku had divulged,
they caught no one except Hsiang Chung-fa, the CCP secretary-general—and he was not at the address Ku had given but
at the house of his mistress.[30] Their grapevine operation
cleanup was, however, rewarded by the arrest and destruction
of over 800 second-string Communist cadres in the next few
weeks. Among the arrested was Wang.

Ku identified Wang as his former henchman from a published photograph and requested a confrontation with him.
It was that which produced Wang's confession of the murder
of the Ku family and of earlier, equally gruesome, Communist reprisals against traitors.

During the next few days the papers in Shanghai banner-
headlined the excavation at the Ku house. The KMT police
and French Concession gendarmes followed Wang to an
empty house at No. 11, Ai-t'ang-li, rue Gaston, where Wang
recognized the thumbtacks he had used to close the window
curtains. After about an hour's digging, an unmistakable
stench arose from the hole. One digger reached in with his
hand and dragged out a leg. Four bodies were brought up,
two male, two female, each tied with arms and legs at the
back, like a newly dressed chicken. Ku identified the bodies
as those of his brother, his wife, and her parents. Ku's son,
Wang said, was spared because, in the process of burying the
others alive, his heart suddenly went soft over the thought

of the only blood lineage of his friend-turned-enemy, and he arranged to have the boy sent back to his ancestral town in Manchuria.[31]

At two other addresses burial grounds were reopened. In a few days over thirty bodies had been unearthed, including those of the brother of a KMT army commander and a Caucasian woman. "They were all on the CCP blacklist," said turncoat Wang, "and any party member, regardless of his position, who disobeyed the orders of Chou En-lai or the Central Committee would meet the same fate. This is the CCP's iron discipline."

With Ku Shun-chang gone, Chou En-lai summoned four other veteran comrades[32] to form a new committee to direct the Red Guard, but the situation in Shanghai was no longer tenable for him; KMT pressure increased steadily and Communist supplies dwindled. In September of that year, he and his wife secretly left for Kiangsi.

Fifteen years later, after the houses of horror in Shanghai had all changed their names and their bloodcurdling history was all but forgotten, Chou returned to Shanghai as the chief CCP negotiator to bargain with the KMT. His residence on rue Massenet was perpetually under KMT surveillance. One day when he was riding in a car, he noticed a suspicious-looking vehicle following him. He ordered his driver to apply the brakes suddenly, forcing the next car to stop immediately behind. He got out of his car, walked around to the driver who had followed him, and said, "Your technique of tailing someone is very bad. You are going to lose your job this way." Too stunned to respond, the driver sat dumb in his car, watching Chou return to his vehicle and speed away.[33]

During the bloody period of the late twenties and early thirties, Chou and his wife, Teng Ying-ch'ao, lived in the house of Chou's foster parents on Seymour Road in Shanghai, one of the quiet havens in the otherwise tumultuous city. His sister-in-law, Shun-yi,[34] the wife of his younger foster

brother, En-chu, has many memories of their family life in
those days.

One night at dinner, the maid brought in the last bowl of
soup. Shun-yi stood up to help her place the large vessel of
scalding hot liquid in the middle of the table. Teng Ying-
ch'ao already had a spoon in her hand, ready to plunge it into
the soup.

"See what I mean, Mother," Chou said to the matriarch
sitting across the table from him. "I said she had put a little
too much salt in the chicken. She wouldn't admit it. Now
she's dying for some soup."

The matriarch smiled, and Teng Ying-ch'ao laughed with
her girlish vivacity. "I know I'll never learn to cook as well
as Shun-yi," said Teng, reaching under the table for Shun-yi's
hand and gently squeezing it. "Don't forget I'm from Honan
where people eat much saltier food than suits your Tientsin
taste. All right, if you think I don't know how to cook, you
show us. Tomorrow is your turn."

"Hsiang-yü [the name by which she called Chou En-lai]
does very well in the kitchen," said the matriarch. "You girls
had better not challenge him. I have tasted his cooking a
number of times before."

With a measure of ill-concealed envy Shun-yi watched and
listened to the merry chatter of her brother- and sister-in-law.
To her, a younger daughter-in-law married into the Chou
family in the old-fashioned way—by parental decree, not of
her own choice—En-lai and Ying-ch'ao were from a different
world. She envied them for their opportunity of having studied abroad, worked in the government (just which government she didn't know and it would not have made any
difference to her even if she did), their new-style marriage,
and, above all, for their obvious affection for each other. And
when the matriarch told her that it was perfectly all right
for En-lai and Ying-ch'ao to go out together because they
were a new-style couple, Shun-yi resented being an old-style
daughter-in-law even more. Her husband, En-chu, was as

temperamental and irresponsible as En-lai was calm and considerate. Even the servants whispered, behind her back but loud enough for her to overhear, that they preferred to have their Seventh Young Master (En-lai) handle such and such a matter instead of their Thirteenth Young Master (En-chu), who was sure to make everybody unhappy without getting it done right. Sometimes she wondered if it could be true that En-lai and Ying-ch'ao had all the virtues, leaving only the vices to her own husband. Yet she could not be bitter toward either as she felt the warmth of Ying-ch'ao's hand over hers and remembered the kind, brotherly solicitude En-lai demonstrated whenever she felt most depressed. She could resent only her own fate.

Noticing her silence, Chou En-lai turned to Shun-yi and asked, "Last night I woke up hearing one of the children cry. Was it the older or the younger one? Are you sure they have enough to cover them at night?"

"It's the younger one," said Shun-yi. "I guess it's just a little stomach upset. He was all right this morning."

"We'd better make sure," said En-lai and turned to his wife. "There is an extra new comforter on our bed. After dinner you take it over to add to the children's bed."

"The comforter won't do, the children just kick it off in their sleep," said Teng Ying-ch'ao. "I am about to finish knitting a sweater, and as soon as I get this one done I will knit another. With a little sweater on, the children will never catch cold at night."

Shun-yi was about to say something more about the children, but the conversation had turned to Teng Ying-ch'ao's knitting and the price of yarns. She sat back in silence again, savoring the warmth of the thought that her successful brother- and sister-in-law, the favorites of the matriarch, took such genuine interest in her children. Now her resentment turned to her husband, the only one missing at the dinner table. It was getting dark outside. She kept stealing glances at the door.

Finally En-chu returned, announcing his entry with a bar of music from an aria in a Peking opera. The matriarch frowned and Shun-yi froze, preparing to stand up. En-chu walked in, his face wine-flushed, but stopped and stood still when he saw the matriarch frowning at him. "Oh, I thought you had finished dinner already," he said apologetically.

Without asking any questions the matriarch launched into a tirade, scolding En-chu for his prodigal way of spending money on a famous singer, a female impersonator in the Peking opera tradition, who had just come to town. En-chu listened with head bent, his face twitching once in a while. Out of habit, Shun-yi left the table to stand against the wall. Teng Ying-ch'ao walked over and stood sympathetically near Shun-yi. Only Chou En-lai remained seated, listening attentively but keeping a smile on his face.

When the matriarch made a reference to En-lai as an example for the younger son to copy, Chou En-lai interrupted her to say to his brother, "Of course, you mustn't squander the family fortune and waste your time on an opera singer." Then he turned to the matriarch, "But it is quite all right to learn the music and poetry of the theatre, isn't it, Mother? All the great scholars and statesmen in the past knew these things." Before the matriarch, her anger already somewhat spent, replied, Chou En-lai turned back to his brother. "I'll go with you tomorrow to the theatre to see just how good the new singer is. Now you'd better go and wash up and eat something. I know those drinking parties. You never get to eat any solid food there."

He stood up and steered En-chu toward his room. And that was the end of that family crisis.

Shun-yi thought that Chou En-lai had said something very clever just to pacify the matriarch, without really meaning it. The next morning, while she was taking care of the children in her room, she heard Chou En-lai sweeping his room with a broom as usual—something she had urged him to let one of the servants do, but to no avail. En-chu was getting dressed.

"Where are you going?" Shun-yi asked her husband.

"To the theatre . . . with Seventh Brother."

"This early?"

"We are going to buy a few things first."

Chou En-lai came out of his room looking elegant in his street dress, a long gray silk gown, leather shoes polished to a high luster. He greeted Shun-yi, asked her again about the children, and went out with his brother. They stayed out the whole day, leaving Teng Ying-ch'ao to try cooking another dish, which she said was the matriarch's favorite. When the two brothers returned, each had an armful of Peking opera costumes. Before the matriarch could say anything, Chou En-lai had already changed into his house dress of a long blue cotton gown, and had involved the whole family in an animated discussion of the art of Peking opera. The matriarch listened, frowning and smiling at the same time, but she never again said a word against the theatre.

Three days later Chou offered to take the whole family to a movie. He let Shun-yi choose one from the ads, took them to the theatre in the family car (quite a status symbol of the Chou family), sat through the show with them, and returned to listen to the matriarch's enthusiastic response to the film. En-chu made a few disparaging remarks about the film, which had been second-rate. But before he had provoked the matriarch into another wrathful harangue, En-lai signaled him to stop. From then on, every so often En-lai took the family to the movie theatre, mostly to humor the matriarch.

The birthday of the deceased grandfather arrived. As eldest son, Chou En-lai took charge of the family preparations for the memorial service. He ordered the supplies and assigned the servants to set up the altar. When the hour came, he went around to inspect everything, adjusting the drapes here, straightening the dishes there, before personally lighting the candles and incense sticks. While trying to keep her children quiet, Shun-yi stood aside to watch how Chou En-lai arranged the cushions and, taking care not to step on his freshly pressed long gown, knelt to kowtow to the altar. He was all reverence as he turned to burn one at a time three pieces of yellow paper, which supposedly bore three messages to the spirits in heaven. The matriarch, too, stood aside and watched. As the third piece of yellow paper burned out, she remarked with pride to Shun-yi, "Hsiang-yü really knows all the rules, and he does everything *just right!*" It was the only time Shun-yi ever heard her mother-in-law, always a sharp and critical person, stress those last two words.

This was in late 1928 and 1929. Shun-yi understood that Chou En-lai was waiting, like all successful sons of the gentry families who had done well in the old imperial examinations, for the next government assignment. Occasionally Chou stayed away from home for several days at a time, and when he did, Shun-yi believed that he was visiting other branches of the Chou clan. Respected and admired by everyone at the house, including the servants, Chou En-lai and his wife gave her no reason to suspect the other half of their double life.

When En-lai and his wife left for good toward the end of the summer of 1931, the matriarch told Shun-yi that they were going abroad, bringing En-chu with them part of the way to Tientsin where he was to take a job. Writing to her husband always in care of a sister in Tientsin, she never knew what he was doing or where En-lai and his wife went. But she had no reason to suspect that, instead of going to the opera house, En-lai had taken his brother to Communist meetings; or that the KMT police had fixed an astronomical price on the handsome head of the gentlemanly filial Seventh Young Master; or that while she innocently gossiped about cooking and knitting, Teng Ying-ch'ao had hidden an indispensable comrade in the CCP's organization department run by her husband.

Even if she had seen Chou En-lai again she would not have recognized him. The moment he left the house he put on a

[5] (above) Neater when in Hankow or Chungking, Chou's creaseless
uniform blended in well with the bleak house in Yenan of 1937. (United
Press International)

[6] (below) Chou, Mao and Chu Teh at their wartime base in Yenan.
(Wide World Photos)

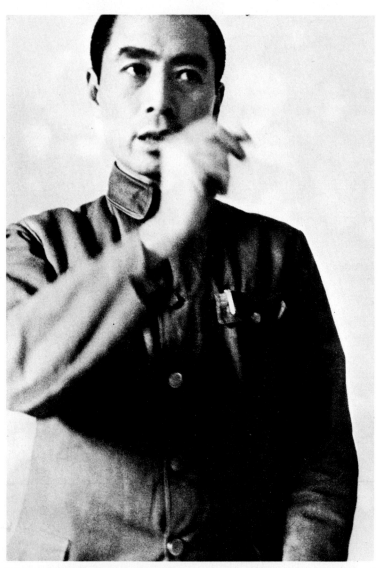

[7] ". . . My fellow students, this is our country. Whatever has happened to cause that fratricidal tragedy must be forgotten. From now on, we must look ahead . . ." (United Press International)

[8] *(above)* Chou with Gov. Chang Ch'un (now Secretary-General of the President's Office) of the Nationalist Government and General George Marshall signing cease fire order at Chungking, January 10, 1946. (Wide World Photos)

[9] *(below)* From right to left: Tung Pi-wu (now Vice-Chairman of the People's Government), Chou, Gen. Lin Piao, Miss Kung Peng (now Director of Information Service in Peking), and unidentified man, April 1943, in Chungking. (United Press International)

[10] Chou and wife at reception given by Communist Party at Chung-king Victory House, February 5, 1946. (Wide World Photos)

convincing long beard and donned a clergyman's black robe to board a small steamer that plied the waters of the China Sea for Ta-p'u on the Fukien coast, thence turning inland toward Juichin, the capital of the Kiangsi Soviet.

CHAPTER 7

THE BEARDED COMMISSAR ON
THE LONG MARCH

AS CHOU EN-LAI REPORTED to the Russian Communist Party
Congress on July 5, 1930, and as he elaborated in his Shao-shan
Report two months later, one of the most urgent tasks for
the Communist movement in China was to strive for the
establishment of a central Soviet regime in a secure area
guarded by a substantial Red Army.

Even while the intraparty power struggle between Li Li-
san, Ch'en Shao-yü (the Moscow-trained clique) and, to a
lesser degree, Mao Tse-tung was in progress, Chou En-lai
on September 12, 1930 called together representatives of
forty-five organizations to plan for the First National Assembly of the Chinese Soviet Republic.[1] But first they had to
find a place for the new regime.

Among the Communist bases scattered over East China,
the Kiangsi Soviet under Mao and Chu Teh with headquarters at Juichin was rapidly emerging as the most promising
Red bastion. It weathered intraparty rebellions, including the
major Fu-t'ien Incident of December 1930, and the following
year successfully repelled three KMT "bandit-annihilation"
campaigns. Chou En-lai and the Central Committee stayed
in Shanghai as long as they could. But when copies of Chou's
photograph, showing him in a smart KMT uniform as chief
political commissar of Chiang Kai-shek's troops in 1925, were
posted at the railroad stations after the bodies had been dug

up in the French Concession, he and his important comrades had to flee, and the only attractive refuge was Kiangsi.

The new Central leadership, which after the Fourth Plenum of January 1931 was headed by Ch'en Shao-yü, first sent delegate Hsiang Ying to Kiangsi, but Hsiang was no match for Mao Tse-tung. In September 1931, Chou En-lai went to Kiangsi to replace Hsiang,[2] only to find himself caught between Ch'en Shao-yü and Mao.

Still speaking for the Central Committee, Chou En-lai told Mao to rid his area of the lingering influence of the now defunct Li Li-san line—extreme leftist adventurism—and to revise his guerrilla strategy. The Red Army, said Chou, had come of age and was ready to mount frontal attacks under a unified Central command of the Party; it was no longer in need of a personalized leadership, which herded a small band of guerrillas in hit-and-run operations.[3] This was a direct barb against Mao.

The Central Committee followed Chou to Juichin where preparations for the First National Assembly of the Chinese Worker-Peasant-Soldier Soviet Regime were accelerated. On November 7, 1931, a Chinese Soviet Republic was born. A Constitution and many bylaws were adopted. In the election of sixty-three Central Executive Committee members, Mao captured the largest number of votes. Chou ranked fourth, while the leader of the Moscow-trained clique, Ch'en, was fourteenth! In the subsequent assignment of jobs, however, Mao was even more clearly ahead. Chou ostensibly slipped down to a mere member of the Military Committee under Chu Teh's chairmanship.[4] Ch'en and his fellow students from Moscow faced an uphill fight to subjugate Mao.

But within the CCP, Ch'en Shao-yü was still the chief, and Chou, as head of the Central Bureau of Soviet Areas, outranked Mao. On January 7, 1932, the Bureau accepted Chou's report entitled "A Resolution Regarding the Measures Taken to Wipe Out Anti-revolutionaries in the Soviet Areas," reviewing the work done thus far in the Kiangsi area

106

CHOU EN-LAI

and characterizing Mao's earlier effort to deal with the Fu-
t'ien and other rebellions as acts of the bourgeoisie who were
quick to panic: such actions, it declared, were inexcusable,
even though they were ostensibly taken to deal with the anti-
Bolshevik traitors. "During the period when the leadership
in the Kiangsi Soviet Area was in the hands of the Secretary
of the Frontline Committee [Mao], the resolute action taken
to suppress the Fu-t'ien Revolt was completely correct," the
report continued, "but mistakes were committed in recognizing the true nature of the anti-Bolshevik group and in
selecting a proper method to deal with it."[5]

Chou's report, which attempted to save some face for Mao,
failed to please either side. Two days later, the Central Committee under Ch'en Shao-yü, with Chou's support, adopted
another resolution calling for Red Army occupation of major
cities to seize the entire Kiangsi Province. This ran counter to
Mao's idea of consolidating the existing Soviet base first.[6]
Chou followed the resolution with a lengthy elaboration, released under the title "Support the Victory of All the Red
Armies in the Country, and Resolutely Carry Out the Policy
of Positive Attack,"[7] which said:

"The fact that the Chinese Worker-Peasant Red Army has
had so far continuous and significant victory has been entirely due to its determination to follow closely the lines laid
down by the Comintern and the Central Committee of the
Chinese Communist Party, both of which advocated a positive and persistent frontal attack. If we review the action
taken by the Red Army in the Central Soviet Regime [Mao's
territory], we must admit that we have made serious mistakes of procrastination. The cause of this rightist-opportunist
mistake was that the Central Bureau [of the Soviet Areas]
in the past [before Chou took charge] was not able to ap-
praise the political situation accurately. Furthermore it lacked
clear vision and did not recognize the validity of positive attack and the importance of the mission to seize one or several
entire provinces as a base of operation.

"All those who regard the seizure of one or several entire provinces as not an immediate but a distant goal; all those who are skeptical about occupying metropolitan centers and prefer to lead the Soviet regime and the Red Army toward remote areas; all those who are hesitant about a positive outward expansion of Communism to enable the Red Army to utilize its full potential, who prefer to tie the hands of our armed comrades with such assignments as propaganda in the villages and raising funds for the army, forgetting that the principal mission of the Red Army is to destroy our enemy through combat; all those who still linger in a past stage for which a gradual expansion of military action and a defensive and conservative strategy were proper and who are consequently unwilling to move swiftly to deal a fatal blow to the enemy in the non-Communist areas; all those who neglect the urgent need to support and respond to Red Army action all over the country in order to distract the enemy, are committing a serious error of rightist-opportunism."

Chou En-lai had spoken. The Central Committee applauded him with a message: "As a result of the arrival in the Soviet area of Comrade Wu Hao [Chou En-lai], many errors have already been corrected. There has been considerable adjustment in party work."[8] A series of resolutions and declarations followed from both the Central Committee (which was under Ch'en Shao-yü and Chou En-lai) and the Kiangsi Provincial Branch of the CCP (which was under Mao). These amounted to the total submission, at least per forma, of Mao-Tse-tung.[9] Ch'en Shao-yü went back to Moscow, leaving the post of secretary-general to the Moscow-trained clique leader next in line, Ch'in Pang-hsien. Meanwhile the KMT set its fourth annihiliation campaign for January 1933, a factor that was at least partially responsible for the temporary settlement in CCP ranks.

To deal with the imminent attack, which promised to be the biggest yet, Chou En-lai was appointed chief commissar of the Red Army, working closely with Chu Teh, the com-

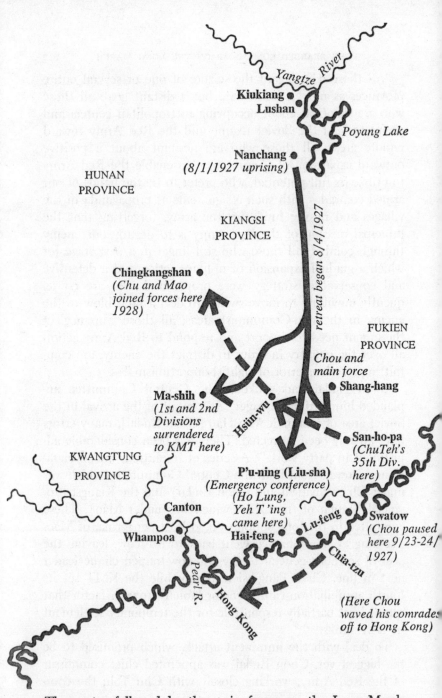

The routes followed by the main forces on the Long March. There was much retracing and crisscrossing by the various units of the Red troops. Dotted lines show Soviet areas.

mander-in-chief. But the serious question of strategy was yet to be settled. Mao insisted on a "scorched land" approach, luring the enemy into the heartland of Kiangsi, where they would be cut off from their supply line and destroyed one by one. Chou supported Ch'in Pang-hsien, the CCP chief, who advocated a swift frontal counterattack before the enemy had a chance to deploy its troops effectively. Chou won, and the Red troops were ordered to move outside the Soviet area and meet the enemy head-on.

On the eastern front of the Kiangsi Soviet defense line, Mao Tse-tung assigned his trusted subordinate, Lo Ming, secretary of the Fukien Province Branch of the CCP, to lead his troops toward Shang-hang and Pai-sha. Lo Ming, however, was not convinced of the wisdom of Chou's strategy. He sent an urgent plea to the Central Command, "The people are running away. What can we do? Even if we invited such and such party leaders to come lecture to them for three days and three nights, they still would not stand up and fight. Under these circumstances, how can we hold a defense line firmly? If we do not switch our tactics to a scorched-land approach, cutting off the enemy's communication and supply lines, we will not win the war. On the other hand, if we did follow a scorched-land strategy, we would be able to lure the enemy deep into our hinterland and destroy him when he is both starved and harassed."

Upon receiving the plea, Chou voted for disciplinary action against Lo Ming and those sharing his views.[10] Among the victims of this purge were a number of Mao's staunch supporters, including his brother, Mao Tse-t'an.

The fourth KMT attack was brought to an end in February 1933, with the Communists still holding their own, but fireworks continued to explode over the Lo Ming Incident. CCP chief Ch'in Pang-hsien criticized Mao Tse-tung for perpetuating personal instead of party leadership in the Red Army.[11] Chou En-lai followed up with a report declaring, "We have struggled forcefully against the defeatist Lo Ming line, and against the policy of only defense but no offensive, and we have overcome many incorrect tendencies . . ."[12] At first Mao listened to these public denunciations in stony silence, then, unable to endure it any longer, he relinquished all his military assignments. For a few weeks he lived at Yü-tu in virtual retirement, holding the titular office of the chairman of the Soviet Government. The bitterness he nursed was visible to his visitors there, and emerged in the open later when his leadership was secure and supreme in Yenan.[13]

Chou's position in the infant Soviet Government (as distinguished from his position in the CCP) dropped lower after the Second National Assembly of the Soviet regime in Juichin on January 22, 1934, but his influence in the army increased with his elevation to vice-chairman of the Military Committee.[14] Mao retained his titular chairmanship of the government.

The fifth and last KMT annihilation campaign forced the Second Soviet Assembly to close before the scheduled date. Chou, Mao, Chu Teh, and other leaders packed away their notes in a hurry and rushed from the conference room to the front line. Chou went to the Kuang-ch'ang front, the line bearing the brunt of the KMT attack, and stayed there under crushing enemy fire until forced back to the second line of resistance at Yi-ch'ien. There he went over the fortifications built with the technical help of the Comintern adviser Albert (Li T'e) several times before deploying some 50,000 men on the line. During a brief lull, he gathered together all the officers above the rank of company commander to have them pledge their lives to the defense of the stronghold.

But Chiang Kai-shek was determined to pry the Reds loose from Juichin. The three-pronged assault on Yi-ch'ien gave Chou and his men no chance to eat or rest for two days and two nights. On August 30, 1934, Yi-ch'ien fell. Ch'en Yi, one of Chou's Paris comrades and now commander of the Kiangsi

Soviet Military Zone, was wounded as he went with Chou among the troops. The fall of Yi-ch'ien exposed other defense positions, which toppled like dominoes, and before the end of September it had become clear that the fruit of seven years of strenuous Communist cultivation was about to slip from CCP hands.[15]

In a small village within earshot of KMT machine-gun reports, Chou, Mao, Chu Teh, and Ch'in Pang-hsien went into an emergency conference. After reviewing the situation, it took them very little time to reach the conclusion that withdrawal was the only choice. "Go north where our comrades have already carved out a base against the Japanese," said Chou, and the others quickly agreed.[16] But how? Ch'in Pang-hsien wanted one last-ditch battle before withdrawal, so that the KMT would not take up the pursuit so readily. Chou En-lai argued that a final decisive battle could last a number of days, giving the KMT that much more time to complete the siege of the Soviet area. Furthermore, after another severe engagement, care of the wounded and the need to regroup the troops would make it too late for the Red Army to retreat.

At this fatal moment, and over this critical issue of Communist survival, Chou En-lai found himself for the first time in agreement with Mao Tse-tung. It was a time when the Comintern was not able to direct the day-to-day combat strategy of the CCP, and Chou was speaking out of his own military experience and individual judgment. It coincided with Mao's judgment and marked the beginning of the Chou-Mao collaboration.

A third opinion held by another group[17] of CCP leaders favored breaking up the Soviet into smaller units to continue guerrilla action in the mountain fastness along the border of Kiangsi, Fukien, Hunan, and Kwangtung provinces. But Chou and Mao won, and the stage was set for the historic Long March.

During his stay in Juichin, Chou En-lai made three major contributions to the CCP: he built up the Red Army, taught it, and maintained political discipline in it.

Wearing several hats, all related to the military, Chou was indispensable in building the Red Army. In addition to being vice-chairman (Chu Teh was too busy commanding the troops to chair the committee) and chief commissar of the Red Army, he was also chief commissar of the Communist Youth Vanguards whose teen-age members were most effective in guerrilla warfare.[18] Normally the Vanguards functioned as merely an auxiliary to the regular Red Army, but in an emergency whole battalions of Vanguards were transferred directly into the army. Besides urging the gullible youth to remember that every privilege they had was a gift of the Soviet regime and that therefore they must defend the regime with their lives, Chou told them, "All able-bodied and youthful voters must be completely mobilized. Wherever the realistic situation permits, there must be at least one battalion of model Youth Vanguards with exceptional standards of training and behavior to each district. These Vanguard units should be ever ready to face enemy fire."[19]

The Central Bureau of Soviet Areas under Chou En-lai adopted a resolution on December 5, 1931 to expand the Red Army. Details of the plan were given in a Central Committee directive on September 21, 1932. Further backed by the Comintern message in the winter of 1933, Chou En-lai set a goal of 1,000,000 men and took immediate steps to implement it. Army dependents received preferential treatment, additional rest periods every Saturday, and assistance in farm work from neighboring families who had no sons in the army. Within the twelve-month period ending in July 1934, Chou reported the induction of 112,105 recruits.[20]

Professor Chou En-lai of the Red Army School in the Juichin woods cut a striking figure with his black beard over five inches long.[21] He lectured on combat techniques, quoting readily from Russian Red Army manuals. His favorite and more impressive subject was, understandably, the political significance of military action. As KMT attacks closed in on the Soviet Area, Chou's voice in the classroom and in the official army journal rose louder. He exhorted "The Worker-Peasant Red Army and the Masses of the Entire Soviet Area to Rise to Fight in Defense of Kuang-ch'ang." He declared, "For Land, for Freedom, and for the Political Regime of the Soviet, We Shall Fight to the End," and "To Commemorate the August First [Nanchang] Uprising, We Must Wipe Out the Enemy at the Threshold of the Soviet Area and Disintegrate the Enemy in Their Own Rear Areas." He analyzed "The New Situation and the New Victory" on the front and reminded the Red Army to keep the KMT troops away from the Shih-ch'eng defense line.[22]

It was easier to whip up enthusiasm among the youth and the lower echelons of the army than to maintain political discipline over the senior comrades. Many troop commanders, having defected from the KMT to join the CCP, had too little formal education and were basically soldiers of fortune with no firm political convictions. In adversity, they were quick to waver and ready to abandon their newly espoused cause. Chou En-lai had to crack his political whip loud and often at "thought struggle" meetings when CCP cadres were brought together to criticize themselves and each other for danger signs ranging from loose habits of private life to disagreement, however slight, with party policies. Those failing to convince Chou by their self-criticism were penalized, sometimes even summarily dismissed from the Party.

Kung Ch'u, who had guarded Chou En-lai's life during the retreat from Nanchang in 1927 and was now the Red Army's chief of staff, was one of the high-ranking comrades chastised by Chou. In May 1933 he argued with Chou in a meeting on the CCP's peasant policy. More punishing than the KMT's military siege of Kiangsi had been their water-tight economic blockade. Two years of complete isolation had forced the occupants of the Kiangsi Soviet to a virtually saltless diet

because salt was one item not produced in their area. The
tax burden on the Kiangsi farmers increased proportionate to
the intensifying warfare, and their morale sank as the Red
Army not only ate up their rice but kept them busy with
the construction and repair of fortifications. Chou En-lai
wanted to persist in land reform, distributing land equally to
the tillers, demanding money from the rich and labor from
the rich and poor alike. Kung argued for a softer approach to
avoid antagonizing the peasantry. "But the mass of poor
peasants are with us," said Chou. "They are willing to give
their lives to defend the land the CCP has given them." Kung
still feared the alienation of even the poor peasants if labor
conscription interfered excessively with farm work. "Step up
our education of the peasants," retorted Chou. "Who told
you to *force* them to build fortifications for *us?* Mobilize
them to build the pillboxes and dig foxholes to defend *themselves!*"

Five months later, Kung failed to complete an assignment
to fortify a section of the Kwangtung-Kiangsi border with con-
scripted labor. This resulted in the loss of a strategic point,
and Kung was summoned one evening in August 1933 to
the office of the Comintern military adviser Li T'e (Albert),
where Chou and Chu Teh were also waiting. Kung was barely
permitted to state his case before Chou En-lai stood up to
deliver a scathing reprimand, charging him with lack of class-
consciousness and failure to subordinate the individual interest of the peasants to the need of the revolution in building
the fortifications. The tongue-lashing concluded with a ver-
dict: Party membership suspended for six months.

The culprit began to serve his probation in the Red Army
School in the woods near Juichin by attending the "thought
struggle" sessions chaired by Chou En-lai. When it was his
turn to speak, Kung again attempted a mild self-defense,
which only aggravated Chou's distrust and caused him to remark at the end of the session, "Comrade Kung has not yet
recognized his mistakes." Realizing that he had to live always

at the mercy of Chou En-lai and the Central Committee, Kung took little comfort in the fact that he was reinstated in the CCP only two months after his dismissal. He defected on May 2, 1935 during the Long March.[23]

Hsiao Ching-kuang, who survived a round of disciplinary action at Chou's hands in the same year (1933) to become chief of the Red Navy in 1950 and later Under-Secretary of Defense in Peking, ran afoul of Chou's iron discipline when he lost a critical battle. He was charged with dereliction of duty and moral turpitude. Chou assembled the officers of the First Front Army and delivered a report describing how Hsiao abused his authority when he used army mules to carry his personal belongings instead of wounded soldiers, and behaved improperly before some village girls.[24] The Supreme Court of the Kiangsi Soviet accepted Chou's prosecution and handed down a five-year imprisonment for the defendant.[25]

Soft persuasion and iron discipline, the book and the sword, between them Chou En-lai held all his comrades, including the ranking generals of the Red Army, answerable to the Chinese Communist Party through the troubled days of the Kiangsi Soviet and the Long March.

In December 1935, when the Communists at long last found themselves safe at Wa-yao-pao, a little out-of-the-way village in Shensi, Mao Tse-tung shouted with his heavy Hunanese accent that the Long March they had just completed was "the first of its kind ever recorded in human history, a manifesto of unconquerable force, a herald of the true Messiah, and a broadcaster of the seeds of revolution!" Chou En-lai, gaunt, tired, and weatherbeaten, altogether a different person from the clean-shaven, gentlemanly son of a rich capitalist family of Shanghai five years before, stood next to Mao, unable to suppress a satisfied smile.

It was not a march to victory; it was a retreat with KMT troops in hot pursuit. But, all the exaggerated Communist glorification aside, the 6000-mile trek from Kiangsi to Shensi through some of the most rugged and uninhabited lands of the world, with enemy (Chiang Kai-shek's troops, other anti-Communist local troops, hostile aborigines, and savage nature) lying in wait all along the route, certainly wrote a remarkable page of military history with, if nothing else, the unbelievable survival of the core of the Chinese Red Army at the end of the journey.

In October 1934 the Kiangsi Communist troops packed their bags ready to break out of the KMT siege. The fifth KMT annihilation campaign had cost the Reds 60,000 men, but a quick count showed that there were still some 80,000 under arms ready to leave. Mechanics and other technicians were needed, and so were the Soviet bank clerks, Soviet factory workers, and the Soviet co-operative staff. The move was supposed to be a military secret, but many farmers, already converted to communism and fearing for their lives in the hands of Chiang Kai-shek's troops, also wanted to go with the Red Army, and soon the whole Kiangsi Soviet was packing.

Under the cover of darkness, battle-tested guerrilla units were rushed to the edge of the KMT encirclement to relieve the regular Red Army units, who were now concentrated in southern Kiangsi for the breakthrough. Spearheading the column was the First Army Corps under Chu Teh, flanked by the Third and Ninth Army Corps. The elite Thirteenth Division was assigned to fight a rearguard action. Mao, Chou, and other CCP leaders moved in the very center of the column, together with the women's political propaganda corps led by Teng Ying-ch'ao. On October 16, 1934 the westward march began from T'ung-lo-wan.[26] The Reds threw their concentrated weight against an unsuspecting KMT unit and broke open a gap in the siege, but once outside they still had to crush three more layers of KMT fortifications in Kiangsi and Hunan provinces before they could reach Kweichow.

The Red armies on the flanks struck out in two separate

directions to distract the enemy while the main retreat column detoured again and again, often retracing their steps and
making loops to elude pursuers and dodge local resistance.
The bulk of the exodus, with 5000 men and about an equal
number of pack animals serving in the transport alone, slowed
down the movement, but they had to move fast if they were
not to perish at the hands of the main KMT forces behind
them or under the KMT air attacks.

After about three months, the Reds entered Kweichow
Province and approached Tsun-yi, a highway hub, which they
occupied for eleven days, the longest rest during the entire
trip. As they had done at each of their stops, the women's
propaganda corps and the political workers immediately
spread out to drum up support among the residents. Money
from the seized banks and supplies from the seized ware-
houses were, after distribution to the troops, handed out
free to the city poor. "The Red Army is carrying out the mandate of heaven," the beneficiaries of this Robin Hood program exclaimed, and those with nothing to lose flocked to
the Red banner and went with Chu, Mao, and Chou, when
they departed.

The brief respite at Tsun-yi also provided Mao with an
opportunity to hold a top-level conference, which resulted in
the decline of the Moscow-trained clique and the beginning
of Mao's dominance in the CCP.[27] At the meeting, supporters of Mao criticized the military strategy implemented during the last days of the Kiangsi Soviet. Ch'in Pang-hsien and
the Comintern adviser Albert were blamed for the defeat,
and Ch'in lost his secretary-generalship to Chang Wen-t'ien.
Chou shared some of the blame, but his name was not among
those criticized in the resolution released subsequently.

Certain highlights of the Long March attained a large
measure of tragic grandeur. All those involved in the year-long
life-and-death struggle, high and low alike, faced the same
grim reality, the same ruthless threat. One day in April 1935,
Chou ordered the unit traveling with him to stop in a one-

street mountain village in northern Yunnan for a brief rest.

The village slumbered in the chilly darkness of an early spring night. A few families had fled to the mountain tops when Chou's unit reached there, but most of them remained. Chou ordered his men to retire early, to recover from travel fatigue and also to save lamp oil. Only his room, a kitchen corner borrowed from a bean-curd vendor, was lighted with a candle. He had a stack of maps to pore over, and his radio man brought him a slip of paper from time to time. The strain of six months of running had begun to tell on everybody, Chou could see; and yet the end was still nowhere in sight. Wearily he pushed the papers aside and walked out of the hut to stretch his legs.

"K'ou-ling! (Password!)" shouted a patrol soldier down the darkened street.

"This is Chou En-lai," responded Chou. Preoccupation had made him momentarily forget his own order, but he did not need to correct himself, for the soldier immediately recognized his voice. Chou returned the soldier's salute and greeted him by name. "When you finish your shift," he said, reaching out a hand to feel the soldier's shivering shoulder under a tattered cotton-padded uniform, "come to my room for a chat. There is some wood in the stove that will warm you up for a better rest."

It was close to midnight when the soldier went to Chou's room. Chou asked him to sit down near the stove and talked to him about his family. The soldier studied the dancing shadows on Chou's face. It was sallow and drawn, almost buried in overgrown hair and beard. The eyes had lost their luster, which the soldier used to see when they were in Juichin.

"You don't feel well, do you?" the soldier said.

"Nothing too bad," said Chou. "The cold I caught shortly after we started last year keeps coming back. It's just a nuisance. Many of our comrades are much sicker than I, yet they carry on."[28]

Their conversation turned to the unit of comrades who stopped at a small hamlet a few miles ahead of them. Earlier in the afternoon a message runner from that unit had brought back a report about the capture of several rich merchants who were kept marching along with the Red comrades. The soldier wondered if they were being held for ransom, since the commander was treating them well, sharing meals with them, and even offering his own good sandals to one of them whose shoes had been lost in the mud.

"It's not so much for their money," said Chou. "Of course, if they have money in excess of their travel expense to contribute, we would welcome it. But it's even more important for us to have friends. They are rich and influential people from Szechwan, where we are going. Cultivating a little good will by showing these people how our Red Army behaves is always a good policy."

"What if they are anti-revolutionaries?" asked the soldier.

"In that case—and if we find out that is the case—we will know how to deal with them. Meanwhile they are getting an education. They are comparing their lily-white soft feet with our commander's feet—your feet and my feet, calloused, chapped, just like those of any one of our comrades. They will watch how our commanders eat and sleep just like any ordinary soldiers, but work harder and do more. Our iron discipline will convince them that we are soldiers of revolution, not bandits."

"That's fine, but I can't help wondering why we add them to our burden when we have trouble keeping all we have got already."

"The commander told me that they choose to walk along with us, at least until they get out of this part of the country. With all the bandits and unruly local reactionary soldiers around, those merchants won't have a chance, now that they have lost their hired bodyguards."

The radio man brought in another message, and Chou moved his stool close to the candle to read it. The soldier stood up to leave. Chou called him back and said, "Tomorrow, when we move on, be sure to remind all the comrades of your squad to return as usual everything they have borrowed—the boards, doors, and what not that they borrowed for beds, and the scissors, needles, and thread borrowed from the womenfolk here—everything back to their owners!"

When the Red Army reached northern Szechwan, they ran out of food. For days they had to forage provisions wherever they could find them, and the nearest cereal field often lay more than ten miles away from their camp. Gathering the half-ripe cereal was a job for everybody, including Commander-in-Chief Chu Teh who, at forty-nine, carried a load of a hundred pounds and marched at the head of the labor column. He chided every comrade with a smaller load, "You young people cannot carry as much as seventy pounds each, how can you call yourselves young people?" At that challenge, Hsü T'e-li, Chou's associate in his Paris days and over sixty years old already, also joined the carrier squad.[29] Only Chou En-lai, because he had to stay up nearly every night to chart the next day's retreat route, often was forced to spend the day taking cat naps on a stretcher.

Finally even the half-ripe cereal was exhausted. When nothing was available, the marchers removed their leather belts, cooked them in water to make them soft, mixed them with two or three kinds of wild vegetable, and served this concoction at the end of a torturously trying day. The broth, euphemistically labeled "The Soup of Three Delicacies," was greeted with enthusiasm.[30]

On and on the marchers pushed, braving all kinds of weather and often marching through the night. The river gorges, cut between sheer rock walls thousands of feet tall, blocked their progress in western Szechwan and Yunnan, and crossing each of them was a test of their ingenuity and courage. The local troops, except the aborigines, had been alerted by Chiang Kai-shek to haul away all the grain in storage and burn what could not be hidden, to cut the bridges wherever they were and sink the ferry boats where there were no bridges. With each crossing the Reds escaped one more KMT trap, and at each moment of critical decision Chou En-lai and Mao Tse-tung were there, studying the map together with the vanguard commander.

After crossing the Tatu River under enemy fire behind a dozen dare-to-die volunteer comrades who crawled along the iron chains (the cross-tie boards on the bridge had been burned by the KMT troops) that spanned the swift stream, they ascended the perpetually snow-capped peaks near the Tibetan border. There was no road, not even a visible woodsman's trail; as they picked their way single-file through the virgin jungle, Chou En-lai recalled the famous poem of Li Po of the T'ang Dynasty on "The Difficult Road to Shu." Adding to their misery was the presence of the Lolo tribesmen who, traditionally suspicious of the Chinese and unable to understand Chinese speech, turned their hostile spears and muzzle-loaders toward Chou. A vanguard commander[31] familiar with the Lolos had to drink a bowl of rooster's blood with their chief and swear brotherhood forever before he obtained safe passage for his comrades.

The darkest days arrived when they reached the immense grassland in northwestern Szechwan. The treacherous swampy soil covered with man-high grass that stretched as far as one could see became the tomb of many comrades and their KMT hunters who, once stepping into it, were never seen again. Food had long since gone, even water was nowhere to be found.[32] The tribesmen confronting them, called Mantzu (savages) by the Chinese, this time would not consent to meet anyone of Chou's emissaries, with or without rooster's blood. They simply hid in the grassland, through which only they knew how to negotiate, and killed every non-Mantzu who came into their view.

On June 16, 1936, the Long Marchers, reduced within the first two months by almost two thirds from their original 80,000, entered Meng-kung in northern Szechwan. Their weary smiles were greeted by the broad grins of the 30,000 well-rested comrades of the Fourth Army under Chang Kuo-tao, one of the original thirteen at the CCP's First Congress in 1921 and senior to Mao Tse-tung in the CCP's central leadership. Chang had cultivated a Soviet base in the border area of Hupeh, Anhwei, and Honan provinces, lost it to Chiang Kai-shek in the winter of 1932, and regrouped and regained his strength in the northern Szechwan mountain bastion where he had been since 1934.

After the initial reunion celebration, Red Army style, a series of top-level negotiations began between Mao and Chang, each with about equal troop strength under his command.[33] Chang favored staying in northern Szechwan; Mao wanted to push on to Shensi in the north to penetrate the area already under Japanese threat.[34] As their face-to-face talks reached an impasse, Chou En-lai and others served as intermediaries to keep trying for a reconciliation, which did not materialize.

Chang and Mao parted, the former heading northwest toward Sinkiang and the latter resuming his northern march toward Shensi. Chou En-lai, speaking for the Central Committee's military department, supported the policy of using the war against Japan to try for another united front, because the Red Army needed relief from the KMT pressure more than from any possible Japanese attack.

A year later, after Chang had moved his troops around and passed up two more chances[35] to unite them with Mao's forces, now well entrenched in the caves of Yenan, he finally walked out on Mao for good. In the subsequent CCP action to oust Chang (April 1938), Chou pronounced the charge, "In the autumn of 1935 when the First and Fourth Front Armies were joined, Chang Kuo-tao estimated that the CCP had already become a political failure. He therefore followed his totally pessimistic rightist inclination to go south against Red Army discipline, and further threatened the central authority with his troops. When his scheme was frustrated, he even dared to set up an illegal Central Committee by himself."[36]

The Long March started as a retreat but wound up a memorable triumph, and considering all it had achieved for the CCP, Chou En-lai, the bearded chief commissar, was justifiably proud of the iron discipline he maintained in the Red Army. Less than half of the marchers reached their destination, but those who did not were not entirely lost. Some were purposely assigned to remain along the route to form Communist nuclei. The Reds made many enemies among the rich, but they won even more friends by their iron discipline. They captured about as many supplies as they had lost, and, above all, they put themselves to a historic test, which only the most stout-hearted survived. Among them were Chou En-lai and Teng Ying-ch'ao, both sick most of the time during the journey.

CHAPTER 8

THE ENVOY FROM
THE CAVES OF YENAN

THE NORTH CHINA PROVINCE of Shensi, Chou En-lai found in 1935, could not be compared to even the bleakest village in rice-rich Hunan and Kiangsi, the "South of the [Yangtze] River" nostalgically described in classical Chinese poetry. Hundreds of years of desiccation had reduced the once-fertile land to deserts—immense stretches of sand, gravel, and loess, that fine powder of yellow soil that could be reconverted into crop-yielding ground if there were water. But there was no water. So the natives dug into these loess walls and carved out caves for dwellings.

Still weak from the Long March, Teng Ying-ch'ao set about to fix up a cave for her husband whom she hardly saw for days at a stretch. In place of the frilled curtains and book-cases that had adorned their rented house in Canton in 1925– 26, she used the locally made rice paper, and once it was pasted onto the latticed window frames, it didn't look too bad at all. She even thought of writing a poem or two on the paper to add a decorative touch, but decided against it because of the very limited space left between the frames and the need to let in as much light as possible—there were not too many windows to a cave. With a borrowed table wiped spotlessly clean and a freshly laundered coverlet on the bed under a mosquito net, the place began to look livable, even luxurious, when she recalled the shelterless mud hovels in which she had spent many a night under the pouring rain on the grassland of northern Szechwan.

Comrades dropped by to admire how well Teng Ying-ch'ao had managed with her interior decoration—they said nothing derogatory about her bourgeois taste. But neither they nor Teng herself had much time to relax in that luxurious comfort. The Soviet base supposedly already developed there by other comrades had since the end of the 1920s been run under inadequate leadership. There was no organized production, no sanitation, and often no discipline among some of the Communist units hastily recruited from bandit groups. Chou En-lai, the political commissar, had hastily to organize a thorough shake-up in political indoctrination and just plain education to make the local cadres fit to lead the villagers. Before long Yenan had become known throughout China, and even abroad, as a kind of new Mecca toward which a constant stream of political pilgrims poured. Older visitors wanted to see what strange social experiments were going on there; younger students wanted to stay and learn. It was Chou En-lai's job to meet and explain to these visitors what the Communists were trying to accomplish, and to make arrangements for those who chose to remain.[1]

Teng Ying-ch'ao had her own jobs. Before there were enough trained women comrades she herself had to make house calls from door to door to help the women straighten out their family problems, learn some rudiments of modern child care without modern facilities, and fight tuberculosis, foot-binding, sales of young girls, and everything else all at once. On top of all this there was the constant threat of a KMT attack. Chiang Kai-shek had instructed the warlords in the neighboring province of Shansi by telegram to "cleanse the map of China of Red stains."

Chou En-lai and his wife rarely shared a meal in their neat little cave. When they did, the conversation was always merry and pleasant, like that between two old warriors looking back over some of their heroic feats. Their faded blue army uniforms looked baggy on both of them, but his beard—a favorite butt of her jokes—was trimmed, and her hair was neatly combed. "Remember how you chided me for putting too much salt in the chicken when we were with Second Aunt in Shanghai?" she said. "Now we'd be lucky if we had enough to salt any dish."

"Well, it isn't quite as bad as it was toward the end of our days in Kiangsi when we really had to save every grain of salt. Anyway, you can always use soy sauce when out of salt." The last was a famous joke that had circulated in Kiangsi, started by some wit who always had a way of making light of even the grimmest fact in the bleak existence of the Kiangsi Soviet in mid-1934. Soy sauce was a luxury because it required an abundant amount of salt to make.

At the end of one meal she surprised him with a cup of pot-boiled coffee; on the can was the popular American S & W brand! "The last bit of the can," she said. "Old Mao brought it over himself. He said a Western visitor gave it to Chu Teh, and it has passed through the hands of many comrades, each taking a few spoonfuls, before reaching us."

But Chou En-lai did not stay to enjoy that rare cup of coffee. From outside the cave entrance someone called him for an emergency conference with Old Mao.

While Chou, Mao, and their comrades were floundering in the swampy mire of the grassland on the uninhabited Szechwan-Chinghai border, Georgi Dimitrov stood before the Seventh World Congress of the Comintern in Moscow praising the Chinese comrades and urging them to turn their attention to international imperialism. "Due to the change in the international and domestic situation," said Dimitrov, "a united front against imperialism has assumed an extraordinarily significant position in all the colonial and semi-colonial countries." The Chinese delegation, represented by Ch'en Shao-yü, was roundly applauded. Ch'en himself was elected to the Steering Committee of the Executive Committee, and Mao Tse-tung, Chou En-lai, and Chang Kuo-tao were elected in absentia to the Executive Committee.

The Moscow pronouncements, including one by Ch'en Shao-yü,[2] encouraged Chou En-lai and Mao Tse-tung to concentrate on the united-front approach, which they had broached before.[3] Quite apart from the threat of Nazism to the international communist movement, Chou and Mao had now come directly under the shadow of Japanese expansion, which since 1931 had started reaching beyond Manchuria into the length and breadth of East and North China, setting up puppet regimes (Japanese-controlled Chinese self-governments) along the way. At the same time, Chiang Kai-shek was still determined to wipe out the Reds; his motto was "Internal pacification before resistance to foreign invasion!"

Nevertheless, Chou En-lai reasoned, the time was ripening for a national united front to resist Japan which would force Chiang to turn his troops away from the Reds. Every day there was some incident in the various parts of China: the arrival of more Japanese troops in North China, Japanese police and bullies beating up and killing Chinese, students beaten and killed in demonstrations against the flooding of Chinese markets with Japanese goods smuggled in under armed protection, Japanese-trained-and-supplied Chinese traitors clashing with patriotic soldiers . . . each incident adding to the nationwide upsurge of anti-Japanese sentiment, which clamored, "Chinese don't fight Chinese! Look, who is our real enemy?"[4]

Through the Central Committee of the CCP, Chou and Mao said in unison, "Even though educating and organizing the masses on the lower social level is critical, it alone is not enough. Our comrades must learn to work with higher echelon and top leaders of all other political parties and factions who can influence the masses. Our Party must be prepared to negotiate and compromise in order to win over elements from other political parties. Our comrades must remain active among all revolutionary segments, petite bourgeoisie and intellectuals as well as peasants, workers, and soldiers."[5]

Chiang Kai-shek personally flew from one major city to another, exhorting the KMT troops in East, Central, and Southwest China to mop up the Communist troops holding out in scattered Red bases. In North China he concentrated his best soldiers to close in on Yenan. On February 21, 1936 as the Chinese Soviet regime called on all the parties and factions in China to convene a national conference to discuss waging war against Japan, one of the elite Communist divisions was being decimated in Shansi.[6] The area under Communist control in northern Shensi was shrinking. For Chou and Mao it was increasingly urgent to make the united front a reality to halt the KMT attacks.

On May 5, 1936, Chou, Mao, and Chu Teh sent a formal truce proposal to Chiang Kai-shek.[7] Chiang assigned Ch'en Li-fu, the KMT's political security chief who had handled the Ku Shun-chang case in Shanghai in 1931, to meet with Chou En-lai. With the blood of espionage and counterespionage still fresh on the hands of both sides, and with the KMT troops still fighting Red soldiers in different parts of the country, Chou made preparations to face his deadly enemy in Shanghai and Nanking.

The moment Chou reached Shanghai, however, he found that not everyone there was unfriendly toward the CCP; there were plenty of people who lent willing ears to his plea for a united front. The neutral groups, the third parties, and many respected independent intellectuals had been hoping for a cessation of civil war. Chou spread word among them that he was ready to come to terms with Chiang, and they responded by forming an "All-China National Salvation League" on May 31, 1936, to support Chou's effort to expedite the realization of a united front. The KMT terms accepted by Chou En-lai included replacing communism with Sun Yat-sen's Three People's Principles, integrating the Red Army in Chiang Kai-shek's command, and converting the

Chinese Soviet Government into a local government under Nanking.[8]

The League cheered the Communists' generous concessions and, offering its good offices for the CCP and KMT to work out a rapprochement, proposed a National Salvation Conference to unify the country against foreign aggression. From Yenan Mao Tse-tung immediately responded with enthusiasm, but Chiang Kai-shek chose to ignore the proposal, thus driving the disappointed League closer and closer to the CCP, until the arrest of the League leaders by the KMT on November 23, 1936 all but turned Chiang into a villain in the eyes of the independent intellectuals and Western observers.

Mao stayed in Yenan and Chou in Shanghai, and together they kept urging a united front—cessation of civil war and the convening of a national conference to fight the Japanese invaders.[9] It was a popular line which catered to the national mood. But Chiang Kai-shek insisted that the Communists must lay down their arms and surrender their army before he would call a truce, and Chou and Mao were not ready to lose "the Red Army's autonomy in organization and leadership."[10] Chiang had his hands full during most of 1936 with one more rebellion in chronically troublesome Kwangsi and Kwangtung where old warlords and his former colleagues raised independent banners demanding "national salvation" and "resist Japanese aggression." Action continued across the no-man's-land between the KMT and CCP soldiers, as Chou En-lai, the chief delegate from the caves of Yenan, continued to run between Nanking and Shanghai, cementing friendship between all non-Kuomintang elements and the Chinese Communist Party.

While Chou was busy negotiating for a united front, an incredible political maneuver occurred. Chiang Kai-shek was kidnaped in Sian on December 12, 1936.

Chiang Kai-shek has declared in his own account of the

incident that the most surprising element was that the prime
mover was not the Communists, but the dashing thirty-eight-
year-old Young Marshal, Chang Hsüeh-liang, who had inherited the Northeastern army from his warlord father, Chang
Tso-lin, and that the actual kidnaping was ordered by General
Yang Hu-ch'eng, head of the Northwestern army. At first
Mao Tse-tung doubted the telegram bearing the news, but
after the third or fourth message repeated the same story to
him, he immediately dispatched Chou En-lai to Sian.[11]

Several behind-the-scenes developments had set the stage
for this melodrama. The Northeastern troops under the
Young Marshal had been ordered by Chiang Kai-shek to wipe
out the Reds in North China. For months only minor skirmishes occurred because the soldiers on both sides, after all,
spoke the same language and had no ancient grievance to
settle. Then in early summer of 1936 a major engagement
shaped up in the Li-hsien area, with over 30,000 Red troops
facing the 106th and 180th Northeastern Divisions. The Reds
won. Numerous Northeastern officers and men were taken
captives and not released until they had received a rich dose
of Communist indoctrination.

Among the returning prisoners Chou En-lai selected a brig-
adier to whom he entrusted a confidential message for the
Young Marshal. In it Chou pleaded with the Northeastern
army chief to turn his guns on his real enemy, the Japanese,
who were ravishing his Manchurian homeland. "The Chinese
do not fight Chinese," said Chou. "Inhuman is he who slays
his own brother to feed the wolf!" The confidential messenger, a Northeasterner himself, watched his chief, whose eyes
began to moisten as he read Chou's letter, and felt a lump in
his own throat.

Chou's political squads—many of them staffed by women
—exercised their well-cultivated persuasive ingenuity and
picked up their chief's theme. They moved within shouting
distance of the Northeastern foot soldiers, who were mostly
farm hands from Manchuria, played up the theme of "Chi-

nese do not fight Chinese," and "For four years now you've been missing your family; why don't you let us help you fight your way home?" The winter of 1935–36 hit both the Reds and the Northeasterners with the bitter freeze of the northland, yet Chou managed to spare some Red Army ration and have it delivered to the already propaganda-indoctrinated Northeasterners who were supposedly besieging Chou's men. The Red food, however meager, warmed their stomachs, and the Red words warmed their hearts. Before long the only thing that remained frozen among these Northeasterners were their rifles.[12]

Communist infiltration in the Northeastern army accelerated. To reach the Young Marshal directly Chou had planted a personal friend, his former elementary schoolmate at Mukden, as chief of the political bureau in the Marshal's "Communist Bandit Suppression Headquarters." Red agents were installed in the city of Sian, and General Wang Yi-che became one of the Communist proponents among the Northeastern field commanders.[13]

Informal communication between Yenan and the Northeastern army began. On at least one occasion the Young Marshal visited Yenan and invited the famed Red soldier, Yeh Chien-ying, to come to Sian to advise him on the modernization of the Northeastern troops. No need for the Communists to walk furtively about Sian now; they swarmed in and out of their liaison office, which was thinly disguised as a clinic run by a German dentist in the newer section of the city. Soon rumors were rife that the Young Marshal and the Northwestern army commander, General Yang Hu-ch'eng, were both negotiating secretly with the Reds.

Formal talks between the Young Marshal and the CCP came about in a devious way. Months before the Sian Incident, a Communist go-between[14] had brought the Young Marshal together with P'an Han-nien (Chou's assistant in Shanghai after the murder cases of 1931) in a Shanghai suburban restaurant, but because P'an was not empowered to

name any specific terms for the proposed truce, the conference
was inconsequential. Then, as a token of faith, the Reds
voluntarily lifted their siege of the Young Marshal's troops
about 150 miles north of Sian but only twenty miles south of
Yenan. Persuaded by General Wang Yi-che, who was already
sympathetic to the CCP, the Young Marshal met an official
representative from Yenan in a city forty miles to the
south.[15] Truce terms were exchanged and initially settled.

With the Young Marshal's friendly attitude assured, Chou
En-lai went to Sian to meet with him in a Catholic establishment one evening. Chou began by cautiously questioning
the Young Marshal on what he knew of Chiang Kai-shek. As
the latter persistently referred to Chiang as his superior
whose sincerity to fight the Japanese he could guarantee,
Chou asked, "What about the three conditions [the Sino-
Japanese friendship alliance, the negotiation for a Sino-
Japanese-Manchurian settlement, and the joint effort against
communism] laid down by Japanese Foreign Minister Hi-
rota?" The Young Marshal's reply was to vouch that Chiang
would never accept them.

After they had agreed on Chiang Kai-shek's sincerity and
stature and that he was the only logical person to lead the
nation against Japanese aggression, Chou explained to the
Young Marshal that most of the Red generals were formerly
under Chiang's command, hence they would be willing to
take orders from him again if they could feel sure that this
time Chiang meant what he said about CCP-KMT co-
operation. The two proceeded to review the truce terms on
which an understanding had already been reached:

"The integration of all Red Army units into national armed
forces would be carried out with a guarantee to keep their
combat strength intact. The Red units to be affected in the
integration would include all those in Kiangsi and Honan
provinces, as well as in the Ta-pieh Mountain Ranges [in
Hupeh and Anhwei Provinces]. Once reorganized, the former
Red troops would receive the same treatment as the Na-

tionalist regular army. The CCP would agree to cease its political agitation within the armed forces and other organized political campaigns, but CCP members as individuals would retain their political rights, except the right of participation in activities against the government or its leader [Chiang Kai-shek]. In exchange for this promise, the Communists held in KMT prisons would be released to go anywhere they chose, including northern Shensi [the CCP base] if they were non-military personnel. At the conclusion of the war against Japan, the Red Army would be rehabilitated in the same way as the Nationalist troops, and the CCP would continue to function as a legal political party."[16]

The last phrase of the agreement was checked; the main business was over. Chou stood up to shake hands with the Northeastern army chief. "Young Marshal," said Chou, using the familiar way of addressing him, which was ordinarily reserved for his subordinates who had served under his father, the Great Marshal Chang, "now that it's all settled, I am ready to take orders from you this very moment."[17]

"That wouldn't be quite right," said the Young Marshal. "We both will wait to take orders from Generalissimo Chiang Kai-shek."

"If you still have any doubt about the determination of my party to join in a united front against Japan, I will gladly stay here in Sian with you and be held as a hostage," said Chou.

"That won't be necessary at all," said the Young Marshal. "We have agreed to this," pointing to the document on the table; "it is as good as done. You know, besides national humiliation, I have a personal account to settle with the Japanese [his father had been killed in 1928 by a bomb believed to have been planted by Japanese]. My determination to fight them is as strong as anyone else's. It is only that being a soldier I shall have to report to my superior, the generalissimo, first and try to persuade him to make our agreement a reality."

After the Young Marshal failed in his efforts to see Chiang

Kai-shek about the proposed truce during the next few days,
he informed Chou that perhaps a local truce could be
achieved pending an over-all decision by Chiang. The CCP
sent Yeh Chien-ying to see the Young Marshal with a detailed
cease-fire plan and a formal truce agreement signed by Mao
Tse-tung, which offered to turn over the command of the
Red Army to the Young Marshal if all future military activities were to be directed exclusively against Japan. At the
Young Marshal's suggestion, the Red troops withdrew northward[18] toward Yenan to create a buffer zone. In return, the
Young Marshal donated a large sum from his personal funds to
the inadequately supplied Red Army to buy clothing badly
needed in the bitter northern winter. Close contact between
the Northeastern army and the CCP was established through
the Communist delegation in Sian, which rapidly became a
leftist city teeming with representatives of such pro-Communist organizations as the National Salvation League and
the National Federation of Students. Through these contacts the Young Marshal also gave financial aid to the Com-
munist-led workers in Shanghai who went on strike in
Japanese-owned textile mills.

Meanwhile resentment rose among the Northeastern
troops against Chiang Kai-shek because their request for additional veteran pension money had been denied, and their
leader, the Young Marshal, had been slighted in the most
recent National Day celebration in Nanking.[19] Red agents
in the Young Marshal's headquarters seized the opportunity to
fan antagonism. Propaganda pamphlets[20] appeared calling
on the Northeasterners and the Northwesterners to unite
against Japan in spite of what Chiang Kai-shek might or
might not decide to do.

General Yang Hu-ch'eng, commanding the Northwestern
armies, had known about the Young Marshal's contact with
the Reds and their secret truce agreement. Encouraged by a
Red agent[21] serving on his staff, Yang became even more
violently anti-Chiang Kai-shek than the Young Marshal him-

self. It was Yang who urged the use of physical pressure on Chiang to force him to come to terms, an action (*ping-chien,* remonstrance with soldiers) with many precedents in Chinese history. Thus the stage was set for Chiang's kidnaping.

The moment Chiang arrived in Sian, the Young Marshal became aware of the possibility that the disgruntled Yang Hu-ch'eng and other Northeastern officers might push the plot to more drastic ends. He feared for Chiang's life and made it a point to be with Chiang wherever he went. Twice he conferred with Chiang, whose words and ideas touched him and made him still more hesitant to act. Unfortunately Chiang somehow saw fit to exclude both the Young Marshal and General Yang Hu-ch'eng from a series of top-command conferences held in his Sian headquarters, which aroused their suspicion that their secret dealings with the CCP had perhaps been leaked. In panic Yang ordered his men to put Chiang Kai-shek under house arrest, a development that took the CCP by surprise.

Sian was thrown into confusion, and the nation was shocked. Yang Hu-ch'eng, having acted rashly, did not know what to do with the tiger in his net. The desperate Young Marshal had to turn to the CCP for advice. Chou En-lai, Ch'in Pang-hsien, and another top CCP leader arrived on the scene. The first thing Chou said to the Young Marshal were words of praise for his courage and intelligence, coupled with criticism for his lack of experience in handling an emergency of that kind.[22]

The next thing Chou did was to visit the incarcerated Chiang, his former boss. What transpired during that dramatic confrontation has never been made known to a third person, and Chiang later would not even acknowledge that the meeting had taken place.

Chou made it clear to the Young Marshal that the CCP had no intention of harming Chiang Kai-shek; instead it was ready to live up to its agreement of supporting Chiang as the national military chief to fight the Japanese. However, he reiterated the CCP's decision to stand by the Northeastern troops, to turn over the Red Army command to the Young Marshal if necessary, in order to resist any effort detrimental to united warfare against Japan. He accepted the Young Marshal's invitation to serve on the Emergency Committee consisting of the representatives of the Northeastern army, the Northwestern forces, and the CCP, to seek Chiang Kai-shek's acceptance of the Eight Conditions[23] for his release. To back up his promise, Chou ordered the Red units to assemble in combat position in the Yao-hsien and San-yüan area a few miles north of Sian.

In this state of nerve-wracking turmoil, the initiative gravitated toward the purposeful, well-organized CCP. The emotionally upset Young Marshal relied upon Chou En-lai to make decisions and to keep peace among the insurgent units. The Young Marshal clashed once with his collaborator, General Yang Hu-ch'eng, over the issue of whether to release Chiang Kai-shek. The Marshal believed that Chiang should be released immediately; Yang disagreed. Chou had to intervene in the violent quarrel by persuading the Young Marshal to leave the room, after which Chou, alone with the hot-headed Yang, pacified him.

Supported by Mao and the majority of the CCP,[24] Chou En-lai, the key person on the Sian Emergency Committee, worked for a peaceful settlement of the incident in the interest of a united front against Japan. This meant not only safety for Chiang Kai-shek but preservation of his dignity and prestige. Chiang's lieutenants in Nanking had issued a warrant to arrest the Young Marshal and declared a national emergency, and full-scale civil war against the Reds, the Northeastern and Northwestern armies would surely result if Chiang were in any way harmed. And with the Japanese already occupying the tip of the Shantung Peninsula, marching on Peking, and attacking the provinces of Chahar and Suiyuan, China could not afford a civil war. Chou En-lai nevertheless had a difficult time explaining this to the extremist Northeasterners and Northwesterners, who had expected him to call a mass meeting immediately to try Chiang Kai-shek.

Through the Emergency Committee, Chou and the Young Marshal tried to make Chiang publicly accept the Eight Conditions, which closely paralleled the secret agreement between the CCP and the Young Marshal, except for including broader terms of political freedom for all "patriotic groups," a condition aimed at opening Chiang's many political jails. Chiang, while indicating that the conditions were not entirely unacceptable, refused to bargain under duress. No written agreement was reached, and the impasse was not broken until December 25, 1936, when the repentant Young Marshal, against the advice of his personal confidants, flew his own plane to escort Chiang back to Nanking. Chiang was out of danger, but the Young Marshal was never again allowed to see his Manchurian troops.

The unfinished and inconclusive negotiations continued in Sian, where Chiang Kai-shek set up a field headquarters with a high-ranking KMT general[25] in charge of carrying on talks with Chou En-lai, assisted by the comrade who had drunk rooster's blood with the Lolo chief a year before. The issue of incorporating the Red Army in the Nationalist forces was the crux of the problem. Chou claimed that 20,000 men were in Communist uniform, but in reality by this time the core of the elite Red Army had been whittled down to no more than 8000 troops.[26] Often the Communist demands exceeded the authority of the KMT field headquarters, and Chou had to journey to Nanking to present the CCP viewpoint directly to the KMT government and Chiang Kai-shek.

The strange circumstances in Sian brought about an unexpected reunion. Chou's high school friend, Han, who had shared the same desk and acted as his protector for four years at the Nankai Middle School and later had kept Chou in his house in Kyoto for a year, was now a member of the Control Yuan in the KMT government. His connection with the

Manchurian forces and his personal acquaintance with the
warlord Chang Tso-lin and the Young Marshal made him a
most suitable envoy between Chiang Kai-shek and Sian. Seventeen years had elapsed since he and Chou had said their
last farewell in Kyoto, and meanwhile they had permanently
parted political ways.

Now in 1937 they were brought face to face again in Sian
by Han's mission to deliver Chiang Kai-shek's revised truce
terms to Chou En-lai. An awkward moment of silence froze
them when Han walked into Chou's office at General Yang
Hu-ch'eng's residence. Then Chou broke out in a smile. The
handshake was a bit strained. Hesitantly Han began by addressing Chou as "Mr. Chou," not knowing whether he
should revive their old first-name familiarity. Chou reciprocated with, "Mr. Han, ah, it's been many years."

"Yes, we both are getting old," said Han.

"Yes, we are." Chou unconsciously passed his hand through
his beard, which he had worn, off and on, depending upon
where he traveled, since his days in Kiangsi.

"How is your wife?" asked Chou.

"She manages all right."

"Any children?"

"Only one."

Then with a twinkle in his eyes, Chou seemed to have
rolled back twenty years as he asked: "Still the same wife?"

Han's reply was an inarticulate humph. He felt heat rising
in his neck as the volumes of Communist vilification against
KMT bureaucrats for their alleged corrupt life in unoccupied China rang in his ears. The insult he felt stiffened him,
and he dismissed from his mind the image of his early high
school friend to finish the rest of the interview in a cold, busi-
nesslike manner.

The mood of many radical Northeastern officers was dark
and ugly. Now that they had freed Chiang, lost the Young
Marshal, and gained no guarantee for their case, they felt that

all they had tried had come to nothing. Some of them directed their resentment against Chou En-lai. Chou nearly lost his life, and his savior this time was a Japanese-trained political adviser to the Young Marshal, Miao Chien-ch'iu[27]—a tall, broad-faced, broad-shouldered Manchurian with a booming voice whose extreme views, expressed in fiery oratory, had earned him the nickname of "Madman Miao" from his associates.

Miao had studied political science in Japan where he, like many other Chinese students there, had seen enough to make him chauvinistically aware of China's plight. He despised the KMT for its corruption and inability to act, distrusted the CCP, and nursed a desperate desire to fight the Japanese. When he became the Young Marshal's political brain trust, he urged him to take action without the CCP. He planned the Sian coup to force Chiang to act, but repeatedly protested against the Young Marshal's overtures to the Reds. Their disagreement exploded when Madman Miao shouted at his boss, who drew his pistol, but checked himself in time to have his political adviser merely locked up in a stockade on Sian's city wall for several days.

What Miao had wanted to see as an organized, well plotted pressure on Chiang Kai-shek turned out to be an accidental Sian Incident. Fear of a mass arrest upon Chiang's release forced Miao to flee to Tientsin. Two days later, he returned to Sian in disguise. The only thing that he believed could salvage the situation was the release of the Young Marshal. He went to see Chou En-lai, who, having heard of his record on the Young Marshal's political staff, greeted him warmly as "our great comrade Miao." Miao retorted: "We only happen to want the same thing for China at this moment; other than that we have nothing in common. I am not your comrade!" Chou tried to persuade Miao to establish a political party to realize his ideal if he disagreed with both the CCP and the KMT. Miao's answer remained the same: "Let's get the Young Marshal out first."

During the subsequent two months Chou conversed with
Miao frequently on the political destiny of China. Clustering
around Miao was a large group of extremist Northeastern
officers ready to offer their lives in exchange for their leader's
return. They clashed with General Yang's Northwestern
troops and CCP agents, accusing both of betraying the Young
Marshal. On February 2, 1937, pro-Communist General
Wang Yi-che was murdered. To check the chain reaction of
personal vendetta, the Emergency Committee placed Miao
in protective custody to isolate him from his diehard followers, one of whom, Wu Chieh-hsia, was his close assistant.
One day Chou telephoned Miao to arrange another visit.

"Let's ask him to make up his mind—either get the Young
Marshal back or no more talk," Wu said to Miao after he
had agreed to let Chou call on him in the afternoon. Wu
had grown impatient with the apparently useless Chou-Miao
conversation.

"What if he again refuses to accept the Young Marshal's
release as a prerequisite to any further truce talks with Chiang
Kai-shek?" Miao asked.

"Then I'll kill him!" said Wu.

"What good would that do?"

"That'll show these hypocrites that we mean business. We
can always go back to Manchuria to fight it out."

"No! You are to do nothing of the kind," said Miao, glaring
at the young officer; and he added as he watched him leave
the room, "You don't have to stay around when Chou En-lai
comes, and . . . leave your gun here!"

That afternoon the guard let in a man wearing a KMT
government-issued cotton uniform, olive green but showing
faded spots because of defective dyestuff. Beltless, it hung
loose and seemed two sizes too large for the slim-looking
visitor. For a moment Miao could not recognize him, but
soon both he and his visitor burst out laughing.

"What happened to your beard?" asked Miao. "Are you
preparing to go to Nanking?"

"No, not for a day or two," said Chou En-lai. "Besides, Nanking can't be worse than it is here these days."

A guard brought in a cup of tea for Chou and refilled Miao's cup on his desk. Chou thanked the guard, calling him "comrade."

Chou and Miao exchanged information on the latest developments in Sian. There had been another clash between loyal supporters of the Young Marshal and some pro-left soldiers of the Northeastern army. Guards had been doubled to insure the safety of the Emergency Committee members. Chou and Miao skirted the subject of the Young Marshal which had frequently stalemated their earlier conversations. Finally, after a long pause, Miao asked, "Still no news from the Young Marshal?"

Chou shook his head.

"You've made up your mind not to do anything about it?" Miao raised his voice.

"Look, Brother Chien-ch'iu, we've gone over this many times already. It isn't that I don't want to help. It is just not up to me to dictate the final terms. Besides, the Young Marshal is only one person, and there is a whole nation to think about . . ."

"But you never told me exactly what terms you and Chiang Kai-shek discussed the day you went to see him!" Miao stood up and walked over to the chair where Chou sat comfortably with his legs crossed.

"How many more times do you want me to tell you? When I walked into his room that day, I offered my hand to him and said, 'Chiang Hsien-sheng [Teacher Chiang], I'm your student. So long as we are fighting the Japanese, anything you say will be acceptable to us.' Then he said . . ."

"I don't believe it!" Miao interrupted him. "I have heard enough from you to know that you Communists believe the Young Marshal, or any one else for that matter, is expendable for the sake of your revolution."

"No, Brother Chien-ch'iu, not for *my* revolution. It's for

our revolution and for those hundreds and thousands of our compatriots who are dying this very minute, either under Japanese bombs or of hunger and disease. You have lived in the Marshal's comfortable headquarters too long. You have not bothered to walk on your own feet for days in western Szechwan and northern Shensi and many other out-of-the-way places in our country. You have not seen how the majority of our people live. They have not lived like human beings for generations. And here you are, fighting for your personal loyalty to one person who, after all, has been taken to Chiang Kai-shek's own house and is sharing his own food . . ."

"Since when did the Communist Party start feeling humane about anybody? You and your ism have long condemned man for his second original sin—the Christians have condemned the first one but you don't recognize that—which is his birth into a landlord family, into what you call 'the lingering poison of feudalism.' That's why you consider the Young Marshal expendable. Tell me, didn't you say that you Communists never shed tears upon the death of a comrade?"

"No. We never shed tears of sadness. We have only tears of anger. And there is a tremendous difference. We are fighting for the people, but we have no use for sentimentalism. Our revolutionary experience has been earned with our comrades' lives, and our policy is written in blood that cannot be washed away with a few drops of sentimental tears . . ."

A guard, concerned about the shouting in the room, peeped in to see what was going on. He saw his boss standing face to face with the visitor who was wiping his eyes with the back of his hand.

Two months passed, and Chou realized that Miao would not do anything to modify the position of the Northeasterners until the Young Marshal's release. Chou was disappointed, but when Miao agreed to sneak out of Sian without alerting his faithful followers, Chou helped him secure transportation and safe conduct through the Communist-controlled area.

Several rounds of negotiation later, on February 10, 1937, Chou offered the KMT a guarantee that the Reds would cease to advocate a violent overthrow of the government, reorganize their army to accept Chiang Kai-shek's orders, carry out general elections in the Soviet Areas, and cease the Communist-style land reform.

On the surface these four promises were so sweeping as to suggest a surrender to Chiang Kai-shek, but the CCP's Central Committee explained them differently to the alarmed comrades. "The Communist Party," said the Central Committee, "was not surrendering to the KMT when it offered the four guarantees. They were indeed a concession, and a compromise (here the KMT observers smiled), but such concessions and compromises in no way diminished the autonomy of the Communist Party's own organization (here the KMT observers frowned). They will not restrict the CCP's freedom in criticizing the Nationalist Government. Nor will they signal an abandonment of the CCP's leadership with regard to the fully awakened revolutionary forces [the Red Army, the aroused peasantry, etc.], and the revolutionary organizations created by the Party through long years of revolutionary struggle."[28]

And when the clarification went on to stress the Communist belief that the ultimate deliverance of the Chinese people and the leadership for a national revolution rested with the CCP, not the KMT, Chiang Kai-shek was loath to respond to Chou En-lai's overture.

The Marco Polo Bridge Incident of July 7, 1937, when the Japanese openly attacked a Peking suburb, electrified the whole country. A week later Chou rushed to Lushan in Kiangsi to see Chiang about expediting the formation of a united front.[29] Chou took Chiang's terms back to Yenan where he promptly developed a compromise, which, as reflected later in the open letter of September 22, 1937 to the Chinese people, offered four specific concessions to the KMT: willingness to fight to implement Sun Yat-sen's Three People's

Principles; cessation of Communist violence and land confiscation; abolishment of all Chinese Soviet governments; reorganization of the Red Army into a National Revolutionary
Army under Chiang Kai-shek's command.

The Japanese, after occupying Peking, Tientsin, and many
other cities in North China, were now attacking Shanghai and
bombing Nanking. With no time left to quibble, Chiang
accepted the Communist offer. The Northern Shensi Border
Soviet Area government was accorded the status of a provincial government under the Nanking regime, and the Red
Army was renamed the Eighth Route Army. Thus, simply by
changing their labels, both the Communist regime and the
Communist army obtained legitimate status in China. And
the chief architect of the united front, Chou En-lai, after
fleeing KMT secret agents for over ten years, was once again
Chiang Kai-shek's ally—at least in theory.

CHAPTER 9

CHIANG'S MAN OR MAO'S MAN?

NOW THAT A FORMAL ARENA had been arranged where Chou En-lai could exercise his prime talent of working with all parties and factions—persuading them, bargaining with them, constantly nudging them unobtrusively toward the left—the Central Committee of the CCP lost no time in setting up a Committee on Liaison with Friendly Forces and putting Chou En-lai in charge.

The new assignment doubled the significance of Chou's other jobs as chief Political Commissar of the Red Army, Chief of Staff of the Revolutionary Military Committee, and Vice-Chairman of the Party's Central Committee; it would in fact have made Chou the sole plenipotentiary speaking for the CCP, if there had been no Ch'en Shao-yü, the garrulous head of the Moscow-trained clique that had risen to power in the Party in 1931 and that had been only partially eclipsed in 1935 during the Long March. Ch'en prided himself on being a Marxist theoretician; he out-argued Chou every time in the Central Committee, and out-wrote Mao Tse-tung in releasing public statements for the CCP. But Mao knew that Ch'en was not Chou's equal in dealing with non-Communists.

It was Ch'en Shao-yü, however, who expounded the united-front line in Moscow in August 1935, and was elected to the prestigious Steering Committee of the Comintern, not Chou or Mao. So in March 1937, riding on the momentum of the united-front political offensive spearheaded by Chou En-lai,

Ch'en went ahead to speak for the Party, urging the political and military unity of the nation to fight the Japanese and establish a "democratic Chinese republic . . . fashioned after Sun Yat-sen's doctrine," and not necessarily based on communism. He pledged that only "traitors and Japanese military fascists would ever attempt to overthrow the Kuomintang," and he talked about insuring "the people's livelihood as well as civil rights."[1]

While all his statements supported the official united-front policy, Ch'en talked a little too much for Mao Tse-tung's liking. And when Mao objected, the question was not whether Ch'en deviated from the party line, but rather how much emphasis he placed on what and with what rhetoric. Like the Li Li-san line dispute of 1928–30 when Li had argued for more action faster and Ch'en Shao-yü for less and a slower pace, Mao now accused Ch'en of going too far in surrendering to Chiang Kai-shek.

This basic argument went on within the CCP from 1937 until the KMT was finally driven off the mainland in 1949, and it was reflected in Chou En-lai's strategy, which blew now hot, now cold, but most of the time was warmly friendly toward everyone except Chiang himself and his few extreme rightist supporters.

Before Chou's could become the only voice speaking for the CCP in the united front, Ch'en had to be silenced. Mao Tse-tung's criticism of Ch'en in the Sixth Plenum of the CCP's Central Committee held in September 1937 in Yenan, gave the signal. The CCP wanted unity in the anti-Japanese national war, Mao said, but there also had to be ceaseless struggle within the nation to maintain the independent policy and action of the CCP. "Not everything can be sacrificed for the sake of a united front!"[2] he proclaimed.

Shortly thereafter Mao sent Chou En-lai, not Ch'en, to deliver a personal letter to Chiang Kai-shek. "We believe that unity at a time like this is more critical than ever," he wrote Chiang. "Only if all parties and factions exert their best efforts, under your leadership . . . can we halt the enemy's advance and prepare our counter-offensive . . . At a time like this when the Chinese Communist Party and the Nationalist Party share the same fate, I believe that a lasting cooperation between us will certainly sustain our war effort and defeat the enemy."[3]

With this symbolic gesture, Mao Tse-tung, head of the Soviet Regime and Chairman of the Central Revolutionary Military Committee, installed Chou En-lai as the only spokesman for the CCP in dealing with the outside world. Ch'en Shao-yü was summoned back to Yenan.

Shanghai fell in November 1937, and a month later the Japanese sacked Nanking, forcing the KMT government to move first to Hankow, then farther west to Chungking. When Chou En-lai arrived in Hankow to head up the Communist delegation, he was already a familiar figure. Clean-shaven now and smartly dressed in a KMT uniform as deputy director of the Political Department in Chiang Kai-shek's National Military Commission, he once again as in 1925–26 found himself a member of Chiang's political staff. He divided his time between the office of the Military Commission, where KMT guards smartly saluted their Deputy Director Chou, and the office of the *New China Daily News*, the CCP organ, where he conferred with his comrades on the main editorial for the day—as in the days of 1919 when he directed the Student League paper in Tientsin. The only difference was that now the united-front policy restrained his criticism of Chiang Kai-shek and the KMT. In fact he bent backward to be complimentary to Chiang. "The Generalissimo is the rightful and the only person to lead the entire nation to victory," repeated Chou in his editorials, "because of his revolutionary experience and dedication."[4]

Teng Ying-ch'ao, who came to Hankow from Yenan in the winter of 1937, added her voice to her husband's in support of the united front. "Since the beginning of the war against Japan," said Teng, "the KMT and the national government under Generalissimo Chiang Kai-shek have had a fundamental policy change to cessation of civil war and alliance with the CCP. Chinese politics has begun to turn toward democracy, and the national government, toward a unified government to carry out the sacred duty of national defense. All Chinese must support the government in fighting the aggressor."[5] She reported on women's contribution to the war effort in northern Shensi, describing how they responded to the call for volunteer guerrillas by encouraging their menfolk and even offering their own services to make winter clothes and round up medical supplies. "Women today are being freed from the feudal bondage of household chores and kitchen duties," she said, commenting on the women's movement in general. "War has destroyed their homes and killed their menfolk and children . . . and to fight the enemy they are now needed to man many posts that are as critical as combat positions."[6]

At the Chou house, Teng no longer had to put up with a borrowed mosquito net and an unpainted table; frilled curtains reappeared at her windows, subduing the sound of mahjong games which frequently rang in her living room. She was not merely an affluent hostess entertaining her socialite equals; together with her husband she had been elected in March 1938 to the People's Political Council sponsored by the KMT, supposedly to funnel ideas and talents from all political parties and non-partisans into the war effort. With just a whisper of a permanent in her hair, enough to show that she cared for her appearance and to modify her rather small eyes and wide mouth, but not enough to offend the advocates of the New Life Movement, an austerity program promoted by the Chiangs, she maintained her own political orbit in addition to that of her husband. Some of the most important united-front decisions were reached at her dinner and mahjong parties when she brought to her house for intimate conversation the women leaders she had befriended in Canton in

1925–26. One of them,[7] who had roomed with her in the Girls' Normal School in Tientsin, joined her frequently. Between rounds of mahjong they reminisced about their school life and exchanged news of the other eight close friends who, together with them, had sworn a ten-member sisterhood, Teng Ying-ch'ao being number nine.

"You've been keeping yourself very well," said the friend to her lively hostess. "I'm exhausted after that tedious meeting this morning!"

"I don't feel nearly as energetic as I used to, since I lost the baby . . . you know, with all the tension and running, and I was six months along with it."

"Oh, what a shame!" said the friend, halting her move in the mahjong game. "You didn't suffer much, I hope."

"It's all right now," Teng said with a smile, "but of course it can never be quite the same again."

A third mahjong partner, impatient with the interruption in the game, urged Teng to concentrate on the chips. Just then a neatly dressed maid came in to announce, "There is the yellow balloon," meaning that the preliminary air-raid signal had been hoisted. As part of Chou household policy, everybody had to take cover at once.

As they filed out of the room toward the air-raid shelter in the backyard, the friend noticed that Teng had changed clothes twice within the past hour. Now she was wearing a summery *ch'i-p'ao* (Chinese lady's gown) made of a colorful print material and trimmed in the latest style. June weather in Hankow was quite warm, but not enough to make one perspire that much.

The Chous were so friendly in those days that rumors began to fly about their real political loyalty. Which was Chou, Chiang's political deputy or Mao's political commissar? If Chou could get along so well with his immediate superior, Director of the Political Department Ch'en Ch'eng (Vice-President of Nationalist China until his death in 1965) who had directed the "annihilation campaigns" in 1931–35 to drive

Chou out of Kiangsi, what problems remained to be solved?

"Chou is about to sever his affiliation with Mao"—the word began to circulate in Hankow, and its credibility increased after Chang Kuo-tao, a founder of the CCP who refused to join Mao in northern Szechwan during the Long March and who was for months the only arch-rival of Mao left in Yenan, defected in April 1938. "It's inevitable that Chou En-lai will be the second Chang Kuo-tao," said a former close comrade of Chou.[8] He saw a fissure between Chou and Mao, which, he said, was all a part of the CCP's internal power struggle; Mao, he predicted, would wait only long enough to recover from the shock of Chang's desertion, and then Chou would get the ax.

Some people even put the question directly to Chou En-lai. "They say that you have already joined the Nationalist Party. Is it true?" Chou moistened his lips before replying. "How could it be true? If I left our party organization I would be useless. What good would it do if I were to join the Nationalist Party?"[9]

As head of the Committee on Liaison with Friendly Forces, the first job Chou undertook was to work on Yen Hsi-shan, the warlord in Shansi which lay adjacent to Communist territory.

In theory, the Communist forces in North China, now dubbed the Eighth Route Army under Chiang Kai-shek's overall command, were placed under Yen Hsi-shan, chief of the Second War Zone with headquarters in Taiyuan, where he operated an Academy of Political Cadres to train commissars for his troops. The director and the key staff of the Academy, all Communists,[10] greeted Chou's arrival with enthusiasm. They informed him that an imminent Japanese thrust at Taiyuan might force them to evacuate, but enough Communist comrades had been working in the Shansi troops to insure their will to fight. Preparations were completed for a huge rally at Linfen, 150 miles to the south by rail, where

Chou was scheduled to be the keynoter on November 16, 1937.

Hundreds of officers, government functionaries, and political workers (KMT, CCP, and local) congregated to listen to the Deputy Director of Political Department, National Military Commission, speak: "The entire North China is no longer controlled by a unified Chinese political authority, but has been seized by either the Japanese or their Chinese collaborators—shame on them!—who have set up 'autonomous' puppet regimes," he informed them. "We must penetrate these areas to mobilize the people for true autonomy, returning the control of the local government to the local people. The local government of North China, being rightfully part of the national government of China, must first establish a democratic system, unifying all the elements willing to fight the Japanese, regardless of their political affiliation or military chain of command. Each of these elements is to be given an equal opportunity and an equal share of responsibility in waging the national war. As to actual strategy, it must be completely and exclusively focused on resistance to Japan. This is the strategy outlined by the Chinese Communist Party. It must be adopted as the basis for all political and military activities in the war zones if we as one nation and one people are to survive."[11]

The CCP comrades in the audience applauded while KMT political workers exchanged puzzled looks. Yen Hsi-shan, who had had a redoubtable army when Chiang Kai-shek was barely beginning to train his Whampoa cadets and who had bargained from a position of strength with the Northern warlords in the early 1920s when Chiang was simply ignored, listened in silence. He liked the ring of "local autonomy" in Chou En-lai's phrases, but he was not sure how much of him would be left if the Reds overran North China. He had already grown suspicious of some of the things going on among the militia he had been trying to organize.

Yen's militia was a Sacrifice-self Save-nation League started

a year before. It collected jobless and homeless youth who
had fled Manchuria and other Japanese-occupied areas,
trained them, and armed them to fight back. As Chou En-lai
spoke on November 16, the first of these dare-to-die Leaguers
had already gone into action against the Japanese, who had
pushed into Taiyuan on November 12, and given a good account of their combat effectiveness. But Yen suspected that
the leaders of the League, particularly Po I-po (later the top
Red leader in North China), were steering the militia toward
communism.[12]

Yen was quite right. After helping to evacuate Taiyuan,
Chou had another round of conferences with his comrades
scattered among the Shansi troops before he returned to Hankow to maintain the united front. Four years later, Yen's
militia declared that they would take orders only from the
Eighth Route Army commander and walked out on the
Shansi warlord.[13] But this was merely one of many similar
incidents that plagued the united front from its very inception.

One major jolt, which nearly wrecked the united front, was
the New Fourth Army Incident in the winter of 1940.

At the time that Mao's troops were renamed the Eighth
Route Army in 1937, the Communist forces under Ch'en Yi
(now Foreign Minister in Peking) who was assigned to dig
in and stay in the area south of the lower reaches of the
Yangtze River, were designated as the New Fourth Army
and placed under Yeh T'ing, a dashing young general with a
Casanova reputation, who had taken his troops to the Nanchang Uprising of August 1, 1927, and Hsiang Ying, who
narrowly missed beating Mao in the Kiangsi Soviet. Ancient
grievances coupled with fresh differences of opinion over
strategy further strained relations between Hsiang and Mao,
and in the winter of 1938 Liu Shao-ch'i (later head of Peking
Regime), was sent to smooth things over with the New
Fourth Army. In the following spring Chou joined Liu to

keep working at the problem, which appeared to be dragging on.

Reports of schism and defection within the CCP were matched by rumors about the KMT's secret plots to liquidate Communist power. Leaflets were circulated among the Red troops describing in specific terms how they stood as unsuspecting targets of KMT coups according to a timetable drawn up in Chiang Kai-shek's headquarters.[14] The mounting tension found expression in increasing "border incidents" and in July 1940 the irritation between the New Fourth Army and its neighboring KMT troops erupted into an extensive engagement, followed by a series of skirmishes in central Kiangsu Province, not far from Chou En-lai's home town. Heated messages of mutual recrimination were exchanged between Chungking, where the KMT government was located after the fall of Hankow in October 1938, and Yenan. The KMT wanted the Reds to move north, beyond the Yangtze by December 31, 1940, and beyond the Yellow River by the end of January. The Reds refused. A showdown during the first week of 1941 resulted in the disintegration of the New Fourth Army, which the KMT ordered abolished on January 17; Yeh T'ing was taken prisoner and faced a KMT court martial.

All of unoccupied China was tense with apprehension over the possible flare-up of civil war. As the news spread, college students and instructors alike were confounded. Then they heard the voice of Chou En-lai in Chungking:

"*Injustice unprecedented in history*
To the south of the River, a lonely leaf [here Chou played on the name of Yeh T'ing, Yeh meaning 'leaf'].
Up in arms in the same room,
Unfeeling is the beanstalk burning under the pot to cook its own beans in [a paraphrase of a third-century poem]."[15]

It was an epigram in classical Chinese consisting of only sixteen characters, but full of literary allusions. It was published in the *New China Daily News*. Chou said nothing more. What else could he say in his position in Chungking, with the evidence and counter-evidence still to be assembled, and with the formal KMT-CCP negotiation over such skirmishes elsewhere already six months old?

Skirmishes like those adding up to the New Fourth Army Incident had never completely stopped, even during the honeymoon period immediately following the Sian kidnaping and the nominal implementation of a united front. By the summer of 1939, it had become evident that the united front was a false front and there would have to be a thorough re-examination of the positions of both sides.

Both sides readied their champions for the talkathon. Because the disputes were largely military—skirmishes and mutual attacks along the vaguely defined but extensive lines separating the CCP from the KMT troops deployed in juxtaposition across China—the KMT first chose Ch'en Ch'eng, supposedly Chou's immediate superior, as their chief delegate, and later General Ho Ying-ch'in, Chiang's Chief of Staff and Minister of War, and before the end of the war in 1945 several others, until the talks were taken up directly with Chiang Kai-shek himself through American Ambassador Patrick J. Hurley.

The CCP, of course, made Chou En-lai their chief delegate, assisted by Lin Piao, the vanguard general to whom the Long Marchers owed much for their survival and now Mao's heir-apparent in Peking, and Yeh Chien-ying, commander of the Eighteenth Army Corps, the new designation assigned the Red forces by the KMT government. When the issues under discussion were considered purely political, such as the convening of a National Assembly and preparations for drafting a national constitution, the battle was usually fought in the People's Political Council where the third parties and independent groups were also represented. There again, Chou En-lai led the CCP delegation, supported by Tung Pi-wu, a scholarly old man who was a carry-over from the Manchu imperial examination and later CCP delegate to the founding of the United Nations in San Francisco; Wu Yü-chang, a steady but quiet senior comrade; the garrulous Ch'en Shao-yü and his close associate the one-time CCP secretary-general, Ch'in Pang-hsien, an impatient and cantankerous fellow; and finally Wang Jo-fei, the blunderbuss of the group, who had been Chou's assistant in Paris.

With these line-ups across the negotiation table in Chungking, the first round began on June 6, 1939 and rapidly developed into a forerunner of Panmunjon, or Dienbienphu, or Geneva.

Chou made the first move with a memorandum to Ch'en Ch'eng, outlining seven major points that would insure the establishment of a border zone government (with its political control to be negotiated later), the removal of KMT troops and security police from this zone, the delivery of KMT supplies to certain CCP forces defending the Yellow River, and the lifting of the KMT blockade in the form of inspection points along the routes to Yenan. Chou further requested participation by the Communists in the local governments being set up in Hopei Province as a counterpoint to the puppet regimes supported by the Japanese.[16]

In submitting the memorandum, Chou took care to preface it with a note explaining that it was his personal statement still to be approved by the Yenan government. This set one pattern of Chou's strategy, which was to provide flexibility for retracting his statements if Yenan found them to be "going overboard in surrendering to Chiang Kai-shek."

On July 16, 1939, Chiang's Chief of Staff, General Ho Ying-ch'in, responded with a counter-proposal to set up a definite line separating the Reds from the KMT troops and with specific demands for reorganizing the Red forces, particularly the New Fourth Army, which was restless in Kiangsu (this was six months before the New Fourth Army Incident).

Chou En-lai took the KMT plan back to Yenan, where it was promptly pigeonholed. After a long wait, Yenan replied to Chungking in September. This time, the KMT did the pigeonholing. Chou waited, watching his comrades making gains in North and East China, the growing militia of Po I-po under the Shansi warlord Yen Hsi-shan, and the expanding New Fourth Army in Kiangsu. A month passed. Chou, without waiting any longer for the KMT response, submitted a revised proposal, demanding a larger border zone and more supplies from Chiang Kai-shek.

This was the second pattern of Chou's strategy—waiting for favorable conditions in the field to up his terms.

The first round of the negotiation ended in a lull, with Chou En-lai depressed over the New Fourth Army Incident and the over-all international situation as victorious Germans marched on Stalingrad. He made mildly conciliatory moves toward the KMT, but devoted more of his attention to winning the sympathy of the third parties and independent groups. He passed up no opportunity to meet and talk to people, any people, to explain the Communist case. One afternoon he appeared before a group of students and reporters who had asked him to discuss the timely subject of the New Fourth Army. His khaki uniform, without belt or insignia, was freshly pressed; his leather shoes polished to a high luster. As he stepped on the stool to mount the table set up in an open yard to serve as a temporary podium, he avoided using his right arm, which he held stiffly bent throughout the talk—the injury he had suffered in a fall from a horse in Yenan two years before had never completely healed. Looking somber and a little pale, he stood quietly on the table, gazing into the space for a long time before he began in a calm voice to analyze the tragedy that had occurred around the beginning of the year. He spoke almost haltingly for a few minutes, then, as the audience packed tightly around him, completely hushed to catch every phrase he uttered, his voice rose and flowed in greater eloquence.

There was another pause at the end of his analysis of the major events. Then, with a restrained tremor in his voice, he added, "My fellow students, this is *our* country. Whatever has happened to cause that fratricidal tragedy must be forgotten. From now on, we must look ahead . . ." Then he made the moving statement about his mother's grave in Japanese-occupied Chekiang, bending his handsome head as though in pain and concluding, "How I wish I could go back there just once to clear the weeds on her grave—the least a prodigal son who has given his life to revolution and to his country could do for his mother . . ."[17]

There was audible sniffling in the audience. Chou had struck an accord with his listeners on the theme of sentimental patriotism, an emotional force that had been motivating high school and college students to abandon their books for rifles, to go to Manchuria, Yenan, and many other fronts where they heard that action against Japanese (not against their compatriots) was in progress. And as diligently as in Yenan, Chou met and talked with everyone who cared to listen to him, encouraging anyone who was ready to go see for himself what Yenan was doing.

This was the third part of Chou's strategy—taking the case to the people when it was stalled on the negotiation table.

Between the first and the second round of negotiations, the CCP bolstered its internal solidarity with a party reform movement that closed the ranks behind Mao Tse-tung. In the spring and summer of 1942, Chou returned to Yenan to assist Mao in a series of top-echelon meetings "to correct the erroneous tendencies in party ideology and discipline." One after another, the CCP leaders who had had some disagreement with Mao lined up with him. Chou's declaration in Yenan set an example for many others to follow:

"The Party's twenty-two-year history has proved that the views of Comrade Mao Tse-tung were formed and maintained with historical perspective, aiming at a sustained effort to Sovietize China. The line he took was the only line Chinese communism could and should take. His line is the Chinese Communist line and is also the Chinese Bolshevik line. Through him and after his effort to develop it and use it, communism has gone beyond being a mere body of ideology suitable to China; it has become rather an ideology that is indigenous and has grown roots in the soil of China. Comrade Mao Tse-tung has integrated communism with the movement of Chinese national liberation and the movement of improving the livelihood of the Chinese people. . . . Because of his leadership, the strength of the party has attained an unprecedented height."[18]

With the Mao-Chou team supreme in the CCP, Chou Enlai returned to the negotiations in Chungking in March 1943, speaking in a voice more confident than ever before. Supporting his confidence was the favorable turn of the war tide in Russia. He took Lin Piao with him to call on Ho Ying-ch'in, presenting him with four new demands: KMT recognition of the CCP as a legal party; expansion of the Red Army to twelve full-strength divisions; establishment of a northern Shansi border zone; and postponement of removing the Red troops south of the Yellow River until after the war.

Chou did all the talking. Lin Piao listened, answering a question on certain military details from time to time. Ho Ying-ch'in merely restated the KMT terms of 1940 without modification. Subsequent exchanges made no progress; both sides held firm. Meanwhile mutual recriminations continued to pour out. The KMT kept charging the Communists with breach of the Four Promises (work for the Three People's Principles, the end of land confiscation and rebellion against the KMT, the abolishment of Soviet regimes, and the abolishment of Red Army systems. Chou kept denying the charges with counter-charges that the KMT was fighting the Communists not the Japanese, was suppressing criticism from neutral and independent leaders by secret arrests and assassinations, and was blockading the Border Zone. The friction led to skirmishes such as the bloody clash in Shantung Province on August 7, 1943, which once again brought the country to the brink of a full-scale civil war.

In Chungking, Chou urged freedom of speech and the practice of democracy as the only way to mobilize the people, while the KMT insisted that military exigency could not tolerate any activity uncomplimentary to the national government and its leadership. In desperation Chou reiterated the CCP's policy of supporting Chiang Kai-shek and the KMT government *because* they were fighting for Sun Yat-sen's Three People's Principles *and* had demonstrated a good beginning of moving forward in the revolution. "The Kuomintang occupies a position of leadership in the nation's political and military affairs," Chou said. "Upon the KMT's improvement hinges the prospect of China's sustained warfare against aggression and the victory . . . The KMT has as its ideological foundation the Three People's Principles, as its revolutionary heritage the 1911 overthrow of the Manchu Regime and the Northern Expedition [to eliminate the warlords and unify China in the late 1920s], and as its leaders Dr. Sun Yat-sen and Mr. Chiang Kai-shek. Furthermore the KMT released the Program for the War of Resistance and National Reconstruction, which has provided a basis for the KMT to move steadily forward. To develop and materialize this basis is not only the KMT's duty but the responsibility of every Chinese citizen. We, therefore, call upon the entire Chinese nation to work, in utmost sincerity, for the implementation of the Three People's Principles and the [abovementioned] Program."

Why did the Communist Party support Sun Yat-sen's Three People's Principles? Chou said, "The Principle of *Min-tsu* [nationalism] in practice will unify the Chinese people to fight the Japanese and call the puppets [collaborators with the enemy] to return to our fold. The Principle of *Minch'üan* [people's rights] includes a respect for the independence of all anti-Japanese parties and factions. Putting it into practice will extend popular participation in the government all the way to the village level . . . which will mobilize and organize the people to join the army, protect themselves, contribute to the war chest, and consequently insure their full *right* to fight the Japanese. Implementation of the Principle of *Min-sheng* [people's livelihood] will insure that 'each contributes all he can' to the country now, toward the future when everybody will be free from material want . . ."[19]

While Chou tried to pin down the KMT and Chiang Kai-shek on their commitment to the Three People's Principles, reserving the CCP's right not to support them if they departed from Sun Yat-sen's doctrine, the KMT took the part of Chou's statement stressing national unity and KMT leadership as a repetition of the CCP's pledge to obey Chiang Kai-shek's command *under all circumstances*. The ideological dispute, then, had become a matter of who was really carrying out the kind of revolution that Sun Yat-sen had wanted— a quarrel that persists even today.

The third round of negotiations brought Lin Tsu-han, a senior comrade of no particular distinction, and Wang Shih-chieh (then chairman of the People's Political Council, later Chiang's foreign minister, now head of the Academia Sinica in Taiwan) representing the KMT, together in Sian on May 5–8, 1944. Chou's absence, an omen forecasting the futility of the talk, did not prevent his style and stature from overshadowing the conference. At the very outset Lin re-presented Chou En-lai's earlier terms, to which the KMT responded with a new set of terms.

Lin studied them with his comrades and came up a month later with still stiffer conditions: instead of twelve Red divisions he now demanded sixteen, and more supplies. In addition Lin asked the KMT to open its political jails as it had done briefly after the Sian Incident. The KMT scaled down its request, but not enough to please Yenan, and two subsequent messages to Lin went unanswered.

The strained situation made Chou En-lai's position in Chungking increasingly uncomfortable. From the very beginning of the negotiations the KMT newspapers withheld all favorable news about the combat record of the Eighth Route Army and the New Fourth Army, and Chou became the only source of information on the guerrilla struggle behind the enemy lines. Under the circumstances, whatever he said was naturally suspected of being pure Communist propaganda.

The Communists, with their experience in Kiangsi during the Long March, and later in North and East China, clearly had an advantage in guerrilla warfare. Their emphasis on political indoctrination of the troops and the villagers as well, now supported by the Japanese atrocities, reaped many times more success than the KMT public declarations emanating from Chungking. The Communist political workers lived like any ordinary peasants, wearing the same kind of straw sandals and eating the same meager fare. They taught the villagers how to fight when the enemy unit was small, and how to take to the hills when the pressure was high; organized the village women to support the men in the guerrilla units; and held classes to train village children to help their parents and know their enemy. Wherever the Reds penetrated, Japanese occupation and control was reduced to within a few miles of the major cities, such as Shanghai and Taiyuan, which they had taken after paying a high toll.

A note of impatience was detectable in Chou's voice when the KMT's propaganda chief[20] told the press on July 26, 1944 that "progress had been made in the negotiations." Chou retorted in a public statement, "There has been absolutely no progress . . . The distance between the two parties on all concrete issues remains enormous!" Then he went on to belabor the KMT spokesman for lying to the Chinese people.

By now it had become crystal-clear that the KMT insisted on unification under Chiang Kai-shek before everything else, while the CCP stubbornly refused to surrender its army and

territory. Everything was back where it had been before the
Sian Incident, except that the Reds were now many times
stronger. With strength came truculence, as Chou declared
on October 10, 1944 in Yenan:

"The orders we can obey are only the orders directed to
strengthen our war effort, issued in a democratic manner. The
orders we must oppose are those following the fascist line
toward defeatism. We demand that the government and the
army be reorganized to permit coalition government and joint
control of the armed forces. The national government must
recognize the legal status of the various levels of popularly
elected local governments and of the troops and units fighting
Japanese behind the enemy lines."[21]

From then on Chou En-lai was to reiterate the demand for
a coalition government, and at each mention of it Chiang
Kai-shek became that much angrier.

Into this deadlocked situation walked an American mediator, United States Ambassador Patrick J. Hurley, who flew to
Yenan, gave his personal guarantee of safe conduct to Chou
En-lai, and brought him back to Chungking together with a
personal message from Mao Tse-tung. Everything in Mao's
letter appeared to be quite in order, but there were the
dreaded words "coalition government" again! More tinker-
ing and quibbling served only to enlarge the area of discord.
Upon Chou's return to Yenan, the expected happened: his
first letter to Hurley was to declare that the Central authority
of the Soviet Regime would not go along with any of the
points agreed upon so far.

The last time Chou appeared as chief Communist delegate
in Chungking was in January 1945. He again requested the
expeditious formation of a coalition government and ques-
tioned Hurley on why the United States delivered arms only
to Chiang Kai-shek's troops. When the American ambassador
said that no United States arms were to be handed over to
the troops of any political party, Chou retorted, "Isn't Chiang
Kai-shek's army serving a political party?" The point was

finally reached where even the most sanguine had to admit that any further discussion would be a sheer waste of time. Negotiations broke off in May.

By this time the lines on both sides were drawn. On March 1, 1945, Chiang Kai-shek had announced his intention to convene a National Assembly on November 12 of the same year to promulgate a national constitution. Less than two months later, on April 23, 1945, the Reds convened their Seventh Congress in Yenan with Mao Tse-tung delivering his historic report, "On Coalition Government," calling on mass assemblies in all liberated areas to demand the formation in three months of a national coalition government. The coalition-government issue was the last straw that broke the People's Political Council in July when Chou for the last time explained to his fellow council members why the CCP would insist that this issue be placed on the agenda. "What's the use of putting it on the agenda?" one KMT member[22] challenged. "You Communists are fighting your way into the government anyway." Chou ignored the challenge and turned to the chairman, "Mr. Chairman, this fellow Council member has insulted the Chinese Communist Party, which is participating in the Council as an equal to any other group. I demand that he be disqualified from Council deliberations."

The chairman did not respond to Chou's request immediately, and soon the need to take action expired—the Communist delegates had walked out of the Council.

"It's fascinating to watch how Chou En-lai operates at a negotiation table," commented a high-ranking KMT official on the scene at the time. "He shifts his line so subtly that it often escapes your notice. Of course, he makes compromises, but only minimal and nominal compromises at the very last moment just to keep the negotiations going. When you study his statements afterwards, you realize that he hasn't made any substantial concession on any important issue at all."[23]

"If Chou is acting," continued the KMT observer, "then he does it so well that after you leave him you carry with you the impression that his emotional reactions to each development in the negotiation process are genuine, and that he is a man of conviction and integrity! . . . If he tells a lie about his party's line and switches to another the next moment, he does it in such a way that nobody can blame him for it." And he added, quite prophetically, "The Communists are winning the mainland not through combat, but across the negotiation table with Chou sitting on the other side!"

Chou's subtle victory over the KMT at the negotiation table was supported by the movement of the "third party" and independent groups who banded together to urge a coalition government. The mainstay in this third force was the Chinese Democratic League, which, two months after its inauguration in Chungking in September 1944, signed an agreement with the CCP pledging never to submit to KMT dominance or even to negotiate with the KMT without prior consultation with the CCP. In return the CCP invited the League to establish branch offices and send its unemployed personnel to work in the Red-controlled Border Zones.

The League and many other non-Kuomintang groups responded warmly to Chou En-lai's call on January 24, 1945 for a national conference to plan for the future, including a coalition government.[24] It set a pattern for political maneuvers during the months immediately following the Japanese surrender in August 1945. The minor parties, whose leaders appreciated Chou En-lai's hospitality in Yenan and admired the CCP's accomplishment in bleak northern Shensi during the dark war years, rallied around the Communists to challenge the KMT's one-party rule of China. The rising clamor for a coalition government provoked the KMT to force the League to disband in October 1947, but the left wing of the League revived their organization in exile in Hong Kong, and from January 1948, they steadily steered away from their earlier position of peaceful democratic reform to drastic revolution.[25]

Chou En-lai maintained close contact with and provided inspiration for left-wing groups in Hong Kong. In addition to the League, there was the left-wing KMT, which remained in exile after Chiang Kai-shek crushed the pro-leftist Hankow Government in 1927. This group, calling itself the Kuomintang Revolutionary Committee to remind the right-wing KMT that it had ceased to be revolutionary, acknowledged that, "It was after the CCP took the lead on August 1, 1935 [the date of the united-front resolution] rallying all parties and factions to resist aggression and save the country that comrades of the KMT Revolutionary Committee found the right road for China's revolution . . . In recording the struggle of the democratic faction of the KMT, one must never forget the leadership of the CCP in the united-front movement."[26]

With statements like this, Chou En-lai needed no more tribute for his contribution to the Chinese Communist victory.

CHAPTER 10

NOW TALK, NOW FIGHT

AFTER HIS FAREWELL TO CHUNGKING in May 1945, Chou flew back to Yenan to prepare for a coalition government without Chiang Kai-shek, while Chiang proceeded to convene a National Assembly without the Communists.

Just as in 1931 Chou En-lai had headed the preparatory committee to plan for a Chinese Soviet Regime, so now he was made chairman of a preparatory committee of 129 delegates representing twenty-six organizations, of which the Communist Party with three delegates was only one. Chou's plan, announced on July 13, 1945, was to convene a National Assembly consisting of 428 delegates from all parts of the country to decide China's future and, more immediately, a grand strategy to prosecute the war against Japan.[1]

The Japanese surrender on August 10 surprised Chou. Within a few hours, Chu Teh as "Commander-in-Chief of the Resist-Japanese Armies in the Liberated Areas of China," issued seven orders to his field commanders to seize enemy territories. This move was followed by his messages to Chiang Kai-shek, protesting against an order to halt all advances against the Japanese, and requesting a prompt national conference to decide a future course of action.[2]

Chiang Kai-shek responded with three telegrams inviting Mao Tse-tung to a face-to-face talk. This brought Mao, Chou, and a number of other Red leaders to Chungking on August 28, 1945, again with American Ambassador Patrick J. Hurley as escort. Chu Teh remained in North China on the battlefield, which, as it proved later, was never completely quiet.

Thus after less than three months' respite Chou was back at the negotiation table facing, most of the time, the familiar KMT delegates. Mao Tse-tung's meeting with Chiang Kai-shek was only a formal gesture. Substantive talks were conducted between Chou and Wang Shih-chieh, the KMT's chief of information, and covered subjects ranging from democratization of the government to nationalization of the armed forces.

One day[3] when the disposition of the anti-Japanese militiamen trained by the Communists was scheduled for discussion, Chou brought with him Wang Jo-fei, who had assisted him in the demonstrations in Paris and Lyon over twenty years before. After a lengthy exchange of views Chou proposed that these militiamen be maintained by the local governments for self-defense and to maintain public security. The KMT spokesman felt that the issue was too complicated to be settled instantly and much study would have to precede a final agreement. Wang Jo-fei, who had been increasingly irritated by each of the KMT's answers, burst out with a remark, "What's the use of this kind of discussion? The Kuomintang doesn't seem to want a prompt settlement, and you don't seem to be able to speak for the Kuomintang. We are wasting our time here! The militia forces in liberated areas are of critical importance to the people there." Wang stood up, gesticulating, his face turning red.

Chou watched the performance of his junior partner with an amused smile. Then, patting him gently on the shoulder, he said, "Sit down, Jo-fei. Don't be impatient and don't hurt our friends' feelings."

Wang sat down, and Chou resumed his detailed, patient analysis of the situation in the liberated areas. He described where the militia came from, how they were trained, and how they fought behind the enemy lines. "It's too bad that in the rear area [unoccupied China] you do not have ready access to such information. Otherwise there would be no need for me to elaborate and emphasize the fact that these militiamen are armed villagers who have been defending their own farms, grazing lands, and families. For months to come they will continue to be needed to maintain local order against any possible traitor-inspired resurgence of pro-Japanese activities, against a revival of banditry, and against . . ." Chou paused as he observed that his listeners' interest in his remarks was waning as two of them reached for matches to light their cigarettes. "Well," he changed the tone and pace of his voice, injecting a note of levity, "I tell you what we'll do. Let's just get the men in the field to stop shooting, and I'll be glad to lead a personal tour for you and your friends—anyone, including Generalissimo and Madame Chiang—of the liberated area. We'll start from Yenan and go anywhere you like to go and see anything you wish to see. We'll go unannounced so that you can eavesdrop on the villagers' private conversations and listen to the farmers' songs from a distance, and you will know that they support Yenan not because we are Communists, but because of what we have done for them. And—forgive the illustration—if you catch a militiaman and a village girl together, I will stake my life that you'll find that they may be committing adultery, but never, never rape. Then you can draw your own conclusions."

Chou En-lai explained the Communist case to his opponents in this manner day after day. Always accompanied by one or two other Communist delgates, Chou did most of the talking, often for hours at a stretch, without showing any need to touch a cigarette or the cup of tea offered to him. The only time he appeared alone was when he called on Chiang Kai-shek.

The forty-one-day negotiation left the world in suspense. Every day new hopes emerged, but they were always mixed with fear. The Communists did not entertain any serious wish to beat their swords into plowshares, thereby exposing themselves to total annihilation (one of the KMT's favorite

Important cities involved in CCP-KMT talks and the civil war during and after World War II.

words) by the Nationalists. They were preparing fully for any eventuality, even before they agreed to return to Chung-king.[4]

The summary of the conference released on October 10 nevertheless added much joy to that National Day. Tentative agreement had been reached on such weighty matters as nationalization of the armed forces to be implemented through a committee including KMT and CCP representatives, reorganization of the government through a Political Consultative Conference to involve delegates from all parties and factions, and maintenance of status quo on the military fronts pending further discussion.

Following President Truman's statement of December 15, 1945, on the United States China policy, General George Marshall sat with Chou En-lai and the KMT representative Chang Ch'ün for four days to work out a cease-fire. At the same time, a Political Consultative Conference involving thirty-eight delegates from all parties and factions was convened in Chungking.

During the next two days, Chou En-lai reported before the Political Consultative Conference that Yenan had ordered all Communist troops to cease fire in deference to the people's will and world opinion. After giving the details of the negotiation, he summarized his impressions: "Personally I have learned four lessons from these negotiations. Each side must approach the other with mutual recognition, not mutual enmity. They must bilaterally discuss, not unilaterally arbitrate; they must give and take, more importantly giving before taking; and they must compete only in bringing about a prompt settlement of the difficulties."[5]

He reiterated the Communist Party's determination to adhere to Sun Yat-sen's Three People's Principles because they outlined the right path for Chinese revolution. "We recognize and accept the national leadership of Generalissimo Chiang Kai-shek," he said. "We did so during the past eight years of war, and we shall continue to do so after the victory.

We recognize and accept the fact that the Nationalist Party is the Number One major party in the country—that's why we gladly accept the arrangement to have the KMT and their supporters represented by twenty-five members in the forty-member State Council to be established, with the CCP and the Democratic League sharing fourteen seats, or slightly over one third, and one seat going to an independent. We shall always respect the position earned by the Nationalist Party through its hard work in recent history. Since the end of 1936, the Chinese Communist Party at no time sought to overthrow the National Government. Since the beginning of the War of Resistance, the Chinese Communists never established a separate central political regime to compete for national leadership with the Nationalist Party. The situation in China today demands a democratic system on the basis of the Three People's Principles. On this conviction we shall not compromise."

An atmosphere of happy reunion surrounded the Political Consultative Conference. The moment it adjourned, Chou[6] flew to Yenan on January 27, 1946. Without pausing to rest, he went straight into a night session with the CCP's Central Committee. Back in Chungking two days later he delivered to the nation the cheerful news that Yenan was deeply gratified by the improvement of the situation.[7] Everything was moving along, he said, as had been hoped, and the Political Consultative Conference was taking long strides toward success.

"I pledge to you in behalf of the Chinese Communist Party," Chou declared solemnly on February 25, 1946, announcing a series of statements agreed upon *in principle* by both sides, "that the basic pattern for the re-organization of the Communist troops will be observed 100 per cent." These agreements, to which both sides had made varying degrees of commitment, described a formula for restoring communication lines between the KMT and CCP areas, and reduction of troops on both sides to a 50–10 division balance within eighteen months.

Three days later (February 28, 1946) the Committee of Three on whom the nation's war or peace depended set out from Chungking to inspect the military lines in North China. En route Chou, Marshall, and the KMT general were all smiles as even the bomb craters seemed to greet the shadow of their airplane with a sigh of relief—now, finally, there was hope for peace and reconstruction. At Kuei-sui, in Suiyuan Province, Chou said to their greeters on March 3, "The unfortunate conflict and hostility between the two Parties have persisted for over eighteen years. The difficulties, I know, will not just melt away because we are here today. But," he added with confident emphasis, "we shall overcome them!"[8] The joy reached its climax when Mao Tse-tung toasted Marshall in Yenan the next day, "All the people of China should be very grateful to Generals Marshall, Chang Chih-chung, and Chou En-lai for their selfless dedication to the firm establishment of a peaceful, democratic, and unified China. Let us all cheer the durable co-operation between America and China, between the Communist Party and the Nationalist Party, and among all the political parties and factions." Yenan outdid itself in welcoming Marshall with a song especially composed for the occasion—an honor no other American had ever shared:

Let us sing for you, for your clear clarion call to peace, and your magnificent influence which extinguished the sweeping forest fire of war. Oh, General Marshall, let the Red Army pay its supreme tribute to you. We of the Communist Party support you![9]

Asked when he would be prepared to go to Nanking, Mao replied, while bidding farewell to Marshall at the Yenan airport, "Whenever Chairman [of the National Government] Chiang Kai-shek wants me to go, I will go." And a visibly

touched Marshall said to a Hankow audience, "I can tell
you in confidence, ladies and gentlemen, that I observed an
atmosphere of optimism everywhere I went. I can tell that
an unprecedented era of progress awaits China."[10] And he
returned on March 11, 1946 to report to his own country
the hopeful excitement generated by his visit to the Com-
munist-occupied areas, which owed much to Chou En-lai's
company, which not only had insured him the kind of reception demonstrated by everyone from Mao Tse-tung down,
but had enabled him to feel the kind of contagious enthusiasm prevailing wherever the Communists had reached and
worked.

But in the midst of all these loud cheers for peace the
cannons of war thundered on. The cease-fire order, supposedly
issued by both Chiang Kai-shek and Mao Tse-tung on January 10, 1946 to take effect at midnight three days later,
did not take effect. The Communists admitted that they
had warned their field commanders, "Shortly before the cease-
fire the Nationalist reactionary units are likely to spring surprise attacks on us . . . Destroy them wherever such attacks
occur."[11] And they reported that one such attack on a large
scale actually took place on January 16 (three days after the
cease-fire was supposed to have taken effect!) on the Chi-
ning front in Inner Mongolia. The Reds duly counter-
attacked.

With many similar clashes taking place all along the front
line, it will probably never be possible to clarify for poster-
ity just exactly who started what first in the early spring of
1946. Whatever the truth, the situation in Manchuria became explosive. The Communists were determined to hold
on to their bases there,[12] and the Russian troops in their
half-hearted evacuation stripped the area of its industrial
installations, carting most of them away and leaving only a
fraction to their Chinese comrades. In Manchuria the Reds
clearly had the advantage of years of infiltration behind the

Japanese lines, but the KMT had the advantage of the mandate agreed upon in the January 10, 1946 cease-fire that "national" troops were to move into Manchuria to take over "the sovereignty."[13]

The race for Manchuria began. Chiang's troops moved in with American trucks and jeeps and ships to take over the cities and railroads surrendered by the Russians and Japanese, but the Communists charged that the Nationalists were taking over everything and chasing and killing their Communist comrades.

Marshall tried again and again to make both sides halt their troops where they were, but neither side listened. He tried to send field teams from the Executive Headquarters in Peiping to inspect, arbitrate, and settle each clash, but the fighting was so intense that the teams could not even get into the area of action.

The military tide in Manchuria was turning in favor of the Reds on March 17, 1946 when they occupied Ssupingchieh, capital of Liaopei Province, placed the KMT governor[14] under house arrest, and fought the KMT troops sent there to assume occupation duty. Ten days later, the Reds took Changchun, a major rail and industrial center in Manchuria 120 miles northeast of Mukden.

From Chungking Chou En-lai continued to plead for a peaceful settlement. "The Manchurian question must be settled through negotiation with all democratic political parties participating,"[15] he declared on April 4. That evening he accepted the offer of a ride back to his residence. There was no third person in the car. Chou said with a weary sigh to the KMT delegate[16] with whom he had maintained almost daily contact for several months now, "I can't say that the position of our side has always been rational. Perhaps we could have made a few more concessions on the deployment of government troops along the Manchurian railways. I really don't know . . . it's such a perplexing thing." And he sighed again.

[11] *(above)* Celebrating the second anniversary of the Sino-Soviet Friendship Alliance, at the Russian Embassy, Peking, February 14, 1952. Chou, Liu Shao-chi, Russian Ambassador N. V. Roshchin, Chu Teh.

[12] *(below)* Visiting the ninety-three-year-old Chinese painter, Chi Pai-shih, Peking, January 7, 1953.

[13] *(above)* With Burmese Premier U Nu in Rangoon, June 28, 1954.
[14] *(below)* With workers at construction site, the Ming Tomb Reservoir, 1958.

[15] (above) Shaking hands with the child of a staff member of the Glass-works of North Africa, in Oran, December 25, 1963.
[16] (below) Explaining agricultural quota to peasants, February 1963.

[17] *(above)* Planting a tree of friendship in Islamabad, Pakistan's new capital, June 1965.
[18] *(below)* Visiting college students from Shanghai assigned to work at the Shihhotzu Farm in the Sinkiang Uighur Autonomous Region, July 5, 1965. (Photo by Tu Hsiu-hsien)

Chiang Kai-shek's troops, equipped with American supplies, continued to pour into Manchuria, which caused Chou to protest to Marshall that the CCP might have to reconsider its position if the United States kept on aiding one side in China's undeclared but real civil war.[17]

One unfortunate development that particularly embarrassed Marshall and impaired his position as an impartial mediator occurred when the KMT troops were fighting bitterly to retake Ssupingchieh and Changchun. Marshall asked for a neutralization of Changchun, which clearly had become the bone of contention, and the acceptance of another Executive Headquarters there to arbitrate the military conflict. Both sides agreed to think it over, with Chou weighing the chances of holding on to Changchun, and Chiang, the chances of chasing the Reds out of it. Then on May 19, 1946 the KMT retook Ssupingchieh after a month-long pitched battle. Marshall again urged both sides to make up their minds about leaving Changchun alone as the only hope to stop the fighting in Manchuria. Three days later on May 22 Chiang asked to borrow Marshall's plane to fly to Mukden to look over the situation because he feared that the momentum of victory might lead his men to march on Changchun, in spite of what he might order them to do or not to do. Marshall reluctantly agreed to the trip, but repeated that any moment's delay in halting the action around Changchun could be fatal. Chiang arrived in Mukden on May 23, the day his men entered Changchun, which the Reds had just evacuated.

Now Chou En-lai was incensed, but it was typical of his tact that he said nothing about his displeasure in the presence of his American friend. However innocent Marshall might be, it looked too much like a conspiracy between him and Chiang to trick the Reds into abandoning Changchun. To make matters worse, Chiang's presence in Mukden only accelerated the advance of his men from Changchun northeastward toward Harbin and points beyond, which was contrary to what Chiang had earlier said that he would permit.

Marshall radioed Chiang in Mukden and Peiping three times, on May 25, 29, and 31, urging him to order a cease-fire, but the signals were crossed and "mistranslated," and no cease-fire orders went out until June 6, three days after Chiang had returned to Nanking.

With the military situation in Manchuria now favoring the KMT, Chou En-lai first requested an indefinite cease-fire against Chiang's proposal of a ten-day truce before the Political Consultative Conference. Then he argued for a complete cessation of all warlike activities, both in Manchuria and to the south of the Great Wall, pending solutions to be developed by mutual agreement. "During the past twenty years," he said, "we have fought almost without stop, but also without any final settlement. I can declare without hesitation that even if we kept on fighting for twenty more years we still would not reach any solution. The fighting must stop!"[18] On June 24, 1946, the Chou-Marshall-Chang Committee reached agreement on the principles for settling the major issues, largely a reaffirmation of their agreements reached on January 10 and February 25 of the same year.

Implementation of these principles was, however, no simple matter. Chou En-lai demanded that political democratization proceed side by side with nationalization of the armed forces. "We must recognize," he said before the People's Political Consultative Conference, "that many political and historical factors were involved in the development of the personal and partisan armies that are still fighting each other today. The troops led by the Communists were forced to take up arms. We agree completely with the motion of the Young China Party delegate that the armed forces must not belong to any individual or party, but be controlled by a democratic government that can truly represent the nation."[19] He urged the inclusion of neutral, objective personnel in all agencies and offices involved in the military reorganization. "Many troop commanders are grossly prejudiced. For example, if the military information service keeps prefacing its reports by claiming that everything said by the other side is fiction, how can we ever work out a fair settlement?"

With each side totally distrusting the other, neither was willing to yield any territory under its military control or allow a situation to develop in the reorganization of the government where one side could dictate to the other. Now that Marshall's impartiality had been cast in doubt, Chou En-lai would not agree to accepting his vote in case of a tie, which made any progress in the arbitration impossible. The pattern kept repeating itself: each side talked tough when the tide of war in the field was in its favor, and toned down its voice when the army of the other side had the upper hand.[20]

While the military tug-of-war could remain indecisive for infinity, the Chinese people, through their articulate and non-partisan spokesmen, were clamoring for a prompt settlement. Intellectual leaders, journalists, and college professors watched in pain as their sons and nephews went to war to kill one another on opposite sides of the CCP-KMT line, and as the recruits, roped together to prevent escape, were herded along by armed KMT guards in Szechwan and Yunnan. As one professor, who was later murdered on July 15, 1946 in Kunming, said, "We must do something about it! Every time I looked at the bodies on the roadside I felt tortured myself . . . Look at those still tied with ropes being dragged along; their legs are only about this big!"[21] And he closed his index finger on his thumb to show his students. He, and many like him, found in the Democratic League a place where they could "do something about it." The League, some of whose leaders had been jailed by Chiang Kai-shek when he disbanded the National Salvation League in Shanghai in 1937, became increasingly critical of the Kuomintang and increasingly loud in its demands for peace and democratization of the government. The balance in the Political

Consultative Conference was shifting slowly but steadily in favor of the Communists, and Chiang Kai-shek felt he, too, must do something about it.

An intensified wave of political intimidation, of arrests and murders followed, the most shocking of which occurred in Kunming in the summer of 1946 and brought a message from President Truman to Chiang on August 10, 1946:

"I would be less than honest if I did not point out that latest developments have forced me to the conclusion that the selfish interests of extremist elements, both in the Kuomintang and the Communist Party, are obstructing the aspirations of the people of China. . . . In the United States, there now exists an increasing school of thought which maintains that our whole policy toward China must be re-examined in the light of spreading strife, and notably by evidence of the increasing trend to suppress the expression of liberal views among intellectuals as well as freedom of press. The assassinations of distinguished Chinese liberals at Kunming recently have not been ignored. Regardless of where responsibility may lie for these cruel murders . . . there is increasing belief that an attempt is being made to resort to force, military or secret police rather than democratic processes to settle major social issues . . . The people of the United States view with violent repugnance this state of affairs . . ."22

Chiang replied to Truman's strong language on August 28, 1946:

"Mistakes have also been made by some subordinates on the government side, of course, but compared to the flagrant violations on the part of the Communists, they are minor in scale . . . The minimum requirement for the preservation of peace in our country is the abandonment of such a policy [to seize political power through the use of armed force]. The Communists attacked and captured Changchun in Manchuria and attacked and captured Tehchow in Shantung after the conclusion of the January agreement. In June during the cease-fire period, they attacked Tatung and Tai-yuan in Shansi and Hsuchow in northern Kiangsu . . ."[23]

Then on September 15 Chou En-lai complained to Marshall:

"From January 13 when the Cease Fire Order came into effect until August, the Government forces in violation of that order have moved as many as 180 divisions and thrown 206 regular army divisions (or reorganized brigades) with a strength of 1,740,000 men, i.e. 85 per cent of its [KMT's] total strength into the offensive against the Communist-liberated areas; they made 6000-odd major and minor assaults, conducted over 300 bombing and strafing raids, and by September 7 had seized seventy-six cities. As a matter of fact, the Nationalist troops are everywhere on the offensive . . ."[24]

Unable to stand the mutual recrimination any longer, Marshall announced to Chiang, on October 1, 1946:

"I am not in agreement either with the present course of the Government in regard to this critical situation or with that of the Communist Party. I disagree with the evident Government policy of settling the fundamental differences involved by force, that is, by utilizing a general offensive campaign to force compliance with the Government point of view or demands . . . On the part of the Communist Party, I deplore actions and statement which provide a basis for the contention on the part of many in the Government that the Communists' proposals cannot be accepted in good faith, that it is not the intention of that Party to co-operate in a genuine manner in a reorganization of the Government, but rather to disrupt the Government and seize power for their own purposes . . . Unless a basis for agreement is found to terminate the fighting without further delays of proposals and counterproposals, I will recommend to the President that I be recalled and that the United States Government terminate its effort of mediation . . ."[25]

And Chiang argued back on October 2:

"The Government is more eager than any other party for an early cessation of hostilities, but past experience shows that the Chinese Communist Party has been in the habit of taking advantage of negotiations to obtain respite and regroup their troops in order to launch fresh attacks on Government troops who have been abiding by truce agreements (attached is a list of important evidences of Communist troops attacking Government troops during the truce periods) . . ."[26]

And so the argument went on, and on.

With Chou En-lai in Shanghai, Mao Tse-tung in Yenan, Chiang Kai-shek in the summer resort of Lushan in Kiangsi, and the American mediator in Nanking where the national government had returned in the summer of 1946, Marshall found a colleague, Ambassador Leighton Stuart, to run up and down the Kiangsi mountain with him to call on Chiang Kai-shek.

Stuart, a respected educator and for years president of the Yenching University in Peiping, took his assignment seriously. He bundled together the thick stacks of negotiation documents and took them up the Lushan mountain to go over with Chiang Kai-shek, then sought out Chou En-lai to clarify the unsettled issues. Chou received Stuart politely, treating the visitor as though he were the President of the Nankai University for whom Chou had much warm affection. For five hours they went over the tentative agreements, item by item, tracing their modifications and ramifications. As Stuart began to describe on what points the generalissimo could not agree with the CCP and why, Chou moved forward to sit on the edge of his chair, listening intently, and then bent his head in depressed silence for a long time. The American took it as a sign that Chou might consider adjusting his position on the issue, and waited, also in silence. But all he got at the end of the depressed silence was a tortured smile from Chou and a gentle shake of his head.[27]

August 1946 saw a turn to the worse in the negotiations. Into the already snarled lines of argument another provocative issue was plunged—the sale of American surplus supplies to Chiang Kai-shek. As soon as negotiations between the U.S. representative and the KMT government reached the final stage on August 23, 1946 Chou sent a message to Marshall:

"In view of past experience when the Government used every last article transferred from the United States in waging the civil war which is currently raging, the proposed sale of U.S. surplus (estimated at 500 million U.S. dollars) to the Government will indeed be pouring fuel onto the flame . . . We feel compelled to stress that the Chinese Communist Party will never accept any Sino-American arrangement of this kind. And if the U.S. persists in concluding the agreement [with the KMT], it will have to bear its share of responsibility for the serious consequence which is bound to ensue . . ."[28]

The United States nevertheless signed an agreement for the sale with the Government in Nanking on August 31. This brought a warning from Chou En-lai on September 14:

"In total disregard of our protest of August 23, [your government] proceeded to complete the sale arrangement. I have, therefore, been duly instructed by the Chinese Communist Party and the 140 million people in the Liberated Area to lodge a formal protest against the U.S. government through you . . ."[29]

Chou had not been seeing Marshall too often since the Changchun fiasco of May; his assistants had been going between his office in Shanghai and Marshall's in Nanking. But the sale of the U.S. surplus to Chiang led him to call on Marshall personally in mid-September.[30] They greeted each other warmly; the arduous task of trying to represent their respective official positions had not diminished the mutual respect they had come to have for each other. After some

cordial preliminaries, Chou said, "I suppose you know what
I am here for this time."

"I think I do, but it's useless. The sale was strictly in accordance with the United States Government policy of handling such surplus material in the interest of a friendly
nation, and China is one of America's friendly nations."

"But, my good friend," said Chou, "how about the policy
statement of your president dated December 15, 1945 which
says specifically, 'United States support will not extend to
United States military intervention to influence the course
of any Chinese internal strife'?"

"There is absolutely no United States military intervention in China!" snapped Marshall.

"Are the United States Marines in North China and
Manchuria not military?" asked Chou. "Are the United States
trucks and jeeps and planes transporting Chiang Kai-shek's
troops not military? Are most of the United States surplus
and war matériel being transferred to Chiang Kai-shek not
military?"

"I know how you feel about Chiang Kai-shek, but in international practice it is the legal government, not the individual behind the government, that we have to deal with. The
National Government of China is the only legal government
with which we can formally conduct transactions."

"Aren't you being a bit mechanically formalistic?" said
Chou. "Isn't there an element of hypocrisy when you know
—and everybody knows—that anything you turn over to the
National Government goes to the front facing the Communist troops? Aren't you . . ."

Chou paused in the middle of his speech when he observed
a change of color on Marshall's face at the mention of
"hypocrisy."

"I have indicated several times that I am ready to recommend that my government terminate its effort to mediate
here," said Marshall slowly and wearily. "Your side has been
particularly critical of me recently, saying that I am unfair

and insincere. And yet, just a while ago you insisted that I must stay on and keep trying this apparently futile job!"

The last time Marshall served the cause of peace in China was after the KMT troops had started an all-out offensive on Changchiakou ninety miles northwest of Peking. Communist build-up in that area had become too great a threat for the KMT to ignore, and because of its strategic location, neither side would yield. Chou En-lai protested to Marshall, "If the Nationalist government does not cease its military action in the Changchiakou area, the CCP will have to regard it as an act signaling a total break." Marshall intervened to bring about the third cease-fire on October 5, 1946, and personally went to Shanghai to persuade Chou to come to the negotiation table in Nanking. In addition to the earlier terms, Chou again raised the embarrassing question of U.S. aid to Chiang Kai-shek. When Ambassador Stuart went to invite him to meet with the KMT representative, Chou's reply was a terse, "There isn't enough time; the Generalissimo cannot be trusted."

Chiang Kai-shek gave up trying to talk to Chou and went ahead with his plan to hold the National Assembly on November 12, 1946 in spite of Chou's threat to boycott it. The date arrived and all the other parties were represented in the National Assembly, but the CCP and the Democratic League were conspicuously absent. Chou pleaded with Marshall on December 3, "In response to the demand by the entire nation, the Communist Party considers that it is still possible to resume negotiations if the National Assembly now in progress is disbanded immediately and the troops returned to their respective positions prior to the January 13, 1946 cease-fire."

Marshall had had enough. He listened to the inflammatory Communist propaganda against the United States, harping on the recent agreements signed with Chiang Kai-shek and the incident of December 24, 1946 involving a Chinese college girl and several American soldiers in Peking, and packed his suitcase.

Chou also packed for his trip back to Yenan. His friends, including many who had quarreled with him in the People's Political Consultative Conference, gave him a farewell party. One member of the Young China Party asked Chou if he remembered how he had looked at his watch and run away when the constitution-drafting committee reached an impasse.[31] "But it was true I had some urgent business to attend to that afternoon," replied Chou. "That's all right," said the other, "but why didn't you show up again, and instead you only sent your assistant who . . ."

A request for Chou's speech interrupted their conversation. As Chou stood up, he caught sight of a non-partisan leader[32] whose opinion he had respected. After a few platitudes Chou directed his remarks at him: "On the eve of my departure, I have only one deep regret. A man of such integrity and wisdom as Mr. . . . cannot find a place to serve our country, and has to bow to the Kuomintang government [the person had consented to join the reshuffled cabinet of the National government] where I am sure he will stand quite alone with his virtue. The thought that some day I may find him, and many other good friends like you, on the other side of the fence, has taken away all the flavor of this cup of good wine you are offering me today . . ."

As he spoke, his eyes turned misty, and the party ended quietly, without any of the traditional Chinese revelry.

A few formalities remained to make the break final. On February 1, 1947 the Communists released their pamphlet, "Greet the New High Tide of Revolution," which declared that "the nationwide struggle against imperialism and feudalism has prepared a new stage for the great revolution of the people." It was a declaration of war, to which the Nationalist government responded by ordering the last Communist delegations to leave Nanking, Shanghai, and Chungking. On July

4, 1947 Chiang Kai-shek ordered "Mobilization for the Suppression of Rebellion."

No post mortem of the peace talks during these years could escape one conclusion: strategically the talks had worked to the Communists' advantage. They gained time for Chou En-lai, when time was critically needed for regrouping and building up the Red Army, and for stalling the Nationalist military pressure, which at times threatened to wipe out the entire Red armed forces. It would be an error, of course, to assume that the Nationalists, down to the last man, were prepared to accept and work together with the Reds in any sort of coalition government. Some of the policy-makers of the KMT were, from the very beginning, convinced that the struggle was going to be a life-and-death fight, and that negotiations were a tool both sides were trying to use to their own best advantage. Other KMT leaders were aware of the danger of Chou En-lai's maneuvering across the negotiation table, but were not able to press for a different course of action. Talk was what the people and common sense dictated; talk was what the Allies (chiefly America) would prefer to open warfare. Not until the very last moment could either party afford to take the initiative to break up the talks.

The busy rounds of serious political negotiations did not completely keep Chou En-lai away from his "feudal past." The moment he reached Nanking in the early summer of 1946 he called on his prosperous sixth uncle who had objected to his attending the Nankai Middle School over thirty years before. From him Chou learned about his foster mother's return to Shanghai from Kao-yu, 150 miles to the north, the home town of Chou's sister-in-law, Ma Shun-yi. Ma and the matriarch had fled the Japanese in 1939 because of a rumor circulating in Shanghai that their relation to Chou En-lai had been discovered.

The day Ma found Chou En-lai in the Nanking office of the Chinese Communist delegation, he dropped everything to greet her and immediately telephoned General Marshall's office to cancel an appointment scheduled for that afternoon.[33] He suggested that they call on the sixth uncle, but knowing the old man's bad temper, she was reluctant. It was only after Chou persuaded her that the younger generation owed their elders such common courtesy that she finally agreed.

On the way to the uncle's house and while waiting for the old man to wake up from his nap, Chou inquired after his foster mother's health, the schooling of Ma's children in Shanghai, and if she had heard anything from her husband, En-chu. She said someone had told her that En-chu was at Huai-an, the ancestral home of the Chou clan, but she had not been able to reach him. Chou said he would try to locate En-chu to give him a message.

Ma told Chou how the matriarch had been unhappy, flying into a tantrum as often as usual and blaming Ma for having driven En-chu away and bringing about one family disaster after another. Over an hour had passed in their whispering conversation outside the sixth uncle's room, and the old man was still not stirring. She thought they should give up disturbing the uncle and leave without seeing him.

"We must not do that," Chou lowered his voice further. "You know Sixth Uncle's temper and his habit of not napping too soundly. He could very well overhear you, and that would upset him to no end."

Finally Chou sneaked into the old man's room alone to announce their visit in a soft voice, and Ma went in to pay her respects to the old man. Chou behaved before the uncle with exactly the same kind of care and reverence that he had demonstrated in Shanghai before his foster mother in 1931.

During the following months Chou called on Ma and the matriarch quite frequently, until news reached Shanghai from Kao-yu about the predicament of Ma's father. The Communists occupying the Kao-yu area had instituted meetings against the rich landlords, and Ma's father, one of the victims, was now locked up in the local jail.

Unable to locate her husband to help her father, Ma sought out Chou En-lai. Chou said merely that there must have been some misunderstanding, and as far as he knew En-chu had something to do with the Communist work in that area. Consequently he, Chou En-lai, did not believe the news to be true.

After several such futile trips, Ma went to see her father for the last time. When she reported back in Shanghai to the matriarch that her father's death wish was that she never see another member of the Chou family again, the matriarch took the younger woman with her and together they stormed into Chou En-lai's office.

Chou was dumbfounded for a moment when he saw the mourning on Ma's hair. "What is all this . . . ?" he said. But the matriarch, without letting him go on, launched into a harangue cursing the heartlessness of Chou En-lai and his Communist comrades. Overtaken with grief, Ma did not stay to hear out the argument and went back alone to live with her brother, a wealthy textile mill owner whose wife blamed her and the entire Chou clan for the death of the elder Ma.

Ma Shun-yi fell violently ill. The matriarch, now feeling close to her daughter-in-law, moved into the hospital to keep her company. She blocked En-chu's visit when he finally showed up to see his sick wife. In her feeble state of health, Ma remembered seeing Chou En-lai quite frequently in the hospital, sitting with the matriarch beside her bed to help her while away the dull passage of time during her recuperation. All three of them avoided mentioning anything unpleasant—En-chu, the Communists, and national politics. They talked only about the children.

When Chou En-lai was packing for Yenan at the end of the negotiations, Ma was still in the hospital, unable to travel. After a tearful good-by at her bedside, she watched Chou En-lai and the matriarch leave, still unable to comprehend exactly what Chou was doing, since she could not see any difference between this man of 1946 and the soft-spoken,

thoughtful, gentlemanly elder brother she used to know some
fifteen years before.

Full-scale civil war resumed. Beginning in March 1947
Chiang Kai-shek's troops marched on Yenan, forcing the
Communists to flee the capital they had held eleven years.
Liu Shao-ch'i and Chu Teh were assigned to lead an *ad hoc*
committee set up as a spare Central Committee in case Mao,
Chou, and the main body of the headquarters were overtaken
by the attackers. Under forced march the Emergency Committee sneaked into northern Hopei Province and installed
itself in a small village.

Chou En-lai, quickly assuming an alias, Hu Pi-ch'eng, rode
in a truck with Mao Tse-tung, known as Li Te-sheng, protected by less than one regiment of security guards. Two days
later the truck broke down and they had to take horses to
continue their flight westward. Another day passed in breath-
less running, and when they paused to rest their horses Chou's
nose started bleeding and could not be stopped. There was
only one litter reserved for Mao Tse-tung and several relatively tenderfooted women comrades who took turns riding
in it. Mao insisted that Chou take the litter. Chou refused,
and it was not until Mao's wife, Chiang Ch'ing, the colorful
figure in the Red Guard movement of 1966, had repeatedly
urged him to rest on the litter that Chou finally agreed.

"How can you walk in those shoes," Chiang Ch'ing remarked, as she noticed the big hole in the sole of Chou's shoe.
"Your sock is showing through."

"That's not sock," said Chou. "I stuck a stack of newspaper in there, and I guess it will hold out for a while."[34]

As they had done on the Long March, only this time with
fewer troops, they zigzagged their route to dodge the pursuers and a month later reached the village Wangchiawan,
in the shadow of the Great Wall, about eighty miles northwest of Yenan, where they remained until June. There were
only about a dozen families in the village, nearly all named

Wang. From one of them Chou, Mao, and two other top comrades borrowed two small loess caves for billeting. Mao alone occupied a rickety wood bed, but Chou and Lu Ting-yi (later chief of the Party's propaganda department) had to share the *kang* (earthen platform used as bed in North China). The benchlike table was too small for two of them to spread out their papers, radiograms, and maps. Chou moved a tree stump close to the adobe stove he used as his desk, and with his padded uniform folded on top of the stump, he found his makeshift stool quite comfortable. The villagers could spare not much more than a quantity of hard-baked barley cakes mixed with some wild greens. Chou took a big bite of it, grinned broadly and said to Mao, "This isn't too bad. I'd say even better than anything we had on the grassland."[35]

But the Nationalists were moving up closer and closer, and soon Chou and Mao had to run again. They turned east toward the Yellow River, which they reached on August 17 after marching for eight nights, hiding from the KMT airplanes during the day. On the same evening, the pursuers caught up with them. Chou pleaded with Mao, urging him to cross the Yellow River. Mao declined and urged Chou to take the radio station and the key staff across the river instead.

Finally Chou and Mao decided that, stay or run, they would stick together. It had been raining hard and even crossing the Lu River, a tributary to the Yellow River, constituted a serious problem. Chou En-lai went ahead to inspect the crossing in the twilight and ordered the guards to borrow all the doors they could find from nearby villages. With these they constructed a temporary bridge. Chou stood on the river bank under pouring rain to direct the operation until every comrade had safely crossed the river. That was one time in Chou's combat experience when he could not have ordered his men to return all the borrowed articles to their owners exactly where they had been found.

Dark days for Chou and Mao were still ahead even after

reinforcements reached them and put a few miles between them and their Nationalist hunters. Time and again the battle became so intense that Chou joined the litter bearers to carry wounded comrades himself.

The tide gradually turned. The Nationalists helped the process by outlawing the Democratic League in October 1947, which drove the League and other "third party" elements to rally around Mao Tse-tung's red banner. The reassembled Central Committee of the CCP in northern Hopei Province announced on May 1, 1948 the plan to call a separate People's Political Conference, bringing together the leaders of all parties and groups to form a People's Republic of China.[36]

Chiang Kai-shek's troops began to lose as economic disorder and political demoralization closed in on them in a pincer movement. Student riots flared up everywhere to demand "rice, not bullets," and even the repeated changes of premiers in Nanking failed to regain the people's confidence. The fateful battle of Hsuchow in northern Kiangsu sealed the Nationalist defeat. Chiang Kai-shek's offer to resign on January 21, 1949 only added another dimension to Nationalist confusion and demoralization.

History was almost written, save for a few last-minute gestures toward another effort to negotiate. On January 14, 1949 Chou En-lai offered eight conditions for resumption of negotiations. This was what humiliated Chiang into offering his resignation. Acting KMT president Li Tsung-jen accepted the proposal and sent Chang Chih-chung, who had sat on the Committee of Three with Chou and Marshall three years before, and Shao Li-tzu, who had spoken for Chou in the 1926 Chung-shan Gunboat Incident, to meet Chou in Peiping on March 26, 1949. The demand Chou presented at the end of a two-week discussion was not acceptable to the KMT, which brought up an all-out Communist offensive, snuffing out the last flicker of hope for a settlement off the battlefield.

On October 1, 1949, Chou En-lai stood immediately behind Mao Tse-tung on the Gate of Heavenly Peace, the entrance to the ancient imperial palace, listening to Mao proclaim in his grating Hunanese accent, "The People's Republic of China is now established!" Chou's beltless uniform, smoothly pressed and neatly buttoned up to the collar, looked fresh, and his hair, shining black. But the contented smile that marked the end of the Long March in 1935 was missing from his face. It was a farewell to dark jails, night flights, worn-out sandal soles, litter-bearing with a bleeding nose, and soups flavored with shoe leather. In their place now stood the awe-inspiring vision of a sea of red flags fluttering over 650 million eager faces whose destiny he and a handful of his comrades must mold in the years ahead.

CHAPTER 11

THE KEEPER OF A KINGDOM

IN THE FIVE HUNDRED-YEAR-OLD Peking palace, relacquered in bright vermilion, Premier and Foreign Minister Chou En-lai could gaze through the latticed window at the marble railing beyond, which reflected a slice of Chinese history—the history of his compatriots struggling for 2500 years through the rise and fall of dynasties, internal revolts, and foreign conquests. Perhaps as he did so Sun Yat-sen's words came to his mind, "For forty years I have devoted my life to a people's revolution for the sole purpose of China's freedom and equality . . ." Chou could say only "thirty years" instead of "forty," and yet the path was clear for him as it had not been clear for Sun. He must now face the task of winning a place in the sun for his country.

With tireless vigor he went about charting the course for Red China's foreign relations, even after he handed the Foreign Office over to Ch'en Yi, his associate in Paris, in 1958. He has continued to represent his country in all important negotiations abroad and at home. He has made nearly all the diplomatic trips himself, and even when Foreign Minister Ch'en Yi traveled with him, he traveled in Chou's shadow.[1]

Several pivotal points underlie Red China's diplomatic stance, with Peking's relation with Moscow understandably the center of gravity. During the past seventeen years Chou has made seven trips to Moscow, from the first three[2] of which he brought back treaties and alliances of political and economic co-operation that might be envied by any diplomat in the world. Through these agreements Russia relinquished some of her historical interests in China, advanced substantial loans to Peking, and sent technicians to help build dams, steel plants, and railroads.

Between his fourth trip in April 1954, which mainly concerned the war in Vietnam, and his fifth trip in February 1959, the Moscow-Peking axis began to show strain. The sweet promises so generously made in Moscow were not nearly so generously delivered in Peking. Not every point of the "revolutionarily advanced technical advice" offered by the well-paid Russian consultants was working out, and even the switch in the nation's foreign-language program from English to Russian was not a complete advantage. Here and there whispers were overheard expressing skepticism, questioning whether Russia was genuinely interested in helping to build up China into an industrial, and indeed, military power.

The split began to come to the surface in 1955 when Khrushchev's bitter denunciation of Stalin fell on deaf ears in Peking. The Russian effort to maintain a strong Moscovite influence in Manchuria and Sinkiang remained a constant irritant. Thus while both sides continued to try to present a united front before the Western world, as witnessed by the joint communique of Chou En-lai and Bulganin in January 1957 over the Hungarian crisis, the conflict was rapidly moving toward a showdown.

The storm finally broke in 1958 when the Russian Communist leadership suggested military control of Red China to keep it in step. Peking's reaction, not revealed until 1963, was violent.[3] Now that Moscow had exposed the iron fist within its glove, it passed up no opportunity to deal a blow to Peking, as it did over the Sino-Indian border dispute. Against Peking's earnest requests that Russia not meddle in the dispute, Moscow issued a statement in June 1959, criticizing Red China's action as regrettable and stupid.

From there on the inevitable followed. The agreement Chou signed in Moscow on February 7, 1959, whereby Rus-

sia was supposed to help Red China build some seventy-eight
large industrial and power plants, was good on paper for only
seven months, and was virtually abrogated in September of
the same year by Russia's refusal to provide technical and
material assistance for Peking's nuclear industry.

The mutual recrimination culminated in a 60,000-word
complaint Moscow filed against Peking at the Bucharest Communist assembly in June 1960. The next month, Russia recalled over 1300 of its technical consultants and terminated
several hundred industrial contracts with Red China. After
this, Chou En-lai no longer was the smiling diplomat who had
brought back a treaty of friendship and mutual aid from each
trip to Moscow.

Yet when he faced the Western world, Chou maintained
his composure. He parried Edgar Snow's pointed questions
on the Moscow-Peking split with his usual grace, admitting
technical difference of opinion but calmly defending the unity
of world communism.[4] Snow asked Chou in October 1960
why Russia had suspended the two Chinese organs published
in Moscow, the *Kitai* and the *Druzhbe;* how Peking had
answered the thirty-two-page open letter addressed to all sat-
ellite Communist parties in which Moscow attacked the Chinese interpretation of Leninism as predicting the inevitability
of war with imperialism; and what justified Peking's refusal
to support the Bucharest Communist report of June 1960.

Chou pointed out the common basis and over-all strategy
of world communism, but admitted that at any given moment
any Communist nation could and indeed should have its own
policy of implementing this strategy. The contrary—that all
the Communist countries saw eye to eye on everything all
the time—would indeed, he said, be rather odd. Then he explained that increased and improved modern mass communication between China and Russia via radio and the press
annulled the need to maintain two special Chinese publications in Moscow. The thirty-two-page denunciation of Peking,
widely publicized in Western nations, was news to Chou. He

dismissed it as simply part of the Western imperialists' continuing campaign to alienate one Communist country from another, with which, he said, he had had ample experience and about which he was therefore not at all disturbed. The Bucharest report, said Chou, had been signed by the Chinese delegation, hence there was no need for Peking to affirm again its support of the statement. Chou indicated to his visitor that whatever the quarrel was between Peking and Moscow, the West would do well not to maximize it as a possible advantage.

Chou quarreled in open meetings with Khrushchev on October 19 over the Albanian issue. He challenged the Kremlin leader by declaring that any public unilateral accusation of that kind "would neither contribute to the solidarity of world communism nor help toward a solution of the problem in point." He condemned Khrushchev's accusation as anything but a "serious regard for Marxism-Leninism," which threatened, much to the dismay of all Communist comrades in the world, to "play into the hands of the enemy." The 22nd Russian Communist Party Congress under Khrushchev's manipulation turned to a collective denunciation of Stalinism. Whereupon Chou En-lai, exhibiting his mastery of Peking's policy, left the assembly on October 21 with his Chinese delegation to place a wreath on Stalin's tomb in open defiance of Khrushchev who, in retaliation, managed a resolution to relocate Stalin's remains literally under the shadow of the Kremlin wall. To this Chou responded by walking out of the conference altogether. On October 24, 1961, Peking greeted its diplomatic hero who played tough in Moscow. Even Mao Tse-tung established a precedent by his personal presence at the airport.

The feud raged, keeping Chou away from Moscow for over three years. During this time verbal skirmishes occurred with high frequency. A futile attempt to sit down to talk it over in Moscow took place in July 1963. Peking's lack of interest

in this effort was shown in its delegation, which was headed
not by Chou, but by Teng Hsiao-p'ing.

But just when Chou first admitted[5] his personal anxiety
about the rift, Khrushchev fell. No analysis of the background
leading to this dynastic change in Moscow can be complete
unless it gives due consideration to Khrushchev's failure to
work with Peking and Chou En-lai. The new leadership in
Moscow greeted Chou cordially on November 5, 1964, and
involved him in high-level conversations, which, however,
produced only a *pro forma* statement from him. Even Moscow's conciliatory gesture of postponing the international
Communist congress in Moscow, planned by Khrushchev to
begin in December of that year, failed to placate the Peking
leaders who cautioned their comrades against a perpetuation
of "Khrushchevism without Khrushchev in person."[6]

Perhaps the wounds will never be completely healed, thus
rendering futile all Western speculations on how intimately
Moscow and Peking could continue to form a solid front in
the future. Chou En-lai's "State of the Republic" report of
1964 reflected a hard-headed approach to the problem. On the
one hand he stressed the need for Red China to stand on its
own feet; on the other he warned against ultra-chauvinism
as a detriment to world revolution.[7] Subsequently the *Pravda*
reprinted the entire report except the short passages where
Chou mildly criticized Khrushchev, "Regarding our relationship with Russia, we have been, through no fault of our own,
confronted with extreme difficulties, and we have suffered
from them. However, we shall continue to stress the importance of solidarity and do our best to maintain a normal relationship." Among the main difficulties, Chou was thinking
of the questions of Manchuria, Mongolia, and Sinkiang.

Next to the Moscow-Peking relationship, Red China's foreign policy under Chou En-lai's tutelage focused on the
emerging pro-leftist and neutral forces in the Afro-Asian bloc.
The guidepost was: win the leadership of this bloc and
through it a bargaining position with the West.

The inauguration of the People's Republic of China in 1949 made it possible for Chou to negotiate formally with the Afro-Asian nations. Within the six months ending April 13, 1950, Chou had already succeeded in establishing diplomatic relations with twenty-six nations, including eight Asian countries.[8] The Korean War dampened the reception of Red China in the United Nations, but the Geneva and the Bandung Conferences of 1953 and 1955 raised Peking's prestige. Through these conferences, Chou, the champion of underdeveloped nations, persuasively encouraged the development of friendly blocs around Egypt, India, and Indonesia, using neutralism as an insulator to cut their ties with the West.

In Asia, one of the first diplomatic offensives Chou launched was leveled at the Viet Minh. He conferred with Ho Chi-minh in July 1954, on "the restoration of peace in Indo-China." Two years later, in November 1956, he met with the Northern Vietnam Prime Minister Pham Van Dong. This resulted in a joint declaration to "develop friendly relations between the two regimes without committing any chauvinistic error." The next time Chou saw Pham was in the spring of 1960, and this time the meeting brought forth a scathing joint attack on the United States and American-supported South Vietnam.

With Burma, Chou En-lai worked out a series of six joint statements between June 1954 and July 1964, focused on non-aggression, mutual aid, and peaceful co-existence. His 1961 visit to Rangoon was a gala affair, with over four hundred Chinese delegates representing nine different interests. He played Santa Claus to the amount of 30 million pounds—a loan to Burma with no interest or any other strings attached. In return U Nu defined the Sino-Burmese borders, which had been an historically irksome issue. The latest Chou En-lai visit to Burma, in July 1964, further strengthened the economic tie between the two nations and reviewed their common approach to the problems in Southeast Asia, particularly with regard to Laos.

With Indonesia, Chou En-lai's diplomatic offensive began

at the Bandung Conference in April 1955, when he signed a
separate treaty with Sukarno to clarify the problem of dual
citizenship of the Chinese settled in that country. For years
there had been frequent reports on persecution of the Chinese
by Indonesians. Chou En-lai had just reviewed the bitterness
of feeling these had aroused when an Indonesian reporter[9]
asked him point blank to state Peking's policy toward the
overseas Chinese: "Will these Chinese accept the nationality
of the country in which they live, or will they be the means
of Chinese imperialist expansion in Asia?" And he went on to
cite examples of Communist activities in Eastern Europe and
South Asia to prove that imperialistic aggressive designs were
a part of communism. Chou En-lai was visibly annoyed, but
he quickly checked himself, allowing only his slightly agitated
hand gestures to betray his displeasure.

Sukarno's agreement in 1955 brought no solution to the
problem, which was further aggravated in May 1959, by his
No. 4 anti-Chinese policy statement. Chou En-lai swallowed
his pride to sign an agreement lending 30 million U.S. dollars
to the Indonesian textile industry, and shortly afterward invited the Indonesian Foreign Minister to visit Peking. When
all these conciliatory moves failed, Chou dispatched ships to
bring the Chinese back from Indonesia, but Indonesia seized
a Chinese boat and one Chinese consul. The uneasy relation
was finally torpedoed in 1965 when the Indonesian army
crushed the Communist Party in their country, and Chou En-
lai's diplomatic offensive suffered a painful setback.

Chou's failure to make the Bandung spirit prevail in India
was dramatically illustrated in the August 1959, border incident precipitated by the Dalai Lama's flight to India. After
the armed clash, Chou, with the new Foreign Minister Ch'en
Yi in tow, went to call on Nehru. Their seven conferences
were rendered fruitless by lack of reliable data on the incident.
The border remained tense while Chou and Nehru exchanged
memoranda—a total of twenty-two—between December 1961,

and March 1962, which merely contributed to the bulk of the inconclusive official dossier on the issue.

The summer and fall of 1962 saw three more clashes on the Sino-Indian border. Between the incidents Chou continued to try to bring other Afro-Asian nations to influence Nehru's attitude. To support his olive-branch gesture, Chou dramatically announced a truce followed by a withdrawal of the Chinese troops for eleven miles to await further negotiation. By that time the Indians had lost over a thousand troops.

Little progress has been made since the Colombo Conference nations agreed to mediate. Nehru died a bitter enemy of Chou, but the Sino-Indian bitterness did not die with him. Even three years later there was still no one in New Delhi who could mention Chou's name without a frown, and in Kashmir every other bus driver kept cracking the joke about how his Chinese brethren across the Himalaya loved him for his Ladek sheep.[10] Many Chinese immigrants, once prosperous in India, complained to Chou En-lai of mistreatment by their Indian friends-turned-enemies, but Peking was too far away and Chou has not yet found a way to recoup his diplomatic losses in India. All he could say was, "If India persists in her refusal to talk to us about the border problem, it doesn't matter. We can wait."[11]

Until the end of 1965 most of Chou En-lai's international junkets were much more successful than his Indian experience. When he reached Cambodia, the natives were so proud of this fellow-Asian hero that one large plywood plant promptly renamed itself after him. In Pakistan, Ceylon, and Nepal he made friends with whom he has been able to renew alliances of mutual aid every so often.

His diplomatic sallies in Africa also began at the Bandung Conference, which he sought to re-enact in 1963. On December 13 of that year Chou brought Ch'en Yi with him on a tour of Africa. For two months they visited ten African nations, drumming up interest in a second Afro-Asian conference and explaining Peking's case in the Sino-Indian dispute. He told his African audience that modern Western civilizaton had been built on the blood and bones of cheap Afro-Asian labor who should, henceforth, rise to overtake the West.

"Once a revolutionary Cuba has appeared in Latin America," said Chou in Algeria, "there will be the second and the third Cuba to appear in Latin America, just as revolutionary Algeria will precipitate a series of revolutionary nations to emerge in Africa." The Chinese policy, Chou declared in Ghana on January 15, 1964, "is to support the African nations to oppose imperialism and all forms of old and new colonialism." In Somaliland, he urged solidarity of the Afro-Asian bloc because "we Afro-Asian peoples share the same pulsation and are involved in the same revolution. Our common objectives are national independence and development of our national economy and culture. Our common enemy is staring in our eyes . . ."

While passing through Pakistan he reminded his enthusiastic hosts that the newly developed "Afro-Asian nations who have just struggled up on their own feet are exerting their increasing positive influence in international affairs." He predicted doom for those neglecting the importance of the Afro-Asian nations, or trying to promote ultra-chauvinism against the natural evolution of world history. Then, at the end of his extensive African swing, he summed up his Afro-Asian policy before a festive reception in the luxurious Great Hall of the People in Peking on March 24, 1964, "The Chinese Communists have shared with you the experience of imperialistic aggression, and therefore are sharing with you the common mission of opposing imperialism and old and new colonialism. Our friendship has been tempered through many an international storm. It is perpetual and indestructible."

Peking's contact with eastern Europe has been rather limited.[12] But when Chou En-lai appeared in Budapest and Warsaw in January 1957, he was accorded the welcome of a graceful peacemaker who helped the Hungarian leader Kadar and Poland's Gomulka to regain a measure of international balance in the wake of their anti-Moscow revolts. For a number of days after Chou had left, the streets of the eastern European capitals continued to sound the praises of Chou's statesmanship.

The Albanians, remembering that Chou had stood by them against Khrushchev in 1961, went wild over the Premier from Peking when he arrived there on New Year's Eve in 1963. For eight solid days he was feted and honored by the leaders of all Albanian circles who, through formal documents, pledged their undying friendship with the Chinese Communist regime.

Outer Mongolia, the smallest and closest non-Chinese state, received Chou's personal attention when he went to Ulan Bator in May 1960. Donning a sheepskin robe several sizes too large for him, he drank repeated toasts with the Mongolian chief to celebrate the Sino-Mongolian treaty of mutual aid, together with a long-term Chinese loan of 200 million rubles, while camelskin drums and bamboo-pipe organs played a jazzed-up version of the Internationale in the courtyard in front of the dining hall.

The Arab nations have been less than completely happy in their relations with the West, and here Chou saw a fissure into which he could drive a wedge. He bought up large quantities of Egyptian cotton, which led to the establishment of regular diplomatic relations with Nasser and Syria. When Nasser criticized Chou for the Communist coup in Tibet (1956), Chou ignored it but promptly apologized for the Syrian leader in exile in Peking who tongue-lashed Nasser at one of Chou's parties.[13] Thus Nasser remained extremely friendly toward Peking when Chou journeyed to Egypt in the winter of 1963.

Castro's rise in Cuba was greeted by Chou En-lai with invitations to over fifty Latin American friendship missions to Peking in 1960. After that Chou missed no opportunity to cite and commend Castro as the model of Latin American revolution. In Japan, which has vital economic interests in

Mainland China, Chou En-lai has found many sympathetic echoes, particularly from the Japanese Liberal-Democratic Party (Jimindo) leader Takasaki Tatsunosuke, and after his death, Matsumura Kenzō. Even though Japan has been veering toward the West politically, she is not likely to antagonize Peking for ideological reasons alone.

Up to the end of 1965 Chou En-lai's high-flying diplomacy worked well, winning friends and commitments of support among the Afro-Asian, the neutral, and the smaller Western countries, some with Peking's money, others with Peking's prestige and potential power, and still others purely with his personal charm. The winter of 1965 saw a sharp decline in Peking's magnetism, largely as the result of its high-pressured salesmanship of communism, which caused even some of the newest small African nations to balk. In the face of such adversity, Chou En-lai has been staying quietly at home, mending political fences for Peking, especially since the beginning of the Red Guard upheaval. But one might predict that the moment Chou has settled the internal party line in Peking, he is likely to be flying around the world again to try to recapture Peking's leadership in world communism.

As to the major Western powers, Chou has not made any serious attempt to sit down with the Americans, either in Korea, or the United Nations, or elsewhere, to discuss anything formally. The only exception was his brief appearance in Geneva in April 1954 to discuss the war in Indo-China.[14] At Bandung in April 1955 he expressed a desire to "sit down with American representatives to discuss ways and means of easing the tension in the Formosan Strait," which led to the Warsaw Conference, which is still fitfully and inconsequentially going on without his personal appearance.

Until the Red Guard problem, which turned his attention homeward, Chou's posture before the Western world was one of confidence. China's being locked out of the United Nations has perhaps worried the West more than it has him. Whatever Peking has been missing by its lack of a UN membership has been amply compensated for by British and French recognition of the regime. The last was particularly a crowning glory in Chou's diplomatic career.

In the ominous rumble of the first nuclear explosion in Red China, Chou cabled the Western leaders for a summit meeting on total nuclear disarmament. He had no illusion about the West's jumping at the very first atomic blast in Sinkiang Province, but the echo to Chou's demand among the Western nations was on the rise until they were temporarily distracted by Peking's domestic difficulties in the latter part of 1966.

Chou En-lai's triumph as a diplomat has been largely due to his personal magnetism. He always has time for a foreign visitor, with whom he frequently chats for hours on end. Through these casual conversations he invariably makes his visitors feel that he can be had as a friend, and, indeed, that he is a friend. By making his visitors feel that he, Chou En-lai, can be influenced by them, he has actually made his own view prevail and has won them over to his side.

When talking to Tachibana Yoshimori, of the Japanese *Mainichi News*, Chou appeared as Japan's best and most understanding friend. Nothing about the serious political and economic conflict, ancient or current grievances, between the two countries disturbed him. He used no Communist jargon and dispelled the stereotyped images of a Communist revolutionary. He was all amity and sincerity. "No visitor could walk away after a talk with Chou En-lai without feeling attracted to him, but at the same time, recalling an irresistible pressure in his presence," said the Japanese journalist. "Isn't Chou's personal character an exact copy of the character of Red Chinese diplomacy? Proceeding with war and peace, resistance and negotiation, toughness and softness, all at the same time. His words may be sweet, but their substance is not."[15]

Another Japanese journalist said, "He always shook hands with every newsman warmly upon departure, with his eyes fixed on the other's face. It was never perfunctory."[16] A third

CHOU EN-LAI

visitor called him "a wise statesman . . . reflecting astute intelligence in his words, however softly he may have spoken." He observed that Chou presented a sharp contrast to Mao Tse-tung's resoluteness as a devout Communist.[17] Raja Hutheesing of India compared his brother-in-law Nehru with Chou. Throughout the five-hour conversation, he found Chou a well-groomed model of Chinese gentility, with a refined eloquence that reflected his complete familiarity with the world situation. "His well-modulated voice," wrote the Indian reporter, "cultured gestures, boyish, infectious laughter and twinkling eyes, held the on-looker in the spell of his charm."[18]

Britain's Lord Montgomery was also among the captives of Chou's personality. He wrote after a visit to Mainland China in May 1960, "He [Chou] is a very different person from Mao . . . One can see from his face that he is intellectual and very clever; indeed, I would describe his brain power as brilliant. He is a quick and clear thinker, very lucid in his speech, with a most pleasing personality and a nice sense of humor. Altogether he is a very intelligent and likeable man, with charming manners . . . I liked him so much that I invited him to come and stay with me in my home in England as my private guest, and he said he would like to do so . . . In all, I talked with Chou En-lai for seven hours, which I was told was a record for any interview given by him. I enjoyed every minute of it and so, I fancy, did he."[19]

The artist of winning friends has put his full talent to good use. He has rolled out the red carpet in Peking to every visitor from abroad. When they did not come fast enough he repeated his invitations. Within a fourteen-month period, from January 1960 to March 1961, ninety-one delegations from African nations alone toured Mainland China. Chou personally attended to the details of these visits to insure that everything would leave a pleasant impression on the visitors. He checked and approved the seating arrangements of every state dinner party. He made certain that the United Nations Secretary-General Dag Hammarskjold was always seated next to his personal assistant, a young American, during their visit to Peking. After they left, Chou remarked, "I knew that the American young man was only a plain-clothes man, yet I paid him special attention. I kept him with us when the photographer made pictures of us, and assigned him a seat at the banquet. He was overwhelmed. We need not be afraid of American secret agents. On the contrary we should work on them."[20]

When provoked, the generous host Chou En-lai had a different way of evaluating his political guests. "The leaders of the imperialist governments are cheap rascals," he said in answer to a challenge about his being over-polite with everybody. "You must occasionally scold them roundly, or even hit them and, if necessary, show a nasty face to them; then you can put them in their proper places."[21]

As chief architect of Peking's foreign policy, Chou's principle is "win friends to isolate the enemy." As chief steward of the Communist Party's extensive political property, his approach is "involve the people and keep them with you." To do the latter job he has two titles: Premier, or *Tsung-li*, of the State Council, and Vice-Chairman of the People's Government of China, which require him to control a mammoth administrative machinery, perhaps the most sprawling in the modern world.

He not only controls it; he created it, out of the united-front mold he shaped before, during, and immediately after World War II.

As soon as the Central Committee of the CCP, still fleeing Chiang Kai-shek's troops in northern Hopei Province in 1948, announced its plan to call its own People's Political Consultative Conference, Chou went to work on the leaders of all political groups in China and in exile in Hong Kong.[22] Six months after he moved into Peiping, he worked as the head of a committee of twenty-three delegates from the various groups to draft a "Common Program," outlining the structure and main policies of the new regime. On September 21,

1949, the first session of the People's Political Consultative Conference involving 682 delegates met to adopt the Common Program and set up the government in Peking, with the Chinese Communist Party in the middle and the other minor parties and groups, held together by Chou En-lai, surrounding it.

Continuing his united-front approach to national unity, Chou worked toward the convocation of the first National People's Congress with delegates from all levels and parts of China, which took place in September 1954. In theory, with the realization of the People's Congress, its scaffolding, the People's Political Consultative Conference should go out of existence. Curiously (and perhaps not so curiously when one recognizes the role Chou is called upon to play) the importance of the Conference increased through an expansion of its National Committee from 180 delegates to 559 in December, 1954, and 1071 in 1958, and 1200 in 1964!

As chairman of the Conference, Chou watched his power grow as the Conference, now a permanent body, streamlined its central committees and added local committees to strengthen its chain of command reaching all the way down to the county level.[23] As the expansion accelerated, more and more local and intellectual leaders were involved, and new committees were created to sponsor an academy of socialism, the highest ideological training center in Communist China, and to take charge of such activities as public health, ethnic minority affairs, and programs for women.

Beginning in the spring of 1958, the Conference, which has in it the most comprehensive representation of all political and professional interests, has been existing and functioning side by side with the elected National People's Congress, holding conventions always simultaneously in Peking because of the joint membership held by many members of both bodies.

The purpose of the Conference seems quite clear: In the current stage of development of education in Mainland China, popular elections may fail to achieve balanced and comprehensive representation in the national government. As a counter-balance, a Conference of the kind led by Chou En-lai can insure selective representation to reflect the sentiment of a meaningful cross section of the populace.

In April 1962, the Conference and the National People's Congress met together to pass a resolution calling for strength-ening the work of the Conference "to revitalize economic ac-tivities and develop the positive elements in the populace." A year and a half later, the two bodies met again. The local agencies of the Conference had already grown to include 1068 units. The central committees of the Conference encompassed nearly every aspect of China's national life, from education to religion to overseas Chinese affairs. According to the Consti-tution of the People's Republic of China, the Conference has no executive power, but because it is an effective machinery to "get people together," through their combination both Chou and the Conference loom formidable.

Whether it is the organization and maintenance of a gigan-tic People's Political Consultative Conference, or the direc-tion of a sprawling bureaucracy, one of Chou En-lai's principal functions in the Peking regime is to keep an eye on the free-wheeling intellectuals.

Mao Tse-tung, himself a verse-writing and library-bred revo-lutionary, rose to power on the strength of his brawny bare-footed guerrilla soldiers, who were mostly peasants, led by such educated and restless members of the intellectual elite as Chou En-lai. Halfway in the Chinese Communist ascendency, both Chou and Mao saw the handwriting on the wall separating the intellectuals from the peasants and workers. The produc-tion quotas could keep the proletariat busy, but what could keep the intellectuals?

The answer was: Get rid of their individual intellectual in-terests, harness their wild imagination, and rechannel their creative energy in the direction of the state. This initiated the waves of thought reform beginning in 1950 with Chou En-

lai's lecture on "Reforming the Intellectuals," delivered at the
workshop of faculties of the institutions of higher learning
in Peking and Tientsin. This was followed by Chou's report
on how to eradicate the capitalist class, presented to the Political Consultative Conference in January 1952. The wheels
of thought reform were thus set in motion, and they churned
furiously until Chou himself put on the brake on January 14,
1956.

On that day Chou presented a full report before a Politburo
meeting called especially to discuss the question of the intelligentsia. Only a small section of his report repeated the party
line concerning the ideological reindoctrination of the intellectuals. The rest of the lengthy document constituted an
apology for and a defense of the intelligentsia.

Chou first declared that the intelligentsia had already become an important element in every aspect of the national
life, and as such it must be protected and cultivated. He urged
improvement of the intellectuals' treatment and increase of
faith in them. There were party members who refused to
accept the guidance of an intellectual in a superior position,
he said, and they must be corrected. In order to improve the
intellectuals' living conditions, he wanted the administrators
of all agencies and institutions to pay respect to them. The
labor unions and cooperatives must recognize their duty to
"serve the intellectuals," by allocating substantial portions of
their funds to the improvement of cultural life among their
members. The pay for intellectuals must be adjusted according to the value of their services, as mechanical equality of
wages would actually contribute to inequity. In his view, Red
China needed a much larger number of higher-quality intellectuals, and he included this need in the third five-year plan
developed by Peking. To implement his proposals about improving the intellectual's life, Chou planned to set up a special
bureau of experts in his State Council.

Coming at the high tide of thought reform and reform-
through-labor movements, Chou's report spelled out a signifi-

cant modification of policy. Ten days later, on January 24, 1956, Chou made a similar plea before the Supreme State Conference, and again before the Political Consultative Conference in the same month. His statements triggered a chain reaction.

Kuo Mo-jo, author-historian, intellectual leader, and vice-premier, released his report on "The mission of the intellectuals in the Socialist revolutionary high tide." In March 1956, the State Council established a Science Planning Commission, bringing together about a thousand scientists from all over the country to develop science-education curricula under the slogan "March on Science." The rising tide in favor of the intelligentsia in Red China received a boost when Mao Tse-tung announced in the Supreme State Conference on May 2, 1956 the new "hundred flowers" direction in literature and science.

The Polish and Hungarian revolts occurring at this juncture gave the Chinese Reds food for thought and nudged the budding "hundred flowers" movement forward. After a bit of watching and waiting, Mao Tse-tung on February 27, 1957, told the State Council "How to handle properly the internal conflicts in the nation," repeating his admonition to "let the hundred flowers bloom, and the hundred schools of thought contend, so that through such healthy competition and mutual vigilance the Chinese people can live forever together in prosperity."

The "hundred flowers" movement unfurled. The *People's Daily* authoritatively expounded on this theme on April 9, and reassured the nation, urging it to have confidence in this new policy—a thaw of significant magnitude. It was certainly a surprise to Chou En-lai, who initiated this new direction, when he realized that in less than six months the movement had begun to tear apart his own carefully nurtured united front.

With the easing of the gag a flood of complaints and protests against Peking's policies and administration appeared.

Most of the critical comments came from the non-Communist elements whom Chou thought had been well corralled in his united-front organizations. A reversal had to be executed, which was the anti-rightist movement launched in July and August of 1957. The pendulum then kept swinging further left until another peak was reached in the People's Commune movement in 1958.

The "hundred flowers" movement was a fiasco, but it did not end in pools of blood. Even the propaganda chief, Lu Ting-yi, who had waved the hundred-flower banner for Mao, survived; Chou, of course, felt no repercussion. On the contrary, his lenient view on the intelligentsia and the need for periodical easing of tension seems to have been appreciated. One could easily see why he needed this policy of "now tightening, now relaxing" to maintain his heterogeneous united front, but it is a remarkable feat in modern politics that he could make it prevail again and again. From September 1959 on, there have been four drives to "remove the rightist cap," or to lift the rightist label too freely affixed on anyone the CCP did not like. There also have been four "amnesties for war criminals," or measures to enable the erstwhile enemies of communism to live outside the constant shadow of persecution.[24]

CHAPTER 12

GOD OF REVOLUTION
AND DEMON OF BLOODSHED

BECAUSE CHOU EN-LAI HAS ALWAYS been overshadowed by a more self-asserting personality in the party hierarchy, his ideas are too often treated as non-original and his quiet strength underestimated. To be sure, he did not invent Leninism, but his interpretation of the revolutionary situation in China on July 5, 1930, had much to do with the Comintern's resolution on how the Chinese Communist Party should behave. This in turn decided, in large measure, the subsequent course of action for Chou En-lai and Mao Tse-tung, as reflected in Chou's Shao-shan Report of September 24, 1930, and later in the Common Program of 1949 drafted under Chou's supervision.

In 1924 when Chou had just returned from France with his political ideas sufficiently mature to form a basis for action and to share an audience with such veteran Marxist writers as Ch'en Tu-hsiu and Ch'ü Ch'iu-pai, he wrote on the nature of imperialism and the role it was to play in China:

"Imperialism, which has appeared only during the past fifty years, is the extreme development, or ultimate product, of capitalism. The economic characteristic of capitalism is free competition, which breeds monopoly as the system develops toward imperialism. When the economic development of a capitalistic country reaches a monopolistic concentration of capital and production, the combined interests of banking and

industry will turn to investment abroad and exportation of
finished industrial products. And as world markets fall under
one or another capitalistic monopoly and the living room of
the world has been parceled out, the capitalistic countries
will inevitably develop into imperialism and come into conflict with each other. Furthermore, during the lulls between
confrontations, the imperialistic countries will form alliances
among themselves to exploit the oppressed nations. This
is the pattern from which China, a semi-colonial nation
jointly controlled by imperialistic powers, cannot expect to
escape . . ." Then he cited as factual proof of his theory the
events that had marred Chinese history, particularly the
stormy and humiliating period between 1880 and 1900 when
the Western powers, Japan, and Russia, each carved out a
chunk of interests in China, and together virtually deprived
China of her last semblance of sovereignty.[1]

Translated by him into Peking's policy, this means that
"the People's Republic of China shall uphold lasting international peace and friendly co-operation between the peoples
of all countries, and opposition to the imperialist policy of
aggression and war," a phrase adopted in the 1949 Common
Program, which is the basic framework for the organization
of the new regime. Throughout the 1950s he stressed co-
existence. "The socialist countries have always advocated
peaceful co-existence and peaceful competition with the capitalist countries . . . In order to ease international tension
[we have] proposed world disarmament, control of nuclear
weapons, and summit conferences . . . and other collective
security arrangements . . ."[2] The emphasis on peaceful co-
existence was dropped from his declarations only after the
Peking-Moscow rift had come into the open, and since then
he has been calling on the Chinese to "hold high the banners
of Marxism-Leninism, of Maoist revolutionary thought, and
of anti-American imperialism . . . to struggle for new gains
in people's democratic and socialist programs, and in world
peace."[3]

The implication of peaceful co-existence has, of course, never been extended to include Taiwan. Taiwan is part of China, and there is only one China as there is only one United States, Chou persistently repeats. And he refuses to sit down and talk to American delegates about any conditional withdrawal of U.S. protection of Taiwan or the seating of Peking in the United Nations.

There is no question in his mind that the world has been divided between the haves and the have nots, or the exploiter and the exploited proletariat. The exploitation of the unpropertied by the monopolizers of means of production is not only morally wrong, but also the source of all evils and strife. Therefore the ultimate solution and progress of the world is a classless society where no individual person owns or needs to own any means of production, but is insured of the provision for a happy life by a state or world system, so long as he contributes his share of labor. Hence the *kung-ch'an-chu-yi*, or common-property-ism, or communism.

Chou read this vision in a 2500-year-old Chinese Confucian classic: "When the Great Way prevails, the world belongs to the public . . . Since one hates to see goods wasted, one does not hoard them for oneself, and since one hates to keep his talents unused, one does not work just for oneself. . . . Thus no robbery or chaos need arise, and no door need be locked. This is the Society of Great Harmony [Uniformity]." He read it in the English Levellers, in the Idealistic Anarchists, and finally in Marx and Lenin. He read it in Sun Yat-sen's Three People's Principles, which at one time Sun himself equated with nationalism, democracy, and communism. Chou, therefore, supported Sun's doctrine (although not necessarily the Kuomintang) from the 1920s through 1949 until the New Democracy was propounded to replace the old Three People's Principles.

But from the very first awakening of his revolutionary fervor Chou has always held that Chinese revolution has to go through stages from an anti-feudal and anti-imperialist revolution to overthrow the warlords and repel foreign aggression in 1920–49 (he considered that the Kuomintang had degenerated into warlordism), to a democratic or modified socialist revolution, and finally to Communist revolution.

The stages are necessary not only because Lenin said so, but because the objective historical conditions in Chinese society dictate such a process of revolutionary evolution. Thus Chou, together with the Comintern, said in 1930 that prior to 1927 the CCP could consider involving the bourgeoisie in the revolution, but "after 1927 the bourgeoisie had turned anti-revolutionary," and the Chinese proletariat had to act without them. But this was not final. Whenever and wherever the petite bourgeoisie and enlightened capitalists joined hands with the proletariat in the revolution, particularly under intense foreign [Japanese, a new capitalist force] aggression, all these revolutionary classes must be united in a common front against the anti-revolutionary forces, foreign capitalists and their Chinese lackeys [the compradores], warlords, and local bosses. The only struggle today, said Chou in 1926, "is to unite the various democratic forces—national bourgeoisie, petite bourgeoisie, and the worker-peasant class—under the Kuomintang leadership to attack our common enemy!"[4]

Even after the 1927 break with the Kuomintang, when Chou had ceased talking about "under the KMT leadership," he continued to urge such a united front of revolutionary forces because "during the interim period of Chinese revolution there must be many preparatory steps."[5] These views of Chou En-lai laid the foundation for the "Chinese People's Democratic Dictatorship" of 1949, which has been accepted by most people as exclusively of the Mao vintage. As it was defined in the 1949 Common Program, the People's Democratic Dictatorship was not yet a proletarian dictatorship but a "people's democratic united front composed of the Chinese working class, peasantry, petite bourgeoisie, national bourgeoisie and other patriotic democratic elements, based on the alliance of workers and peasants and led by the working class."[6]

Chou accepted the Leninist doctrine that industrial workers, the most exploited and politically awakened class capable of action, must form the cutting edge of revolution; he kept repeating the phrase "led by the working class." But in 1929 he was painfully aware of the "weakness of the proletarian basis in the CCP," whose less than two thousand worker-members, inadequately indoctrinated and educated, looked upon revolutionary uprising as the same old "burning houses and murdering people" type of banditry.[7] He had to stress that the center of revolutionary gravity was in the country-side where "the peasants formed the solid basis for a peasant-worker alliance and rallied around the proletariat."[8] This Chou said in 1929–30, anticipating the worker-peasant-soldier alliance led by the CCP that remains the foundation of Chinese socialist revolution today.

But, Chou warned in 1959, "the Chinese socialist revolutionary process is a continuous process, while keeping a definite step-by-step development. . . . We recognize that there is no, and we cannot permit, a Great Wall to separate democratic revolution from socialist revolution, or socialism from communism. At the same time we recognize that each of the various stages of revolutionary development reflects its own qualitative change in man and the things around him. We must not confuse or mix up these qualitatively different stages."[9]

The argument is reminiscent of the Li Li-san line dispute of 1930–31 when some comrades insisted that the revolutionary high tide had come, while others shouted to stop violent insurrections because the conditions were not quite ripe. The flexibility, seemingly double-faced, provides Chou with a powerful leverage to achieve the "three steps forward and two steps backward" rhythm of ebb and flow, movement and quietude, freezing and thawing—the pattern of organic life traditionally accepted in the Chinese mind. In December 1964 he urged his fellow countrymen to be forever on guard against the possibility of a bourgeois reactionary resurgence: "Underestimating the danger of such a resurgence is completely wrong. . . . But since over 95 per cent of the Chinese people want revolution, want socialism, and are resolutely supporting or can be made to support the policy of the CCP, so long as we adhere to the mass-line, confidently mobilize the masses and organize them, . . . [our enemies] will be smashed, and the proletarian dictatorship will stand unshakable."[10]

This is drawing a line between the revolutionary and the anti-revolutionary, but in the next breath Chou proclaimed the continuing validity of the united front. "The Chinese people's democratic united front, led by the proletariat through its vanguard, the CCP, is based on the worker-peasant alliance, and comprises national bourgeoisie, the various democratic parties and groups . . . and patriotic overseas Chinese. . . . Further consolidation and development of this united front is extremely important to the successful progress of the socialist program."[11]

"No destruction, no construction; and only when there is destruction can there be construction!" Thus Chou repeated one of his favorite epithets in December 1964.[12] And only the Chinese Communist Party, or its leaders like Chou En-lai, have insight into this undulating rhythm of revolution. Each time Chou presses the brake or the accelerator, his enemies (if there are any who are strong enough) can easily criticize him for revising the party line, but, interestingly, he has managed to escape such criticism. That he can revise the party orthodoxy without being called a revisionist is due partly to the built-in ambiguity of the party line itself, as was shown in the Li Li-san dispute, and partly to his ability to out-argue his less eloquent opponents, but largely to the fact that, to the Chinese mind, the important thing is not whether one remains true to an abstract label, but whether one's actions bring about the desired result. Every Chinese prime minister during the past two thousand years called himself a Confucian scholar while promulgating laws based on economic determinism and writing poetry that reflected Buddhist and Taoist ideas. They all got away with it and died Confucian scholars. There is no reason why Chou cannot end his political life as a Leninist or Maoist in name, but a revisionist or Chou-ist in fact.

Responsible for overseeing the process of revolution moving step by step from a democratic, national revolution to communism, Chou En-lai developed an economic policy of "forcibly seizing the enterprises of the Kuomintang and foreign capitalists" in the 1930s,[13] nationalizing all enterprises that "exercise a dominant influence over the people's livelihood while encouraging active operation of all private economic enterprises beneficial to national welfare" in the 1940s and 1950s[14], and concentrating on the build-up of socialism in China in the 1960s.[15] In industry, there has been a forced march toward early completion of five-year plans, stressing bigger and bigger output of steel, coal, food grains, and cotton.

In agriculture, Chou started with a policy of equal distribution of land but not nationalization of ownership. "The farmers have not yet abandoned their idea about private land ownership," he said in 1930, "and in organizing the poor and tenant farmers, winning over the middle peasants, and overthrowing the rich farmers, care must be taken to enable the rich farmers to live on, though without their traditional privileges, after land redistribution."[16] In the 1960s agriculture had gone through "land to the tiller" and "rent reduction" to various types of collectivized farming with private land ownership retained.

The key to Chou En-lai's economic policy is an insistence not so much on a unified organizational mold of production as on the final outcome. Now that the distribution of the fruit of labor has been more or less equalized, or at least quite thoroughly controlled, private ownership of the means of production—or of what little is left after nationalization of major industries—is a psychological comfort to those incapable of forgetting their economic past. Chou announces an economic goal of so many tons of steel, coal, grains, and cotton, and the economic planning boards go to work to drum up enthusiasm in whatever way possible to fulfill and surpass these quotas—through communization of farming and industry in areas where conditions are ripe for this development, or some other form of farming and industry where it is most appropriate. By the end of 1964, Chou's report on the nation's economic progress included no mention of how many farms had been collectivized, but rather of how many fertilizer plants had been added and how much the output had exceeded that of the previous year.

How did this economic transformation of China fit into his theory of revolutionary stages? "Suitable steps have been adopted," said Chou in 1959, "to fit the gradual evolution of relationship among the segments in the economic production process, and the gradual maturity of the awakening of the masses. That the broad masses of the peasants have been able to move voluntarily from private enterprise toward the people's commune system has been due to their experience of going through seasonal mutual-aid teams, all-year-round mutual-aid teams, preliminary agricultural production cooperatives, and an advanced agricultural production co-operative, and then they were ready for the commune. . . . Capitalist-type industry and business have moved through government contracts and consignments, total purchase and distribution by the government, and individual government-private joint operations, until they have become ready for large-scale government-private joint operation. . . ."[17]

And the rhythm has been, like that of the political and ideological struggle toward socialism, "in conformity with the realistic and concrete situation of the time, rising and falling, alternating like waves, but forever going forward and in deeper penetration."[18]

"We want *to* (much) *k'uai* (fast) *hao* (good) and *sheng* (thrifty) all at once," declared Chou of his principal approach to economic reconstruction, "and some of our critics say, 'You want your horse to run fast, and you want your horse to eat nothing!' [the Chinese equivalent of to have your cake and eat it]. We are confident that we can have both because we have the most precious 'capital'—the 650 million people who are, after all, makers and users of means of production!"[19] "Furthermore, we use the 'walking on two legs' approach, or the combined approach of old methods and modern methods of production, whichever is the most efficient under local conditions of a given time."[20]

Controlling this revolutionary rhythm has become Chou En-lai's chief concern because it applies to all aspects of China's national life, including cultural and educational activities. He sought to release the pent-up energy of the intellectuals in the early 1950s with the "hundred-flower" movement, and in December 1964, he was still repeating, "We must continue to implement to the full the 'let one hundred kinds of flowers bloom together, and let one hundred schools of thought contend' policy, in the direction of serving the workers, peasants, and soldiers and serving socialism. For this is the only correct policy for the development of science and culture. Only through grappling with bourgeois thought can proletarian thought be developed, and only by fighting the poisonous weeds can the fragrant blossom of socialism bloom luxuriantly."[21]

This echoes his stern injunction against the behavior of timid yes-men in the Party in the 1920s as he once criticized them, "Even though within the Party there are problems and divergent views, our comrades are afraid of argument, afraid of any heated debate that they think might cause a schism within the Party . . . and afraid of offending friends, and therefore avoid discussion and tend to gloss over the differences. . . . But so long as we keep our political discussion impersonal, the more intensely we argue the closer we can come to the truth!"[22]

The way a bourgeois intellectual can learn proletarian thought is not just by going to spend a few days in a factory or on a farm. "Cadres of all levels must participate in collective productive labor in order to overcome fundamentally their tendency of becoming bureaucrats, and to convert themselves into true laborers who can share the life of the masses with all its sweetness and bitterness."[23] To a young college girl who asked, "How can we become proletarian intellectuals?" he replied, "It is not to be determined by sitting for an examination or being judged by the leaders. It comes only when your thought and feeling are in accord with those of the laboring masses, and when you realize that you are wholeheartedly serving the laboring masses. It is judged by the masses. . . . There are still many people who think that having been in the countryside for several months, thus having been 'gold-plated,' they must already be proletarian intellectuals. This is like the way in the old days that a man thought of himself as educated simply because he had just graduated from college with a mortarboard on his head—sheer formalism, and downright bourgeois thinking."[24]

The girl was one of a group of co-eds participating in agricultural production in a commune or agricultural association outside Shanghai. She had graduated from the chemistry department of the University of Nanking and had been doing research in the Science Academy of China. After three months of manual labor, she and her schoolmates excitedly greeted Chou En-lai's visit. She did not quite know what to say about the portion of time she continued to devote to reading, as she was supposed to be learning from the proletariat. Some of her friends had said that they should continue to read whenever they had time to do so; others maintained that they should keep completely away from their books for the duration of their period of learning from labor.

Chou solved their dilemma. "You are not yet accustomed to labor," he said. "Once you get used to it, you will know how to budget your time [between manual work and reading]."

"Practice should be constant," said Chou. "After you have finished a certain period of manual work here, you may go back to your office or laboratory and think it over for a while, then come back here to work physically for another period of time. When the farmers are busy, you should try to come here and help." Then he turned to the secretary of the Shanghai branch of the CCP. "How are these girls doing here?" "Oh, they are just like professional farmers," was the reply. "No," said Premier Chou, shaking his head, "they can't be. They've been here only three months; they can't be exactly the same as regular farmers. If you say so, you are inflating their ego." The secretary said, "They are much more like regular farmers now than when they first came." "That sounds more like it," said the Premier.

With touching paternal solicitude the handsome Premier inquired of one after another about their life on the commune. Noticing the mud all over them he asked, "Did you cry when you first arrived on the farm?" "No," was the answer. "It would not have mattered if you did. It's only human to cry when you are not used to something." Then he went on to find out how the self-criticism program had been started. "Everybody progresses from backward to forward," he said. "Take me, for instance. Once I was much more backward than you girls. In my young days I had a pigtail on my head, which was so full of the old, old stuff that there was no room even for capitalism—which got in there later. And it was a long time before I found Marxism-Leninism. . . . I had two brothers at one time. One of them rotted away along with the old society and died a decadent, never awakened. I helped the other join in the revolution, but after working with us for some time he also fell on the wayside. . . .

The road to revolution is not easy; it takes constant self-awakening to stay on it."[25]

Chou En-lai has seen most of his ideas translated into reality, although without his always getting the credit for them. The chances of their perpetuation in China will depend less upon Chou's political survival than upon whether man has enough wisdom and ability to prove to the Chinese that the dialectical destiny of humanity is not inevitable and that peace and prosperity can come to all men without exploitation and to all nations without imperialism.

As to the chances for Chou's political survival, he has indeed done well so far and the end is not yet in sight. China stands on the strength of three forces—the youth and intelligentsia, the army, and the party apparatus. He who can work with all three forces on the national scale will remain the indispensable figure to hold China together.

We have seen how Chou could appeal to the sentimental patriotism of the youth as far back as 1919, the patriotism that brought them out of their classrooms to parade down the streets of Peking shouting "Down with the Warlords!" The same force brought out the students during the war to exchange their books for rifles, to go to the battlefront, or to march on Japanese stores and smash them. The same force sustained the students immediately after World War II to demand "Rice, not bullets" from Chiang Kai-shek, and most recently to drag out the anti-Maoists wherever they were and spit on them. The Red Guards of 1966–67, over 90 per cent of whom were young students under twenty, adored Mao, not because they had grasped any profound truth from Mao's teachings, but rather because they had identified Mao as a symbol of the state around whom they could rally their sentimental, therefore impulsive, patriotism. The very fact that the Red Guard movement could be generated into a movement in Mainland China proved that the Chinese revolution had not yet outgrown the stage during which students con-

[19] (*above*) With workers in a tire factory, Alexandria, Egypt, June 1965.
[20] (*below*) Getting acquainted with delegates to the Afro-Asian Writers' Emergency Meeting in Peking, June 1966.

[21] The rally of 1,000,000 Red Guards at the Gate of Heavenly Peace on August 18, 1966. The four principal speakers of the day (from right to left, front row). Mrs. Mao (Chiang Ching), Chou, Lin Piao, Mao.

[22] Watching fireworks with Mao at the Gate of Heavenly Peace, October 1, 1966.

[23] Ma Shun-yi, Chou's sister-in-law, during interview in Taipei, June 28, 1964. (Photo by Kai-yu Hsu)

tinued to provide the fire and dynamism. Chou En-lai, who had been one of these students himself and has retained his ability to speak their language, is the only one today among the top Communist leaders in Peking capable of kindling this fire and guiding this dynamism.

On a more sophisticated level, we have observed how he seems to have had a greater measure of empathy with the adult intellectuals, authors, artists, and college professors, although he does not pretend to be one of them. He initiated the thawing in the hundred-flower movement with some broad policy statements; later he participated in the freezing, also with some broad policy statements, after the hundred-flower movement had gotten beyond control. But in no instance has he involved himself in the hair-splitting, often ridiculously demogogic vilifications waged by party-line defenders to knock down an author by finding fault with one of his novels or poems. Among the top leaders in Peking today, he exhibits a most wholesome respect for the integrity of a true intellectual. This alone is enough to help him retain the respect of the intelligentsia.

He claims no undying glory for his record in the Red Army, and yet his political cultivation of some of the ablest soldiers trained at Whampoa, who later fought under the Red flag; his leadership in the earliest armed insurrections; his successful direction of strategy in Kiangsi and during the Long March; and his perpetual position as a guiding light on the Military Committee of the Party, are not easily forgotten. As we have noted, Defense Minister Lin Piao was at one time his student at Whampoa, and later fought under his command during the Long March. The most respected commanders in the Red Army are not necessarily merely combat heroes, but political soldiers who can converse with equal eloquence on political strategy and military tactics. Chou En-lai is such a combination, which will keep him a respected general even though he has no soldiers under his direct command.

In party apparatus, Chou, the infallible Bolshevik, was

never the chairman or secretary-general for any length of time, and yet he was always the indispensable number two who came just in time to save the Party from disintegration and defeat. He worked conscientiously under Ch'en Tu-hsiu, Li Li-san, Ch'ü Ch'iu-pai, Ch'en Shao-yü, until, one after another, these leaders were disgraced because of their departure from the party line. Ch'en Tu-hsiu and Ch'ü Ch'iu-pai are dead. Li Li-san since his last abject confession of political error in 1956 has been given a secondary assignment in the government and the eighty-ninth seat in the Politburo. Ch'en Shao-yü has been working, of all things, in collaboration with Teng Ying-ch'ao for the promulgation and practice of the New Marriage Law since 1950, and has been given the very bottom seat in the Politburo.

Chou En-lai's stature in the Party has grown not by knocking others down, nor by staying away from controversy, but by taking the orthodox party line and sticking to it until the tide was really turning. Then he plunged into the deadlocked controversy to cast his deciding vote.

His strength lies in the fact that when he teamed up with another leader, he was still not his man; and he is not Mao's man now. He is popular without being the subject of jealousy because he can yield gracefully whenever another leader, either because of his merit or ambition, appears to be ready for the number one position. When he returned from Moscow in 1928, he did all the work of reviving the Party from the brink of extinction, but he gave Li Li-san the honor of being the party chief. In 1930 Ch'ü Ch'iu-pai had already lost the Comintern's blessing, and yet Chou yielded the honor of calling the Third Plenum of the CCP's Central Committee to Ch'ü, even though everything pointed to Chou as the most popular leader in the Party at that moment. At the Fourth Plenum of the Central Committee in 1931 he quietly pushed Ch'en Shao-yü to the forefront to take the secretary-generalship; Ch'en then proceeded to steer the Party along the lines prescribed in Chou's Shao-shan Report of 1930, which was supposedly condemned by party orthodoxy. In the Kiangsi Soviet of 1931–34, everybody knew that Chou was the real voice for the Central Committee, and yet Ch'en Shao-yü's men occupied seats of higher honor than Chou.

After Chou helped Mao Tse-tung establish his leadership in the Party in 1935 during the Long March, time and again Chou yielded without rage or rancor to comrades of much less distinction and seniority. When Liu Shao-ch'i, an obscure partisan working with the students and labor unions first in Hunan, then in North China when Chou had already been number two man in the Central Committee for years, revised the party bylaws and emerged as Mao's heir with his popular pamphlets on communism in 1945, Chou smilingly stepped down to the number three position. When Teng Hsiao-p'ing rose as the CCP's secretary-general in 1956, Chou again graciously yielded the number three position to his former clerical assistant who had run a mimeographing machine for him in Paris. The latest example of his lack of megalomania occurred on March 22, 1967, when he referred to Lin Piao as "the comrade at arms closest to Chairman Mao," and "deputy leader," honoring him as the new number two. Something of the traditional Chinese philosophy of yielding, of recognizing ebb and flow as an organic part of any life, is reflected in this man. The important thing is that, after he has yielded, his comrades know that he is still indispensable.

In the 1966–67 Red Guard tumult he attacked nobody personally and was called upon to intervene in the disputes and pacify the mobs.[26] At various times he represented Mao, Lin, the Party and the military in addressing Red Guard rallies when things appeared to be deadlocked.[27] Chou anticipated the Red Guard movement in his December 1964 reports, when he urged vigilance against any possible slipping back to bourgeois thinking and re-emphasized the constant need for cadres of all levels to learn and relearn from the proletariat. But he, above all people, knows that the socialist reconstruction of a country as large as China cannot be accomplished

with slogan-shouting and parades. "Work on the farm a period, then back to your office and schools to think it over a
period, criticize yourselves and each other when needed, and
then back to the farm or factory to work for another period,"
he said to the students. This, too, is part of the ebb and flow
rhythm Chou has been striving to maintain in China's revolution. And when all the hundreds and thousands of anti-
Maoists have been exposed and disgraced in varying degrees,
Chou En-lai may once more pull the pieces together, for
neither ex-actress Mrs. Mao, nor Defense Minister Lin Piao,
nor speech-writer Ch'en Po-ta alone could run the huge
country.

In sharp contrast to the Russian pattern, the party purges
in Communist China have been noticeable for their relative
lack of bloodshed. Even Li Li-san and Ch'en Shao-yü still
remain in the Politburo, and after months of harassment by
the Red Guards, Liu Shao-ch'i and Teng Hsiao-p'ing at this
writing still hold their respective top posts as chairman of
the government and secretary-general of the Party. The only
exceptions were the case of Kao and Jao in Manchuria in
1949, and the case involving P'eng Teh-huai, one-time deputy
chief commander of the Red Army, in 1959. Once these three
or four well-known rebels faded out of the limelight, even
their accused followers seemed to survive the ordeals without
any appreciable damage to their careers. Whatever the outcome of the current Great Cultural Revolution in Mainland
China, Chou En-Lai's lack of an identifiable loyal clique
around him need not be to his disadvantage.

There is, of course, factionalism in the Chinese Communist Party, but any assumption that the party hierarchy is
supported by hard-and-fast cliques and that a member of a
clique lives and dies for his big brother on top as the members of the secret brotherhoods did in ancient times is totally
unfounded. Liu Shao-ch'i had been chosen by Mao to succeed him,[28] yet the Red Guards pointed out that Liu is not
a member of Mao's loyal clique. Lin Piao, for years rumored

to be one of the Whampoa clique rallying around Chou and said to have teamed up with Chou to overthrow Mao in 1958,[29] turned out to be the sole supporter of Mao in 1966–67. Indeed, if the cliques had any real influence in the party hierarchy alignment, Mao Tse-tung today would be the loneliest man in Peking, and Chou En-lai, because of his multidimensional connections with so many different groups within and outside the Party, the most powerful.

Chou, the multi-faceted man, has impressed his visitors and associates in so many different ways that they invalidate any single characterization. Perhaps the patterns, as they appear from different angles, should be left the way they are—kaleidoscopic, not to be telescoped together.

"Chou En-lai, oh, that rascal!" said Han,[30] Chou's high school friend. "You can't help liking him, even though at times he exasperates you with his damned patience. Yes, he is always patient with me. No matter how angry I get, he always smiles and goes back over the same ground covered in our argument, only in a different way—different enough to make you feel as though he were presenting a new point. . . . Take that time in Kyoto, for example, when I smashed the bottle, almost hitting him. Anyone else would have given it back to me, or at least walked out of my house. But he just turned and quietly went to look—for a broom! And the next day he went to get a bunch of flowers for my wife. Mind you, that was when he was totally broke. How can you get really angry with a man like that?"

Another high school friend,[31] however, had a strong aversion to Chou. "He was too effeminate. He liked make-up, the stage, and that sort of thing, which gave me creeps. My brother got along with him all right, but I had no use for a boy like him."

A Kuomintang high official,[32] a seasoned scholar of law and administrator who was friendly toward Chou in private life, declared, "At first I was completely convinced that he was right, and there perhaps should be more concession on both sides of the negotiation. Then, as days went by, I began to wonder if this man, however sincere he might be, was not totally blinded by his political prejudices. Finally I came to recognize that there was not a grain of truth in him. He spoke beautifully—I don't mean his voice is beautiful, but his art of presenting arguments is beautiful, including the calculated effects of his stammering and incoherence at times —and he convinces everyone. But in the end I realized that it's all acting. He is the greatest actor I have ever seen. He'd laugh one moment and cry the next, and make all his audience laugh and cry with him. But it's all acting!"

A leader of the Young China Party,[33] who had become acquainted with Chou over the years and had visited Chou during the Yenan period, thought that Chou might not be brilliant, but was the best the Chinese Communist Party could offer. "He is at least very clever," he said, "and he has polish. He does not pretend to know much and—this is his virtue—he listens and learns, and he is always asking questions about everything he wishes to know. There is no one else among the Communist leaders who can listen, or, when they rarely do, can understand what you are saying. This goes for Mao Tse-tung as well. I remember once in Chungking there was a general, a self-styled genius of military strategy. We listened to him a couple of times and knew that he didn't have much to offer. Chou En-lai kept going to him with all sorts of questions on the war situation. Whether Chou felt he was really learning something, or simply keeping up a front to please that general, I don't know. But Chou En-lai is the only man the Communist Party has now [spring of 1967] and, survival or collapse, the Peking regime depends upon him."

This view on Chou En-lai is supported by another writer and teacher of political science,[34] who has been involved in China's politics since the 1920s, except that he spoke of Chou with greater enthusiasm, "There is no doubt that Chou is next in line after Mao [this was in 1964 when Liu Shao-ch'i was at his most popular]. After the Chinese Communist Party ousted Ch'en Tu-hsiu and the downfall of Ch'ü Ch'iu-pai, there was no intellectual among the Communist leaders except Chou, who is at least half intellectual and certainly has been around and seen the world. He has exactly what Mao Tse-tung needs—practical and sophisticated political craftsmanship—which makes him number one administrator and diplomat in Peking. Mao has only the brute force of the guerrillas, and the Moscow-trained Bolsheviks have only empty talk. Only Chou En-lai can pull them together and make something of them. Now that he has built upon his early following with fifteen years [by 1964] of unblemished premiership, his strength in Mainland China is most redoubtable."

"Chou En-lai is rather weak in his mastery of political theories," said one of his close comrades[35] in Paris, "but he can summarize my ideas and re-present them much better than I can. We depended on him to prepare all our public statements, either orally or in writing, because once he handled them they were sure to be accepted by all groups involved."

Of all those who have known Chou En-lai well, his sister-in-law, Ma Shun-yi[36] knows best his non-political life. She still does not believe that he can be bad. Repeatedly she said, "Unlike my husband, Chou En-lai is so understanding and nice to everybody. I don't believe he personally had anything to do with my father's death because I know he really respects our traditional Chinese ethics about family relations. It's communism that made people do such awful things in China."

"But, no!" disagreed Madman Miao Chien-ch'iu,[37] who spent many long days with Chou in Sian in 1936–37. "Everything that appears to be human in Chou En-lai is false, absolutely false! And he is sharp and capable—that is what's terrible about him. He has too many tricks, and yet he can appear so touchingly innocent. He is the god of revolution, and the demon of bloodshed, but never a man!"

Chou En-lai at sixty-nine lives the life of neither a god nor a demon, but a man.[38] In between meetings, conferences, and State of the Republic reports, he goes home to chat with Teng Ying-ch'ao about her work on the Standing Committee of the National People's Congress, over a cup of the famous Shao-hsing wine produced in his home town, or occasionally a cup of coffee—no more left over from a can of S & W, but the choice brew delivered from the Cuban legation in Peking. Then he goes to the Central Park where children watch him with wide, beaming eyes (they have seen him before, in parades, in photographs, and on the streets of Peking), as he walks up to them. He pats their heads, and his crisp, silver-gray beltless uniform brushes against their backs as he leans over to watch the famous Peking goldfish cavorting in a huge porcelain tub. He exclaims with as much excitement as do the children, and for a long time he stands there, hemmed in by the little heads with their beribboned pigtails.

And he strolls down a side street in Peking where housewives momentarily pause in their daily chores to watch him enter a noodle house. He sits down by himself at a corner table. While waiting for his order of noodles in soup with meat sauce he chats with the old waiter about the weather, the quality of wheat this year, the wage he earns, and his family. "This table is clean," he says to the waiter upon leaving, "but you can wipe it once more."

He goes to visit the Woman's Association Headquarters in Shanghai where a large crowd of anxious faces, old and young, surround him, each eager to get her turn to say something to the Premier. He asks a nineteen-year-old girl about her job and marvels at her ability to learn to drive a tractor in thirty days. He checks on how well the children are cared for when their mothers, wives of soldiers and workers assigned to distant stations, go to the countryside to assist farm production.

He wonders if the women cadres, all unpaid volunteers working in the neighborhood, hear any complaints in their families when they make calls on their neighbors and sometimes
pay their own streetcar fares, all without financial compen-
sation. From the director of family planning he learns that
birth-control devices are of sufficient quantity, but, she says,
"They don't always work." "Ah," he says, "you know it's not
always the fault of the devices. Too often it's because their
users are careless." "Some men comrades don't want to co-
operate. Some don't even want to hear anything about birth
control," says another woman in the crowd. "That's the problem," comments Chou. "There is a great deal more educating we all have to do. Our country is leading the world in
population. I guess we will always be in the lead, but we have
to work toward a balanced development between production
of supplies and population increase." He makes everybody
laugh when he remarks on how well the secretary of the
association is doing in her own family planning, in addition
to being a well-known expert on planned economy. He reminds his women audience that motherhood and family management are important everywhere and any time. "Family
is still extremely important in Socialist society," he says. "You
must not look down on household chores. After all, each of
you is running a one-person cabinet. Each of you has in her
hands both the Department of the Interior and the Department of Foreign Affairs in her family. How much more important can anyone's job be?" More laughter, more cheers . . .

He goes to inspect a commune, a collectivized co-operative
farm outside the city of Chengchow in Central China, where
he asks a seventy-year-old farmer if the 5600-pound-per-acre
wheat yield is an accurate prediction as claimed by the commune director. He squats down with a seventeen-year-old
farm girl on the dirt partition in the field to count the grains
in one spike. He asks her where her *ai-jen* (boyfriend, or
lover, or husband) works and when they plan to get married.
He takes a steamed bread from a lunching farmer nearby,

breaks it open, and tosses a piece into his mouth to taste
the mixture of wheat and sweet potato flour, and he smacks
his lips. He stops at the co-operative store, asks about the
prices of the various items, and says, "That's too bad" when
informed that the store does not sell wine.

When he arrives at the famed Yangtze River Gorges to inspect the hydraulic engineering projects in that area, he sits
up at night in his river boat to review the engineer's maps
and reports to prepare for the next day's visit and discussion.
The next morning when the chief engineer emphasizes with
an exaggerated gesture the need for a 180-mile wiring system
for the trunk power line, Chou remarks, "Maybe not quite
so long." And they open the map to check. Surely Chou is
right—it's less than 130 miles! Still in his crisp silver-gray
beltless uniform, he treks up and down the rocky hills along
the river bank together with the young workers, many of whom
have just taken a break from their city jobs, white-collar jobs,
to "learn from labor." A little boy passes them on the path.
Chou stops the boy and shows him the map in his hand to
see if the boy can read the large characters printed across the
top of the paper. "That's very good," he says, patting the little
boy on the back, "but try to pronounce it with a falling tone.
You know, we all are learning to speak the same accent now
—Mandarin."

The boat stops at Tzu-kuei shortly before it proceeds
through the first of the Gorges. He walks out on the deck
to point out to his traveling companions that it is the birthplace of the patriot-poet, Ch'ü Yüan, who lived 2300 years
ago. "Comrade Mao Tse-tung often reminds us to read Ch'ü
Yüan's poems," he says. "They are really inspiring poems."
A little later the boat reaches the Goddess Peak in the Gorge.
He asks the engineers to pause for a few minutes in their
discussion to go to the front of the boat for a good view of
the famous scene.

"Look there," he says, "that rock standing on top of the
peak—that's the goddess whom a king is said to have met in

his dream when he passed the night here over two thousand years ago."

The rock, standing erect, tapers gracefully on both ends and, with just the right amount of green clustering around it, resembles at a distance a silk-draped dancer balancing herself in the wind. As Chou recalls for his younger companions the ancient legend of a romantic fantasy, perhaps two lines of the poet Ch'ü Yüan keep coming back to ring in his ears:

> Often do I heave long sighs
> To hide my tears, silent tears,
> Sorrowing for the lives of my people
> That are so full of grief and fears.

Near the river bank a farmer with his water buffalo pauses in his strenuous job to wave at Chou En-lai. A group of children and some adults from the nearby village have gathered close to the docked boat, chattering and watching, and when one schoolboy exclaims in joy of his discovery, "Chou *Tsung-li!* Look, there is Chou *Tsung-li!*" a wave of applause rises above the din of the river current, to which Chou responds with pleased hand-clapping. For a while the river valley resounds with hand claps, like the firecrackers Chou used to hear in Huai-an when he was a child, and the haunting rifle reports in the still of the night at the Shanghai suburb of Lung-hua in 1927, and the thunderous cheers at the Gate of Heavenly Peace in Peking in 1949 . . .

And on his head, for years well known for its pitch-black hair, the setting sun picks out a few strands of gleaming white.

NOTES

(For full identification of sources, see Appendix B at end of book.)

CHAPTER 1

1. *The Liberation Daily* (Yenan, October 9, 1945), and *The Ta-kung-pao* (Chungking, same date).

2. Liu Shao-ch'i and others, *Comrades Liu, Chou, and Chu in the Midst of the Masses*, p. 27.

3. Some sources say that Chou En-lai's grandfather was once magistrate of Huai-an. Su Chi-ch'ang, *Noted Persons of This Era*, p. 66. Chou's sister-in-law, Ma Shun-yi, however, identified the brother of En-lai's grandmother as having served on this post. Ma's father was at one time an official of transportation on the Grand Canal. After 1949 Ma managed to reach Taiwan by way of Shanghai and Hong Kong. She subsequently testified before a fact-finding committee of the International Commission to Abolish Concentration Camps which was studying Communist persecution, meeting in Brussels, Belgium, on April 24–30, 1956.

4. Chou admitted that Huai-an was his birthplace. Liang Sou-ming, "Who is Responsible for the Civil War in the Past?" *The Chinese World* (San Francisco, February 4–9, 1949). Other sources give different places as Chou's home town. Hatano Kanichi, *History of the Chinese Communist Party*, Vol. 1, p. 34, gives Hunan. *The Events of Modern China*, p. 257, gives Huai-an. *The Yearbook of New China*, p. 462, has Huai-an. Hatano Kanichi, "A Biography of Chou En-lai," gives Hunan, Huai-an, and I-wu in Chekiang Province as three equally possible places.

5. "A Report on the Investigation into the Visit to Chekiang by Chou En-lai, member of the Chinese Communist Party's Central Committee" (mimeographed), Bureau of Investigation.

6. The exact time of death of En-lai's own mother cannot be as-

certained. Su Chi-ch'ang, *Noted Persons of This Era,* p. 66, gives it as when En-lai was four years old. Other information indicates that the death must have occurred before En-lai reached ten when he left with his fourth uncle for Manchuria. Many popularly cited sources identify Chou's father as Yün-liang (otherwise pronounced Wen-liang). See Union Research Service, *Index to Biographical Service,* No. 3 (July 1, 1956–December 31, 1957).

7. According to Informant No. 3, Chou's schoolmate at the Nankai Middle School.

8. *New China Daily News* (Chungking, July 15, 1942).

9. *Chou En-lai Grows Old as a Negotiator* (July 1946).

10. *Ibid.* One was identified as Kao Erh-wu, the other, Fan.

11. According to Tuan Mou-lan, diplomat and contemporary of Chou.

CHAPTER 2

1. Information on Chou's life in his Nankai Middle School days has been obtained from Informants No. 1 (a teacher), No. 2 (Han is an alias), and No. 3, who were all with Chou.

2. According to Chih-kang Wu, who recalled of Chang's description in a speech in 1945.

3. *Symposium in Honor of the 80th Birthday of the Late President of Nankai University, Chang Po-ling.*

4. One source relates that Chang finally moved to Tientsin where the Communists continued to approach him, urging him to take an active part in the "Oppose-America-Aid-Korea" campaign. Chang's death was at least partially attributable to these ceaseless harassments.

5. According to Informant No. 2, among the five students who supported Chou En-lai financially in Japan were Yen Chih-k'ai, the son of the founder of the Nankai School; Ts'ai Shih-chieh, a student from northwest China who was trying to enroll in the Military Academy in Japan; and Chang Jui-feng, a student of the Waseda University.

6. Ma Chün came from a rich Manchurian Moslem family. During the May 4 Movement Ma made speeches in front of mass rallies to agitate for a general strike. Police forces were out several times after him. He was arrested at least once, and was released upon petition by many civic leaders. Later Ma went to Russia where he joined the Communist Party. Upon his return to China he continued his Communist activities until 1927, when he was arrested by the warlord Chang Tso-lin and executed together with the first Chinese Communist leader, Professor Li Ta-chao.

7. The source of the information on Chou's activities during the May 4 Movement (Informant No. 3) worked together with Chou in the Student League and collaborated in publishing the daily. According to him, the League's headquarters was set up in the Nan-shih District in Tientsin. The daily, which lasted exactly one hundred days, first appeared in August 1919.

8. According to Chang Hsi-man, "There was another Russian professor at Peking University who went under the Chinese name P'ai-lieh-wei and claimed that he was a specialist on the Chinese classic *Book of Poetry*. He came to China with the express purpose of working on his vernacular Chinese speech. After the October revolution, he was appointed Cultural Liaison for the Third Comintern in Tientsin." Shen Yün-lung, *The Origin of the Chinese Communist Party*, pp. 2–3. The same Russian agent is identified as Pao-li-wei in *China Yearbook* (1948), Vol. 1, p. 771, and as Sergei A. Polevoy in Chow Tse-tsung, *The May Fourth Movement*, p. 244.

9. According to Informant No. 1, who was imprisoned at the same time with Chou En-lai.

10. Chou did not show much interest in girls, which was not unusual for Chinese students in those days. One story about his falling in love with a high school classmate from Manchuria and his secret betrothal, is not confirmed. He did meet Teng Ying-ch'ao, but not in jail, as has been erroneously reported by some Western sources. Informant No. 3, Chou's Nankai schoolmate, and Informant No. 23, Teng's high school roommate, both stated that Teng never attended Nankai, and was never arrested. Chou and Teng became acquainted through the student activities, but they did not develop any serious attachment to each other until they started correspondence across the world, while Chou was in Europe. More about Teng Ying-ch'ao in Chapters 5 and 7.

CHAPTER 3

1. One former schoolmate of Chou En-lai (Informant No. 3), said that Chou was writing only for the *I-shih-pao* of Tientien. Another schoolmate (Informant No. 2), however, recalled that Chou was at the same time also a correspondent for the *Ta-kung-pao* of Tientsin and the *Hsin-wen-pao* and *Shih-shih-hsin-pao*, both of Shanghai. In view of the fact that Chou did not really write too extensively, it seems unlikely that he was serving all four newspapers at the same time. The name of the school where Chou and about thirty other Chinese students studied French was offered by Informant No. 12.

The name of the ship carrying Chou to Europe was confirmed by Informant No. 6, who was on the same boat with Chou.

2. Informant No. 5 related that Chou first went to Germany and stayed there until the organization of the Communist group in France became imminent. Although this source was in France during the stormy days of Chinese politics there, he did not follow Chou's activities closely from the day he left China for Europe. The information used here (according to Informant No. 6) seems more reliable in that the source went to France on the same ship with Chou.

3. Li Shih-tseng (French-trained biologist) and Wu Chih-hui (d. 1953).

4. The early group life of the Chinese students in France was described by Informant No. 8, who went there in 1918 and remained close to the students for many years. The source had personal contact with Chou and was acquainted with Chou's activities. Also, I Chai, "Report on the Sino-French Education Commission in Paris and the Hunanese Students in the Work-and-Study Program," *Hunan Historical Data*, No. 4 (1959).

5. Informant No. 2.

6. Chu Ch'i-ling.

7. Ch'en Lu.

8. Information on Chou En-lai's participation in the demonstration at Lyon, his imprisonment, and his escape, has been secured from Informant No. 7, who was with Chou during the event and was also imprisoned. He himself escaped after the ship carrying the deported students had reached the Suez Canal Zone. A fellow student in the group somehow still had his residence permit with him, apparently an oversight on the part of the French police collecting these papers at Marseilles. Since this student had run out of funds and was willing to return to China anyway, Informant No. 7 persuaded him to give him the permit. He took the permit, got off the boat, and approached the local French consulate to let him go back to France, saying that it was a mistake to have included him in the exodus. The French were actually quite indifferent to the whole affair and the consulate at Suez permitted Informant No. 7 to return to France. Informant No. 5, however, maintained that in his recollection, Chou was not personally involved in the Lyon imprisonment. Evidence supporting the version adopted here seems to be strong. For example, *Martyr Hsiang Ching-yü* (Peking, The Women's Magazine Editorial Office, December 1958), p. 2, relates: "She enthusiastically participated in the struggle led by Comrades Chou En-lai, Wang Jo-fei, and others, which opposed the monopoly of the Lyon

University by the Sino-French Educational Commission and the Chinese Legation under the Northern Warlords." As to the Communist leaders among the deported, Hsiao San, "Comrade Mao Tse-tung Founds Communism," *Chinese Youth*, No. 62 (1951), says: "Ch'en Yi and Li Li-san were sent back to China under guard." Chou En-lai is not mentioned.

Another record of good authority also relates: "On February 28 (1921), the financially embarrassed Work-and-Study Chinese students in France, over four hundred in strength, besieged the Chinese embassy in Paris to demand the issuance of monthly stipends amounting to 400 francs per person for at least four years." See *The Eastern Magazine*, Vol. 18 (March 25, 1921), No. 6. The same journal, Vol. 18 (December 25, 1921), No. 24, further reports: "Talk was afoot last March to return all the Work-and-Study students now in France. Subsequently the French government, feeling that this matter had great cultural significance, approached the Chinese Minister Ch'en Lu to organize a Sino-French Educational Commission to solve the problem. While the commission was studying the problem, the students went on strike protesting a proposed French loan to the Chinese government. This development changed the mind of the French authorities who decided to cease any effort to help the students by disbanding the commission. On September 10, [1921] the construction of the University of Lyon was completed. The students demanded that the university open its doors to them. They dispatched a vanguard group of over a hundred students who left Paris on September 21 for Lyon and proceeded to occupy the university buildings. The president of the university, a Frenchman, unable to check the onrush of the Chinese students, reported to the Lyon Municipal government which removed the demonstrating students to a nearby army camp. Later the French government secured the consent of the Chinese Legation to deport this group of over a hundred students. On October 13, French agents arrived in Lyon, rounded up the 104 Chinese students and escorted them to Marseilles to board a ship for China. They reached Shanghai on October 23."

9. Including Ch'u Min-yi (executed by the KMT as a collaborator immediately after World War II), and Chang Shih-chao (Minister of Education, 1925, now member of the Standing Committee, People's Congress, Peking).

10. Ts'ai Ch'ang, "In Memoriam of Comrade Wang Jo-fei," *In Memory of the Martyrs of April 8*, p. 195.

11. Informant No. 10 moved into the same house immediately after Chou En-lai left.

12. Informant No. 3.

13. Assisting Chou was Liu Hsin.

14. *In Memory of the Martyrs of April 8*, p. 242.

15. Informant No. 5. Also see Ho Ch'ang-kung, *Reminiscence of the Life of Work-and-Study in France*, pp. 74–75.

16. Wang Ching-ch'i.

17. Informant No. 11 worked for this journal. Informant No. 5 said the publication was named *San-min chou-pao* (*The Three People's Weekly*).

18. Informant No. 8. Also see *The Works of Tseng Mu-han*, pp. 418–19, 437, and 420.

19. Ho Lu-chih, now a member of National Assembly, Republic of China, but living in semi-retirement in Hong Kong.

20. Hatano Kanichi, "Biography of Chou En-lai," relates that at the founding meeting of the Chinese Communist Youth Corps in France, Chou proposed a compromise with the Young China group, which was criticized by Chao Shih-yen as opportunism and voted down. It is impossible to ascertain how Chou phrased his proposal, but judging by his basic "united front" approach, some exchange of this kind could very well have taken place.

21. Liang Shih-yi, for one month premier of the warlord-controlled Peking government toward the end of 1921.

22. Informant No. 5, who was Chou's comrade in Paris, and Informant Nos. 7, 8, 11, and 12, who were in the KMT and the Young China groups.

23. Some authors, however, have attributed too much significance to the "clique" nature of the Paris group around Chou. See Ku Kuan-chiao, *The Chinese Communist Party during the Past 30 Years*, p. 64.

CHAPTER 4

1. Informant No. 11.

2. Pavel Mif, *The Fifteen Years of the Chinese Communist Party's Heroic Struggle*, pp. 30–31.

3. Ch'en Chiung-ming rebelled on June 16, 1922, May 9, 1923, November 12, 1923, November 30, 1924, and January 15, 1925.

4. Liu Chen-huan and Yang Hsi-min rebelled, June 5, 1925.

5. Sun Yat-sen received such reports on November 29, 1923, June 1, 1924, and June 18, 1924.

6. July 7, 1924.

7. June 2, 1924.

8. August 9–25, 1924.

9. Some say that Chou first went to North China upon his return from France.

10. Liu Ning, *The Autobiography of a Proletarian*, p. 4. T'ao Hsi-sheng and others, *A Compendium of Historical Documents of the Communist Betrayal of the Nation*, Series I, Vol. 1, p. 325. Chou Fu-chen, "The Golden Era of the Kwangtung District Committee," *Contemporary Historical Data*, Vol. 2, pp. 312–15.

11. Ch'en Kung-po. Wen Shu, "Ch'en Kung-po and the CCP," *Contemporary Historical Data*, Vol. 1, p. 65.

12. Many early Whampoa Academy graduates (for instance, Informant Nos. 16 and 19) recall that Chou En-lai was deputy director of the Academy's Political Department in the winter of 1924–25, but none could give exact dates. Mao Ssu-ch'eng, *Chiang Kai-shek Before 1926*, Vol. 9, p. 84-A, records: On May 10, 1924, Tai Ch'uan-hsien was appointed Director of the Political Department; two days later, Chang Sung-nien was made Deputy Director of the same department. On March 29, 1925, Chiang Kai-shek recommended that the Executive Committee of the KMT appoint Chou En-lai Chief of the Bureau of Court Martial. The same book, Vol. 10, p. 65-B, further states that on May 25, 1925, Chiang Kai-shek and several other offices jointly recommended Chou En-lai again to serve as chief of the Court Martial. On September 13, 1925, Chou was appointed to the reviewing committee for the editorial board of the Academy's official history (*Ibid.*, Vol. 12, p. 17-B). Nowhere in the same source is there any written evidence of Chou's official appointment as deputy director of the Political Department. The directorship of this department was subsequently transferred several times, all properly recorded, but nothing was said about removing Chang Sung-nien from the deputy directorship.

Draft History of the Central Military Academy, Vol. 7, Chapter 7, p. 17-B, states that during the Second Eastern Expedition, the director of the Academy's Political Department Chou En-lai was recommended to serve as chief of the First Army's Political Department, concurrently the KMT representative in the First Division. This is the only source identifying Chou as head of the Academy's Political Department. The Whampoa Academy was the predecessor to the Central Military Academy.

Edgar Snow, *Red Star over China*, p. 46, "To Chiang Kai-shek, then president of Whampoa, the youthful Red (Chou En-lai) was anathema. But Chiang was nevertheless obliged to appoint him Chief of Whampoa Academy's political department, because of Chou's great influence with the radical cadets." Judging by the course of events in those years, Chiang Kai-shek had not yet identified Chou as his deadly enemy, when he gave him such important political assignments in the KMT Army.

13. Tai Ch'uan-hsien.

14. Including Yün Tai-ying, Hsiao Ch'u-nü and Hsiung Hsiung.

15. Feng Yü-hsiang.

16. Tuan Ch'i-jui.

17. Li Ang, *The Red Stage*, p. 42.

18. Wu Hao, "The Most Recent General Political Situation in Canton," *The Guide*, No. 92 (November 19, 1924).

19. Wu Hao, "Kwangtung Province, After Sun Yat-sen's Departure for the North," *The Guide*, No. 98 (January 7, 1925).

20. T'ao Hsi-sheng and others, *A Compendium of Historical Documents of the Communist Betrayal of the Nation*, Series I, Vol. 1, pp. 325 ff. The comrade was Pao Hui-seng.

21. Chiang Hsien-yün came from Hunan. His membership in the Communist Party dates back to 1922. Mao Tse-tung assigned Chiang to organize the workers at the An-yüan Coal Mine near the Hunan-Kiangsi border under the guidance of Liu Shao-ch'i and Li Li-san. In November 1922, he was dispatched to lead a strike of the lead and zinc miners at Shui-k'ou-shan in Ch'ang-ning, Hunan Province. In his entrance examinations to the Whampoa Military Academy, he scored the highest and soon emerged as an active group leader of the Academy's first class. Bright and eloquent, he was Chiang Kai-shek's personal secretary during the first few months of the Northern Expedition. Later he was sent to Hankow to take charge of a regiment in the Fourth Army. He was killed in action in Honan Province.

22. Informant No. 13.

23. Russian agreement with warlord Chang Tso-lin, September 20, 1924.

24. Special Officer Miao Pin of the Whampoa Academy.

25. Li Chih-lung came from Shangtung Province. After graduation from the Naval Academy at Cheefoo, he enrolled in the First Class of Whampoa, and there he became a Communist Party member. When he was involved as a key person in the Chung-shan Gunboat Incident, he was in reality only the political chief of the Navy Department. A rather involved personnel difficulty made him acting chief of the department, a post far beyond the normal aspiration of the Whampoa cadets. The chief of the Navy Department was a Russian named Smirnoff who took leave of absence to go back to Russia. According to the normal procedure, the Chief of Staff of the Navy should have served as the acting head. However, the Chief of Staff, Ou-yang Lin,

had fled to Hong Kong after his involvement in some illegal dealings was discovered. The National Military Commission Chairman, Wang Ching-wei, therefore made Li Chih-lung temporary head of the Navy Department. The man who framed Li Chih-lung was said to have been Ou-yang Ke, brother of the escaped Chief of Staff, who had his eye on his brother's vacated position. After the incident, Li Chih-lung declared that he was ready to abandon communism and went north with the Expedition troops. Subsequently he was sent back to Canton where he was arrested and executed by the Nationalist leader Li Chi-chen.

26. Li Hsia-kung's message reads: "I have arrived with the First Division at Shih-t'an for three days, yet this is the first chance I have had to write a report. I am surrounded by non-comrades, sharing the same room (including the Division Commander and the Chief of Staff). The Political Department has its separate office, but there are also outsiders around. . . . Among the officers, Division Commander Ho recognizes the importance and value of political work, thus he does not present a problem. We can proceed undercover and use the opportunity to spread our ideas." *Factual Records on the Elimination of Communism*, pp. 24–25.

27. Shao Li-tzu, now member of the Legislative Committee, People's Congress, Peking.

28. The delegation included Ch'en Ch'eng, late vice-president of the Republic of China, Ho Chung-han, one-time Minister of Communications; Huang Chen-wu, one-time National Guards Commander; and P'an Yu-ch'iang.

29. On the Chung-shan Gunboat Incident and the factional strife in the Whampoa Academy, the following sources are among the most important: Chiang Kai-shek, *Russia in China*, pp. 40–43, recounts what appeared to him to be a kidnap plot intended to take him to Vladivostok. P'eng Shu-chih, "After Reading the February 21 Speech by Chiang Kai-shek," *The Guide*, No. 192 (March 18, 1927), blames the incident on the Sun Yat-sen Society's enmity against the CCP. Chou En-lai himself clarified about the persons actually involved on the side of the Sun Yat-sen Society, in his letter to the editor, *The Guide*, No. 193 (April 6, 1927). Another version of the story told by Chiang Kai-shek is in T'ao Hsi-sheng and others, *A Compendium of Historical Documents*, Vol. 1, pp. 99–133. Another CCP story of the incident is Chih Chung, "A Study of the Canton Incident," *The Guide*, No. 148 (April 3, 1926), collected in T'ao's *Compendium*, pp. 1379–81. A rare document on this subject is Li Chih-lung's hand-written account, in *Documents on the KMT-CCP Cooperation*,

Party Purges, and Worker-Peasant Movement (Hoover Collection, 2980/6482, Vol. 1), which gives details on the political conflict between Chiang Kai-shek and Wang Ching-wei, and the internal problems of the navy.

It appears quite certain from these documents that several developments contributed to the Incident: 1. There was a growing rivalry between Chiang Kai-shek and Wang Ching-wei, partly because of personal ambitions on both sides and partly because of their different approaches to the grand strategy for China—Chiang was increasingly suspicious of the CCP while Wang stressed the need to continue working with it and with the Russians. It was only a year after Sun Yat-sen's death; his advocacy of co-operation with Russia and acceptance of the Communists still rang in many ears. The moment Chiang decided to check the spread of Communist influence in the KMT and the army, he ran the risk of being labeled a traitor to Sun Yat-sen and an anti-revolutionary—a most cursed label in those days. As Chiang's intention became known, he had to take drastic action to avert a possible mutiny against him. 2. The cliques in the Navy Department were complex, incorporating many rather uneducated and unprincipled elements who fought among themselves, more for personal gain than to serve the cause of revolution. Some of them bore a grudge against Wang Ching-wei who, as head of the National Government and the Military Commission, had prosecuted some unruly naval officers. Others were attacking Li Chih-lung and his friends in order to get their jobs in the Navy Department. As Chiang Kai-shek got ready to crack down on the CCP of which Li Chih-lung was a member, Li's enemies were ready to carry out Chiang's orders even though they seemed to be fratricidal. 3. The KMT army officers loyal to Chiang Kai-shek had grown increasingly uncomfortable with the CCP commissars and Russian advisers who acted more and more truculent, overriding and browbeating the troop commanders, as the Stepanoff reports cited on p. 57 openly admitted. In order to protect his men in the army, Chiang had to take action against the commissars and many officers whose first allegiance belonged to the CCP.

These main threads in the intrigues behind the Gunboat Incident were echoed in Chiang Kai-shek's speech of April 20, 1926—a month after the Incident—before the political commissars and CCP members he had ordered to withdraw from the army. (*Chiang Kai-shek Before 1926*, Vol. 15, pp. 38–47) "I could not reveal the full detail even if I wanted to. . . . Only after my death can the whole story be told." He admitted that someone had informed him of a plot by the Russian adviser Kissanka to kidnap him and take him to Russia, but said that he could neither accept the story as complete truth, nor ignore it as pure imagination.

Informant Nos. 13–22, all on the scene at Whampoa, contributed information on the Gunboat Incident.

30. Naval rebellions, May 31, 1923, October 30, 1923, and April 24, 1925.

31. Ou-yang Ke, Hui Tung-sheng, Wang Po-ling, and Ch'en Chao-ying (or Miao Pin).

32. *Red Archives* (Hoover microfilm, 2984/2371), pp. 157–59. A CCP resolution says, "The right-wing and middle-of-the-road KMT elements attack us because we have adopted a wrong approach toward them. We have excluded the KMT left wing from active participation in the task of combatting the right wing. Consequently we have made all KMT elements our enemies. . . . We should stay in the KMT, helping but never replacing their left wing in dealing with their right wing. If there are still comrades who believe that we should move in to take over the KMT altogether, the mistake made in Kwangtung (the Chung-shan Gunboat Incident) is a clear warning. Therefore at this Enlarged Central Committee meeting (July 1926) it has been resolved to cultivate the left-wing KMT and correct our strategy so that these left-wing elements can share the common political tasks, including fighting the right-wing influence."

33. Chang Shu-shen, "Ch'en Tu-hsiu and the CCP," *Defense Against Communism* (Hoover microfilm), p. 80. Hua Kang, "The CCP in the 1925–27 Great Revolution," comments on the CCP reaction to the Chung-shan Gunboat Incident as follows: Before the Incident the Reds in Kwangtung felt that they failed to act where they should have, while the Reds in Shanghai felt that they should have backed up where they did not. After the Incident, the Kwangtung CCP preferred to stay within the KMT, while the Shanghai CCP wanted to withdraw from the KMT. Only Ch'en Tu-hsiu had the last word, and that was, "seize control of the situation, but withhold overt action; back down from an aggressive position, but remain within the KMT framework." This explains the CCP intraparty dispute and Chou En-lai's peace-making role quite accurately.

34. Tsou Ts'ui-fen, "The Central Committee of the KMT during the Kwangtung Period," *Contemporary Historical Data*, Vol. 2, p. 105.

35. The CCP offered Chou and Wu Yü-chang; the KMT offered Tai Ch'uan-hsien and Shao Li-tzu.

36. Sun Ping-wen, director of political affairs in the rear areas; Chu Tai-chieh, department of organization; Kuo Mo-jo, chief of propaganda; Li Fu-ch'un, director of the political department, Second Army;

Lin Po-ch'ü, director of the political department, Sixth Army; Yün
Tai-ying, chief of the political department, Central Military Academy,
Hankow.

37. Later Mao Tse-tung repeated the same advice when he said, "If
we speak of revolution in China without armed forces, the proletarian
class cannot make any headway, neither can the Communist Party."

38. Mao Ssu-ch'eng, *Chiang Kai-shek Before 1926*, Vol. II, p. 730.
According to an eyewitness, the repercussions of the left-right strife
within the army caused a demonstration in the Central Military Political Academy in Hankow in the summer of 1927. Yang Ying-chih,
sent by Chiang Kai-shek to work in the Academy against the Communists, was shot by the leftist cadets.

39. Tsou Ts'ui-fen, "Unofficial History of the Political Department, General Headquarters," *Contemporary Historical Data*, Vol. 2,
pp. 135–42. Ch'en Tu-hsiu, Chou En-lai, and others, *For What Are
We Struggling Now*, pp. 10–30. Hu Ch'iao-mu, *The Thirty Years of
the CCP*, p. 12.

40. Yü Shu-te.

41. Among them was Ho Hsiang-ni, wife of Liao Chung-k'ai, considered Sun Yat-sen's successor until his assassination in August 1925.

42. Informant Nos. 24 and 25, actively involved in KMT politics in
Canton.

43. Li Ssu-shan and others.

44. Ch'en Tu-hsiu, "On the National Government's Northern Ex-
pedition," *The Guide*, No. 161 (July 7, 1926). *Compendium of Doc-
umentary Evidence of the Soviet Russian Plot*, Vol. 5, p. 23-B. "A
Brief History of the CCP" (mimeographed, Bureau of Investigation).
The Eighteen Years of the Chinese Communist Party, p. 6. Chang
Han-ch'ing, *Personalities in the Great Era*, pp. 49–50. Wang I-p'ing,
The CCP Before the War of Resistance, pp. 30–33.

45. The CCP man was Chao Shih-yen, Chou's associate in Paris.
The KMT sent Niu Yung-chien.

46. Sun Ch'uan-fang.

47. Many accounts of varying accuracy are available on the Shang-
hai Revolts. See Hsia Chih-hsü, "Fragments of Reminiscence," *The
Fluttering Red Flag*, Vol. 5 (December 15, 1957), pp. 5–13. Wu
Yü-chang, "Remembering Martyr Chao Shih-yen," *The People's
Daily* (July 19, 1962). Chao Yü, *Armed Revolt*, pp. 61–68. Ma
Ch'ao-chün and others, *A History of the Chinese Labor Movement*,
pp. 642 ff. T'ao Hsi-sheng, *Compendium*, pp. 255–56. W. Woodhead,
China Yearbook (1928), pp. 819–23. Edgar Snow, *Red Star Over
China*, pp. 47–48. *The Chinese Communist Party* (Tokyo, 1956), pp.

47–50. "Remembering the Shanghai Revolts," *The Red Flag*, No. 86 (March 22, 1930). Hsin-k'e-lai and others, *Profile of the Cadres of the 8th Route Army*, p. 59. Po Hsin, "Unofficial History of the Shanghai Labor Movement," *Contemporary Historical Data*, Vol. 1, pp. 299–300. Ho Sheng, "The Three Revolts in Shanghai," *Contemporary Historical Data*, Vol. 3, pp. 182–86. These accounts vary in their exaggeration of certain aspects of the revolts, but the most debunking account has been furnished by Informant No. 9, a former CCP Central Committee member who personally took part in the insurrections. He described the action as more like child's play than any serious armed violence. Even for the third, most serious, uprising in 1927, the CCP order at the beginning was but to welcome the arrival of the Northern Expeditionary army. The factories were instructed to stop work that day. On March 20, 1927, a number of active union workers were brought together at about 3:00 p.m. near the Chapei district. Since wire fences had already been erected around the foreign concessions, the concession police did not interfere with the strikers' action. The strikers marched into the Chapei district and disarmed the Chinese police. The "victorious" strikers then pushed on to the railroad station. Such rather confused skirmishes continued for a day and a half.

48. Pi Shu-ch'eng.

49. Under Generals Hsüeh Yüeh and Pai Ch'ung-hsi.

50. These included Li Yi-mang, chief of the political department, P'an Han-nien, Chang Po-chün, and Chu Tai-chieh.

51. Hatano Kanichi, *A History of the Chinese Communist Party*, pp. 539–40.

52. Ts'ai soon yielded the post to Chang Kuo-tao.

CHAPTER 5

1. Li Ang, *The Red Stage*, p. 42. Wang Wei-lien, "Wang Ching-wei Arrives in Wuhan from Marseilles," *Contemporary Historical Data*, Vol. 1, p. 6.

2. Ho Chien.

3. Hsü K'e-hsiang. The incident has become known as the Ma-jih Incident.

4. Liu Ning, *The Autobiography of a Proletarian*, p. 8.

5. Wan Ya-kang, *A Short History of the CCP*, pp. 16–17.

6. Robert North, *Moscow and Chinese Communists*, pp. 106–7.

7. Ch'en Tu-hsiu, *To All the CCP Comrades*. North, *Moscow and Chinese Communists*, p. 108.

8. Chang Tso-lin.

9. T'ao, *Compendium*, p. 594.

10. Ch'ü Ch'iu-pai, *Controversial Problems of the Chinese Revolution*, pp. 67 ff. P'eng Shu-chih, "Statement Before the Enlarged Conference."

11. Wang Min-chao, "All Depends on the Party and the Masses," *New China Daily News* (August 7, 1951).

12. The traitor was identified as Chao, who reported to General Chu P'ei-te.

13. Sun Fo, Chang Fa-k'uei, and Chu P'ei-te.

14. Yu Chi-yü, *The August 1 Uprising in Nanchang*, pp. 10–11. "The Events of Nanchang," *Contemporary Historical Data*, Vol. 4, Section 3, pp. 141–43.

15. Wei Hung-yüan, *The August 1 Uprising*, shows the Steering Committee as composed of Madame Sun Yat-sen, Ho Lung, Kuo Mo-jo, Yün Tai-ying, Teng Yen-ta, and two others. Shen Tzu-min, "The August 1 Uprising in Nanchang," *The Progress Daily* (August 1, 1952), has T'an P'ing-shan on the Committee. Chao Chün-hui, *Ten Years in the Red Army*, includes Chang Fa-k'uei on the Committee. The staff corps under Chou's direction included Liu Po-ch'eng as chief of staff, Ho Lung, Yeh T'ing, and possibly Ts'ai T'ing-k'ai. These sources vary somewhat in the detailed assignments of the committee members. Also see Liu Nung-ch'ao, "Odds and Ends About the August 1 Uprising," *The Progress Daily* (July 27, 1951).

16. Liu Ning, *Autobiography*, pp. 8–9.

17. And Chou Shih-ti, commander of the 25th Division.

18. The First Division under Ho Ching-chai, and the Second Division under Ch'in Kuang-yüan.

19. Wei Hung-yüan, *The August 1 Uprising*, p. 23.

20. Led by General Yü Han-mou.

21. And Chou Ch'i-chien.

22. *In Memory of the April 8 Martyrs*, p. 248. Jung Tsu, "The Rise and Fall of Kao Yü-han," *She-hui News*, Vol. 2, No. 22 (Shanghai, March 6, 1933), p. 308. In the afternoon of October 15, 1927, Ho Lung, Yeh T'ing, Wu Yü-chang, T'an P'ing-shan, Lin Tsu-han, Yün Tai-ying, Chang Kuo-tao, and Chou En-lai held an emergency conference in the Queens Hotel, Hong Kong. It was decided that Chou must stay in Hong Kong for medical care.

23. P'eng Pai.

24. Fan Shih-sheng, whom Chou En-lai had severely criticized while in Canton in the winter of 1926.

25. Wu Yü-chang, "In Memorium of Comrade Po-ch'ü," *The Peo-

ple's Daily (June 2, 1960). Kung Ch'u, *The Red Army and I*, pp. 76–78.

26. Yu Chi-yü (Footnote 14 above), and Liu Nung-ch'ao (Footnote 15 above).

27. Liu Ning said that of the thirteen attending, only three were Central Committee members.

28. The party leadership then involved also Hsiang Chung-fa, Li Li-san, Li Wei-han, and Liu Shao-ch'i.

29. CCP writers react to the so-called Putschism differently. Lo Fu (Chang Wen-t'ien), *The CCP during the Past Ten Years* (January 1938), claims that "The August 7 Conference was not at all the beginning of putschism in the Party." Hu Ch'iao-mu, *The 30 Years of the CCP*, pp. 21–22, however, insists that "Under Comrade Ch'ü Ch'iu-pai's leadership, from the winter of 1927 to the spring of 1928, the Party made the mistake of leftist putschism. It opposed temporary withdrawal and persisted in its offensive. The result was continued depletion of the revolutionary force." The role played by the Comintern in these revolts has been described in Chang Fa-k'uei (the KMT general who first supported the leftist Hankow government but then turned against the CCP), "Reminiscence of the CCP Canton Commune 30 Years Ago," *The United Review* (Hong Kong, December 26, 1958 through January 2, 1959), has this to say: "On June 1, 1927, we captured some Third Comintern documents. Among the Communists killed in action in the Lung-yen-tung, Yen-t'ang area, six were Russians. We searched the Russian consulate in the Eastern Hill district, the consular staff was burning documents. What was seized on the scene proved that the consulate was instrumental in plotting the revolt." Chiang Kai-shek, *Russia in China*, p. 54, "The December 11, 1927, Canton Commune was directed by Heinz Neumann and Gerhart Eisler from the Russian consulate."

30. Hsia Hsi.

31. Formerly an officer under warlord Sun Ch'uan-fang.

32. Ma Tung-lin.

33. Liu Ning, *Autobiography*, pp. 14, 18, 19.

CHAPTER 6

1. Informant No. 9, who was at the 1928 Moscow meeting. Hatano Kanichi, "A Biography of Chou En-lai," may be in error about Chou's failure to build up a Red army of 70,000 men because it was a Comintern instruction given before Chou became CCP's military department head in May 1927. Kuei Nien, "Chou En-lai during the

Wuhan Days," gives inaccurate statistics to prove Chou's failure. It states that there were 10,000 rifles in the Wuhan Military Political Academy which had, actually, fewer than 2000 cadets altogether. Wang I-p'ing, *The CCP Before the War of Resistance*, p. 55, is wrong in describing a verbal exchange between Chou and Ch'en Tu-hsiu in Moscow because in fact Ch'en was not in Moscow. The same error appears in Ku Kuan-chiao, *The CCP During the Past 30 Years*, p. 65. About the ouster of Ch'en Tu-hsiu, *The Red Flag*, No. 57 (Shanghai, November 27, 1929) quotes the CCP Politburo resolution of November 15, 1927, "In accordance with the Comintern directive, it was decided at the August 7 Emergency Conference that Ch'en Tu-hsiu report to the Comintern to discuss Chinese revolution. Ch'en disobeyed. Furthermore he expressed dissatisfaction with the Comintern. The CCP authority and the Comintern both urged Ch'en to attend the Sixth CCP Congress in Moscow, but he repeatedly ignored the order. During and after the Sixth Congress, the Comintern cabled Ch'en time and again to go to Moscow. The new CCP leadership explained the need for his presence in Moscow. At first he agreed to go, then he changed his mind, finally he procrastinated saying that he would go in the spring afterwards." Ch'en Tu-hsiu acknowledged the enmity between him and the emerging Li Li-san clique which included Chou, Hsiang Chung-fa, and Hsiang Ying, in his response to the Comintern dated February 17, 1930. He said that the Li Li-san group had already denounced him as a Trotskyite, an abolitionist, an anti-revolutionary, and a new labor traitor. *Central Military Communique* (Hoover microfilm 4292.9/5640).

2. For instance, at the end of the two-day Canton Commune, December 11–12, 1927, directed by the Comintern agents Heinz Neumann and Gerhart Eisler (some say, Lominadze), over 6000 were rounded up and executed.

3. Chou En-lai, *The Organization Problem of the CCP at Present*.

4. *Central Military Communique* (January 15, 1930). *The Red Flag*, No. 97 (Shanghai, April 26, 1930). By the spring of 1930, Chou had built up considerable military support, including the First Army under Hsü Chi-shen, the First Army Corps with Ch'en Yi as its chief of staff, the Third Army Corps under Wu Chung-hao, the Tenth Army Corps under Liu Ch'ou-hsi, the Sixth Route Army under Chou I-ch'ün, the Fourteenth Army under Ho Wei, the Thirteenth Army under Hu Kung-mien, the Eleventh Army under Ch'en Keng, and Chung Ch'ih-hsin as commander-in-chief of the southeastern front of Kiangsi Province, Nieh Jung-chen as secretary-general of the Central Military Affairs Committee, Li Fu-ch'un as secretary of the Kiangsu

Provincial Military Affairs Committee. Hatano Kanichi, "A Biography of Chou En-lai." Otsuka Reizo, A History of the CCP, Vol. 1, p. 88.

5. Chou En-lai, "The Central Task and the Basic Problem of the Red Army," Central Military Communique, No. 1 (January 15, 1930).

6. Informant No. 9.

7. Chou En-lai, The Organization Problem of the CCP at Present, pp. 19–20.

8. Tso-liang Hsiao, Power Relations within the Chinese Communist Movement, pp. 107 ff.

9. The Struggle, No. 47 (Juichin, Kiangsi, CCP Central Committee, February 16, 1934). This was the second time Mao was reprimanded. The first time occurred after Mao Tse-tung's failure in the Hunan-Hupeh insurrections in the autumn of 1927.

10. Li Ang, The Red Stage, chapter 12. "The Chinese Communist Party during 1931–1933" (Bureau of Investigation). "The Story of the Rift in the CCP during the Fourth Plenum of Its Central Committee" (Bureau of Investigation). Informant No. 9. Ho Meng-hsiung founded the Railroad Workers' Union on the Peking-Suiyuan Railroad, became Communist leader in Kiangsu Province, assisted by Hsü Hsi-Keng and Wang K'e-ch'üan. When Mif was sending the Ch'en Shao-yü group back to Shanghai, Li Li-san learned of the intention of this move from his close friend, Yü Fei, in Moscow. As a result Li was determined to resist the Ch'en Shao-yü group, assigning them only minor jobs when they reached Shanghai.

11. Hsiao, Power Relations, p. 52.

12. Informant No. 9 disagrees with many published sources on the initiative behind Chou's visit to Moscow in the summer of 1930. Hatano Kanichi, A Study of Red China, p. 55, suggests that Chou and Ch'ü Ch'iu-pai returned to China together in the fall of 1930. This is questionable.

13. The Red Flag (Shanghai, September 7, 1930). Hsiao, Power Relations, pp. 61–63.

14. North, Moscow and Chinese Communists, p. 137.

15. Chou En-lai, The Shao-shan Report. Brandt, Schwartz, and Fairbank, A Documentary History, pp. 200–8. Lu Chieh-shou, "Chou En-lai Flees to the Red Zone," Contemporary Historical Data, Vol. 3, p. 343 contains much inaccuracy.

16. "Ho Meng-hsiung's Statements" (Hoover 4292.23/2214).

17. Informant No. 9.

18. T'ieh-chiang, "The Development of the Struggle against the Li Li-san Line," Building the Party, No. 3 (February 15, 1931). As late as December 1, 1930, Chou was still apologizing for Li Li-san.

19. Hsiao, *Power Relations*, pp. 96–97.

20. Among them was Lo Chang-lung, who had been close to Chang Kuo-tao, now Ho's chief supporter.

21. "Background Information on Intraparty Matters" (mimeographed documents, Bureau of Investigation).

22. Chou En-lai, *The Shao-shan Report*, p. 1.

23. Li Chih-kung, *A Brief History of the CCP*, pp. 46–47. Kuwashima Shukei's report (Hoover microfilm J315.51/Jr42, p. 68) cites a man named Yang Yin as having succeeded Chou as the military department chief for a period. Hatano Kanichi, *History of the CCP*, Vol. 1, pp. 291–305, cites a full report by Chou in the capacity of the military department chief.

24. Informant No. 9.

25. For Li Wei-han and Ch'ü Ch'iu-pai's self-criticism, see *Building the Party*, No. 3 (February 15, 1931). One Politburo resolution criticizing Chou, apparently the only one of its kind, appears in *Building the Party*, No. 4 (March 8, 1931).

26. *Selected Works of Mao Tse-tung* (one-volume edition), pp. 1433, 1438.

27. Wang Chu-yu came from Kiangsu. After spending a period as a student in Russia, he returned to work under Ku Shun-chang. Most of the time he disguised himself as an herb doctor, peddling special cures in the street. After his arrest, he turned against communism and worked for the KMT Bureau of Investigation. During the Sino-Japanese war, he took charge of a garment factory at T'ang-chia-t'o where he died of illness.

28. Hsü En-tseng, *My Memoirs*. Informant Nos. 27, 28, and 29. These sources were directly involved in the Ku case, and their information is at odds with *Time* (May 10, 1954), pp. 31–32.

29. *The Red Stage*, p. 156.

30. Informant No. 27 tells of Chou's narrow escape. Police and Security Department, Japanese Government, *The Present Situation of the Communist Movement in China*, p. 5, and Osaka Taishi Economic Alliance, *The Communist Movement in China, Manchuria, and Russia*, p. 395, give very questionable reports on Chou's arrest. Bureau of Investigation documents show that the KMT executed Hsiang Chung-fa at Lung-hua on June 24, 1931, in spite of the fact that Hsiang had agreed to turn against communism. T'ao, *Compendium*, confirms this report. On July 4, 1931, the Chinese Communist Youth Corps issued a statement denouncing any "rumor" about Hsiang's defection before his execution.

31. Ku later married the beautiful daughter of a tailor in Nanking.

Her name is Chang Yung-ch'in. The surviving son, Ah-sheng, also returned to Nanking. Ku was subsequently executed by the KMT for his
continued dealings with the CCP.

32. Chao Yung, P'an Han-nien, Liao Ch'eng-yün (also known as
Ch'en Yün), and K'uang Hui-an.

33. Informant No. 27.

34. Information in this section of the chapter has been obtained
from a series of interviews with Ma Shun-yi in Taipei, Taiwan, in the
summer of 1964.

CHAPTER 7

1. The organizations included National Labor Union Federation,
the Central Committee of the Communist Youth Corps, the Labor
Union Federation of Shanghai, the Freedom League, the Anti-
Imperialist League, the League of Social Scientists, and the League of
Left Wing Writers.

2. Kung Ch'u, *The Red Army and I*, p. 256. When the Central
Committee of the CCP moved to Kiangsi in September 1931, the
Central Bureau of the Soviet Areas abolished its Kiangsi branch office
because it had become unnecessary. Chou represented the Central
Bureau and published many articles in its organ, *Honest Talk. Red
China* (February 10, 1932).

3. "The First Enlarged Meeting of the Central Bureau of the Soviet
Areas" (mimeographed, Ch'en Ch'eng collection).

4. On the Central Executive Committee, Mao was chairman,
Hsiang Ying and Chang Kuo-tao, vice-chairmen. Wang Chia-hsiang
headed the Foreign Affairs Committee; Chu Teh, chairman of the
Central Revolutionary Military Committee, with P'eng Te-huai as
vice-chairman.

5. Hatano Kanichi, A *History of the CCP*, Vol. 5, p. 572. Yü Ming,
"The Development of the Cheka System in the Communist Area,"
Contemporary Historical Data, pp. 306–7. These sources report some
detail on the friction between Chou and Mao during the first months
of Chou's arrival in Kiangsi. Kung Ch'u has a slightly different version
of the story.

6. *Honest Talk*, No. 3 (Juichin, 1932).

7. *Honest Talk*, No. 5 (Juichin, 1932).

8. "Directives from the Central Committee (Shanghai), and the
Decisions by the Central Bureau (in Kiangsi) Relating to the Task of
Expediting Victory in Kiangsi and Its Adjacent Provinces" (Ch'en
Ch'eng collection).

9. Hsiao, *Power Relations*, pp. 164–69.

10. Yang Shang-k'un, "Oppose the Rightist-opportunist Policy of Fleeing and Escaping," *Red China* (February 19, 1933). Yang was a key member of the Ch'en Shao-yü faction. He criticized Lo Ming for upholding the Kiangsi Soviet government (headed by Mao) above the CCP (headed by Ch'en).

11. At a meeting on July 24, 1933. *Red China* (August 4, 1933).

12. *The Struggle*, No. 24 (August 29, 1933).

13. *Selected Works of Mao Tse-tung*, pp. 955–1002.

14. Hsiao Hsiang, "The Soviet Zone Today," *The Struggle* (Shanghai, April 15, 1934).

15. Chao Chün-hui, *Ten Years in the Red Army*, pp. 35–38.

16. Huang Feng, *The Journal of the Eighth Route Army on the March*, p. 113. Chu Li-fu, *The 25000-li Long March*, pp. 69–70.

17. Advocated by Ch'ü Ch'iu-pai and Hsiang Ying.

18. Chou En-lai and Chang Ai-p'ing, "Expand the Communist Youth Vanguard by 1,500,000 Persons in All the Soviet Areas in the Country," *Red China* (March 1, 1934). Chang was commander of the vanguards, now a member of the National Defense Council in Peking.

19. *Red China* (June 26, 1934).

20. *The Red Star Daily* (July 20, 1934). The CCP's Central Committee and the Central Revolutionary Military Committee jointly announced that in May–July 1934 the Red Army was to be expanded by 50,000 men. Chu Teh's statement in *Red China* (May 18, 1934).

21. Liu Tao-sheng, "The Red Army Academy in the Woods," *The Unfurling Red Flag*, Vol. 3.

22. *The Red Star Daily* (April 22, 29, May 5, July 20, August 20, 1934).

23. Kung Ch'u, *The Red Army and I*, pp. 372–84. This is an important source, but not without inaccuracies. It erroneously describes (p. 226) Chou as secretary-general of the CCP in April, 1931, and distorts the facts about the defection of the commander of the Ninth Red Army (p. 384).

24. On November 23, 1933.

25. *The Red Star Daily* (April 3, 9, 1933, January 14, 1934).

26. Chao Wen-hua, *The 25000-li Long March*, pp. 31–32.

27. *Selected Works of Mao Tse-tung*, p. 971.

28. Hsiao Ying-t'ang, "The Clever Crossing of the Gold Sand River," *The Unfurling Red Flag*, Vol. 3. Yang Ch'eng-wu, "Chairman Mao Guides Me to Cross the Grassland," *A Spark Sets the Entire Plain*

Aflame, p. 170. Informant No. 46, who was one of the merchants accosted by the Long Marchers.

29. Chao Chün-hui, *Ten Years in the Red Army*, p. 93.

30. Liu Ya-lou, "Crossing the Great Grassland with Only a Handful of Ching-k'o Barley," *The People's Daily* (March 3, 1961).

31. Liu Po-ch'eng.

32. *Look*, Vol. 25, No. 3 (New York, January 1961), pp. 85–104.

33. The conferences were at Liang-ho-k'ou, Sha-wo (August 5, 1935), and Pa-hsi (August 24, 1935).

34. Kan Yu-lan, *Mao Tse-tung and His Group*, p. 91.

35. In the summer and October of 1936. Yang Shang-k'un, "The Grand Reunion of Main Red Forces," *Struggle* (August 15, 1936).

36. "Outline of Report on Smashing the Anti-revolutionary Activities of Chang Kuo-tao" (hand-copied Yenan document, Hoover 4292.3/1356).

CHAPTER 8

1. Informant No. 42. Tso Lin, "Fragments of Reminiscence of the Hsin-an Tour," *Fighting Experience*, pp. 84–95.

2. Pavel Mif, *The Fifteen Years of the Chinese Communist Party's Heroic Struggle*. A declaration by the Central Government of the Chinese Soviet People's Republic and the Chinese People's Red Army Revolutionary Military Committee published in the *Struggle*, No. 104 (July 3, 1936), however, continues to criticize Chiang Kai-shek and the KMT for not resisting the Japanese.

3. During the summer of 1935 when Mao and his Long Marchers reached northern Szechwan to confer with Chang Kuo-tao at Mao-erh-kai, the united-front policy was thoroughly discussed. North, *Moscow and Chinese Communists*, p. 176.

4. Yang Chia-lo, *The Main Diplomatic and Military Events Between China and Japan Since 1894*, pp. 144 ff.

5. CCP Politburo resolution dated December 25, 1935 (Bureau of Investigation).

6. The division was under Liu Tzu-tan. Kao Yin-tsu, *Chronology of the Republic of China*, pp. 417 ff.

7. The message was sent from the Red Army Revolutionary Military Committee to the Military Affairs Commission of the Nationalist Government.

8. Chiang Kai-shek, *Russia in China*, p. 73. Most of the documents referred to in this section are included in U. S. State Department,

United States Relations with China: with Special Reference to the Period 1944–1949.

9. The CCP request was dated August 15, 1936.

10. CCP Politburo statement of September 17, 1936.

11. Huang Feng, *The Journal of the Eighth Route Army on the March*, p. 127. Information from this and other sources on the initial impact of the kidnap news on the CCP has been checked with Informant No. 30 who served in the KMT headquarters in Sian in 1936–37.

12. Lee T'ien-min, A *History of the Communist Betrayal of the Nation*, pp. 40–41. Huang Feng, *The Journal of the Eighth Route Army on the March*, pp. 33–34. Eye-witness accounts have been checked. Propaganda leaflets in Bureau of Investigation.

13. Chou's schoolmate was Lu Kuang-ch'i. Another leftist activist in Sian in those days was Ch'e Hsiang-ch'en. Informant No. 30.

14. Named Li Tu.

15. Li K'e-nung, at Lo-ch'uan.

16. Chang Hsüeh-liang, "Chang Hsüeh-liang and the CCP," *Prospect*, No. 69 (Hong Kong, September 1964), originally released as "A Confession about the Sian Incident" in the Taiwan magazine *Hsi-wang (Hope)*, which was confiscated by the KMT authorities the moment it appeared on the newsstands. Also see Fan Ch'ang-chiang, *Journey Beyond the Great Wall*, pp. 24–30, 311–38.

17. Chang Hsüeh-liang's own account, cited above.

18. Red troops pulling back from Wa-yao-p'u (later known as Chih-tan-hsien).

19. Feng Yü-hsiang received a medal.

20. Kao Ch'ung-ming, *The Life-line* (pamphlet, Bureau of Investigation). Kao is currently a high-ranking Communist in Manchuria.

21. Wang Ping-nan, later Chou's assistant during the 1946–49 CCP-KMT talks.

22. Similar accounts appear in *The Works and Speeches by Chou En-lai and Teng Ying-ch'ao*, the *Journal of the Eighth Route Army on the March*, and Edgar Snow's *Red Star Over China*. Other accounts relate that Chou and Yeh Chien-ying attempted to dissuade the radical Northeastern officers from harming Chiang Kai-shek. Chou En-lai is said to have flown from Yenan to Sian on the Young Marshal's personal plane.

23. U. S. State Department, *U. S. Relations with China*, pp. 46–47. Hatano Kanichi, A *Study of Red China*, pp. 119–20 reports on extensive conversations between Chou and Chiang. Among the points discussed were the renaming of the Soviet Areas into Socialist Experi-

mental Districts (Chou's proposal), and Chiang's proposal of exiling Mao and Chu and renaming the CCP as the Ta-chung-tang (Populist Party). This is rather dubious.

24. Chang Kuo-tao, upon his defection in April 1938, accused the CCP of trying to overthrow Chiang in the Sian coup. Mao counter-charged Chang with the same. *Selected Works of Mao Tse-tung*, pp. 269 ff. Liu Shao-ch'i admitted on March 2, 1942 that the views among the CCP leaders had been divided on the Sian coup. "Some comrades were opposed to a peaceful settlement of the Incident. Their feeling was that however it was settled or even not settled, it would not pre-vent the CCP from cooperating with the KMT later. . . . This was a mistake on their part which, fortunately, involved only a few comrades and was quite easily corrected." *On Intraparty Struggle*, undated pamphlet in Bureau of Investigation, not to be confused with another work of the same title in Brandt, Schwartz, and Fairbank, A *Docu-mentary History of Chinese Communism*, pp. 356–72.

25. The KMT was represented by General Ku Chu-t'ung. Chou was assisted by Liu Po-ch'eng.

26. Informant No. 32, who participated in the Sian talks.

27. Interview with Miao Chien-ch'iu in Tokyo, August 22, 1964.

28. T'an Ts'en (ed.), *Documents on the KMT-CCP Cooperation against Japan*, pp. 95–101.

29. Okubo Hiroshi, *Red China*, p. 23. Nakayasu Yosaku, *Most Re-cent History of the CCP*, reports that on July 9, 1937, Chou called on Chiang Kai-shek at Lushan, proposing some revision in the rules of the planned National Assembly. On July 18 and 19, Chou went to see Chiang again and this time he suggested that the Communist armed forces in Manchuria, North China, and Korea be mobilized. While it is true that Chou did call on Chiang twice, these reports on the subjects of their confidential discussions remain rather speculative.

CHAPTER 9

1. Report on the CCP's Politburo meeting, March 1937 (Bureau of Investigation). The relative position between Chou En-lai and Ch'en Shao-yü in the CCP can be seen in the official Communist statements during this period. Chou alone signed a statement on a relatively un-important issue, in *The Masses*, No. 20 (1938). On more important issues, Ch'en, Chou, and Ch'in Pang-hsien signed statements in that order, of which one was in the same issue of *The Masses*, and another in *Liberation*, No. 45 (1938). But in 1941, Chou alone signed all the

important statements for the CCP, such as the one in *The Masses* (June 10, 1941).

2. Mao Tse-tung, "The CCP's Position in the National War" (speech at the CCP's Central Committee, Sixth Plenum; Bureau of Investigation).

3. Letter in Bureau of Investigation.

4. *New China Daily News* (Hankow, October 7, 8, and 9, 1938).

5. *Chou En-lai and Teng Ying-ch'ao*, p. 75.

6. *Ibid.*, p. 83.

7. Informant No. 23.

8. Liu Ning, "A Comprehensive Report on the Current Situation of the CCP" (handwritten manuscript, Bureau of Investigation).

9. "Report on the Investigation into the Visit to Chekiang by Chou En-lai, Member of the CCP's Central Committee" (Bureau of Investigation).

10. Director, Liang Tun-hou; dean of political studies, Po I-po, now vice-premier in Peking.

11. Informant No. 31, who was in the audience.

12. Besides Po I-po, there was the Red leader Niu P'ei-tsung.

13. Informant No. 31, then on the staff of Yen Hsi-shan's head-quarters.

14. In the Bureau of Investigation there is an original document identified as a propaganda broadside issued by the political department of the New Fourth Army stationed to the north of the river dated January 29, 1941. Under the title, "The True Story of the New Fourth Army Incident," the document includes fourteen points, all anti-CCP actions the KMT was allegedly planning to take. The sixth point is: "Find pretexts to declare that the Eighth Route Army refused to take orders, consequently it must be disbanded and its leader Chu Teh and P'eng Te-huai arrested without delay." The seventh point is: "Abolish the offices of the Eighth Route Army now functioning in the cities of Chungking, Sian, and Kweilin, arrest Chou En-lai, Yeh Chien-ying, Tung Pi-wu and Teng Ying-ch'ao." Point eight charges the Nationalist government with preparing to close all the *New China Daily News* offices in the Nationalist areas. Point nine states that the Nationalist Army was ready to move on Yenan to take over the Shensi-Kansu-Ninghsia Border Zone. The twelfth point accuses the Nationalist government of treason and collaboration with the enemy, saying that the Japanese armies would retreat from Central and South China to give the Nationalist government a chance to declare victory and at the same time a new policy stressing the necessity to obtain an honorable peace. Point fifteen of the document describes

a secret treaty between the Nationalist government and Japan. The document was one of the propaganda measures taken by the Communist Army to prepare the people to react to the Nationalist action against the New Fourth Army.

These charges have been made a permanent part of the CCP's official archive. Mao Tse-tung, *The Selected Works of Mao Tse-tung*, Vol. 2 (Peking, February 1962), pp. 770–71, reproduces a statement Mao gave to the press on January 22, 1941, in behalf of the CCP Central Revolutionary Military Committee. It reiterates most of the charges listed in the foregoing paragraph, and adds such details as: (The KMT) appointed Generals T'ang En-po, Li P'in-hsien, and others to take charge of the anti-Communist campaign in Central China, and the specific strategic direction to follow toward a complete annihilation of the Red troops.

About the Hsiang-Mao difficulty involved in the New Fourth Army case, see T'an Hsi-lin (a division commander in the New Fourth Army), "Spring Awakens over the Lower Yangtze River," *The People's Daily* (Peking, August 22, 1961). The exact date of the formation of the New Fourth Army is given in Kao Yin-tsu, *Chronology of the Republic of China*, p. 493. According to Informant No. 37, who was KMT chief of the political department, the Third War Zone, Chou En-lai went to Anhwei to smooth over the differences between Yeh T'ing, who had been away from the CCP for many years because of his stay in Germany, and Hsiang Ying. Yeh was actually a compromise candidate for the post of the New Fourth Army's commander because his relationship with the CCP had been alienated and consequently the KMT felt that it could work with him.

Yoshioka Bunroku, *Personalities of Modern China*, pp. 161–63, explains a personal grudge between Yeh T'ing and Chou En-lai. It is said that in 1927 Yeh was a regimental commander on the instructional staff of the Wuhan Military and Political Academy. He secretly ran away to Shanghai with a woman, where he led a decadent life for a period. Because of this Chou wanted to dismiss him from the CCP, and was persuaded to keep him for six months on probation on account of his brilliant combat record. This story is suspect in that Yeh did not disappear from his post at the Military Political Academy in 1927, where Tien-min Lee was a cadet.

15. *New China Daily News* (Chungking, January 18, 1941).

16. The document is in the Ch'en Ch'eng collection.

17. Told by a college student who was in the audience.

18. *The Liberation Daily* (Yenan, August 6, 1943). Ch'in Pang-hsien's "surrender" statement is in the same daily, July 12, 1943.

19. Chou En-lai, *On the Present Situation of the War of Resistance*, p. 10. Chou's editorials in *New China Daily News* (October 7, 8, and 9, 1938).

20. Liang Han-ch'ao. *New China Daily News* (Yenan, August 13, 1944).

21. *New China Daily News* (Yenan, October 10, 1944).

22. Informant No. 36, who was a member of the People's Political Council. Chou's opponent that day was K'ung Keng.

23. Informant No. 35, who participated in the talks.

24. The women's organizations in Chungking responded with a joint statement on February 13, 1945. The cultural circles of Chungking did the same on February 22, reprinted in *The Liberation Daily* (Yenan, April 6, 1945). Similar actions were taken by the cultural circles in Kunming on May 11, and in Chengtu on May 12, 1945. A subsequent examination of the signers of these statements reveals that most of them were leftists.

25. *The Masses*, Vol. 3, No. 3 (Yenan, 1948). New China News Agency dispatch (Northern Shensi, March 6, 1948).

26. *The People's Daily* (January 11, 1952).

CHAPTER 10

1. *The Liberation Daily* in Yenan published a stream of reports on these preparations until the eve of the Japanese surrender. At the same time the paper also released one after another charges condemning Chiang Kai-shek, for example, see March 3, 1945.

2. *The Selected Works of Mao Tse-tung* (Peking, 1960), Vol. 4, pp. 1141–46, carries the two telegrams (August 13 and 16, 1945) with a footnote identifying them as having been drafted by Mao Tse-tung but signed by the commander-in-chief of the 18th Army Corps, Chu Teh. These were addressed to Chiang Kai-shek as chairman of the Military Affairs Commission of the National Government. In addressing the Red forces, Chu Teh used the different title as cited in text.

3. Informant No. 35.

4. Mao Tse-tung urged his men to be prepared on August 26—just two days before he went to talk to Chiang Kai-shek—so that he could negotiate in strength. Immediately upon his return to Yenan, he addressed his men on October 17, 1945, indicating that he did not expect much to result from the talks. *Selected Works of Mao Tse-tung*, Vol. 4, p. 1158.

5. Informant No. 35, who was at the Political Consultative Conference meeting.

6. Accompanied by Lu Ting-yi, CCP's propaganda chief until the Red Guard upheaval of 1966.

7. *The Ta-kung-pao* (Chungking, January 30, 1946).

8. *The Liberation Daily* (Yenan, March 28, 1946).

9. Wang Ssu-ch'eng, *Mao Tse-tung and the Red Disaster*, p. 355.

10. *The Liberation Daily* (Yenan, March 29, 1946).

11. Ch'en Cheng-hsiang, "The Struggle to Prevent the Enemy (KMT) from Seizing the Strategic Points before the Cease-fire of 1946 Took Effect," *The People's Daily* (December 20, 1960).

12. "The Situation and Our Mission in the Northeast," by the Northeast Bureau of the CCP, quoted in the *Compendium of Chinese Communist Rebellious Mobilization Documents*, p. 23. "Persist in following the guideline on creating bases of operation as it was laid down by the Central Committee. Establish such bases so that we can fall back on Russia, Korea, Outer-Mongolia, and Chahar."

13. Chiang Kai-shek, *Russia in China*, pp. 168 ff.

14. Liu Han-tung, who was released the next day.

15. *The Liberation Daily* (Yenan, April 6, 1945).

16. Informant No. 35.

17. Dallin, David J., *Russia and the Far East*, p. 345.

18. *The Masses* (August 31, 1946). *The Liberation Daily* (Yenan, June 7, 21, 22, July 7, 1946). About Chiang's trip to Mukden, see *United States Relations with China*, pp. 155 ff.

19. Chou En-lai and others, *On Nationalizing the Armed Forces*, p. 6.

20. There is evidence that the Reds were more serious in plotting for military conquest than working through the Political Consultative Conference for a peaceful settlement. In the *Selected Works of Mao Tse-tung*, Vol. 4, the period from January to July 20, 1946, shows only one article, "Several Estimates of the International Situation at Present," released in April. It is incredible that Mao for six months did not give any direction to his men on such serious matters as the reorganization of all Chinese troops and the progress of the Political Consultative Conference. The only possible conclusion would be that whatever he said was not for the record. After July 20, 1946, the documents in Mao's work relate only to military preparations and action, with no mention of the truce negotiations. On the other hand, during the same six months the CCP issued many policy directives, one of which deals with the land problem (May 4, 1946), instructing an intensified course of Sovietization. On the other hand, the archives of the negotiation contain many accounts of the unreasonable attitude of the KMT leaders observed by the "third party" and non-partisans

involved in the Political Consultative Conference. For example, Liang Sou-ming, one of the Democratic League leaders, summarized the negotiations immediately after their termination with a scathing indictment which charged the KMT with the responsibility of forcing the Reds to resort to arms out of desperation. See his article, "Who Is Responsible for the Civil War in the Past?" in *The Chinese World* (San Francisco, February 4–9, 1949).

21. Kai-yu Hsu, *Wen I-to*, p. 152.

22. *U. S. Relations with China*, p. 652.

23. *Ibid.*, p. 653.

24. *Ibid.*, p. 655.

25. *Ibid.*, pp. 662–63.

26. *Ibid.*, p. 663.

27. Informant No. 35.

28. *Important Documents on the KMT-CCP Talks During the Past Six Months*, pp. 25–26.

29. *Ibid.*, p. 27.

30. Informant Nos. 42, 43. *U. S. Relations with China*, pp. 186–87.

31. The Young China Party man was Ch'en Ch'i-t'ien.

32. Interview with Wang Yün-wu, independent intellectual leader, in Taipei, January 1966.

33. Interview with Ma Shun-yi, Taipei, summer 1964.

34. Yen Ch'ang-lin, "The Great Turning Point," *Reminiscence of the Liberation War*, pp. 117–18.

35. *Ibid.*, pp. 92–93.

36. *Selected Works of Mao Tse-tung*, Vol. 4, p. 1301.

CHAPTER 11

1. Since 1949, the only other statesmen from Peking who appeared in foreign capitals with any significant missions were Mao Tse-tung, Chu Teh, and Liu Shao-ch'i who visited Moscow at different times. Liu Shao-ch'i alone once also toured Burma, Cambodia, and Indonesia in 1963. All the other important trips were made by Chou En-lai.

2. The dates of Chou's visits to Moscow: January 1950, to sign treaties of friendship and mutual aid regarding railroad rights in Manchuria, Dairen and Port Arthur; August 1952, further treaties of Russian aid to build Chinese railroads; March 1953, to extend the Russian aid items to a total of 141; April 1954, on the Vietnam war; February 1959, on Russian aid to build seventy-eight industrial and power plants; October 1961, to quarrel with Khrushchev; November 1964, on the plan to hold an international congress of Communist delegates.

263

3. Nine editorials, beginning with "The Origin and Development of the Split between the Soviet Russian Leadership and Us," published in *The People's Daily*, starting on September 6, 1963.

4. *Look* (January 31, 1961), pp. 85–104. Edgar Snow, *The Other Side of the River*, pp. 97–101, 758–64.

5. Interview with Iwamoto Kiyoshi of the Japanese Kyodo News Agency, May 16, 1964.

6. *The People's Daily* (November 21, 1964).

7. *Important Documents of the Third People's Congress*, pp. 30–38.

8. Russia recognized Red China on October 2, 1949. This was followed by Bulgaria, Romania, Hungary, North Korea, Czechoslovakia, Poland, Outer Mongolia, East Germany, Albania, Northern Vietnam, Yugoslavia, Burma, India, Pakistan, Britain, Norway, Ceylon, Denmark, Israel, Afghanistan, Finland, Sweden, Switzerland, Holland, and Indonesia—in this chronological order. Then after a long wait came the recognition by Nepal and Yemen in 1955 and 1956, and by France in January 1964.

9. Raja Hutheesing, *The Great Peace*, pp. 50–54.

10. My visit to India including Kashmir, December–January 1966.

11. *Important Documents of the Third People's Congress*, p. 36.

12. Mao accepted, but did not go through, the invitation from the Polish Premier Cyrankiewicz who toured Mainland China in 1956. After September 1959, Liu Shao-ch'i also received invitations from seven eastern European nations without actually using any. *The People's Daily* (November 8, December 22, 1959, January 21, February 7, 17, March 26, and April 10, 1960).

13. On October 1, 1959, the Syrian Communist Party chief exiled in Peking quarreled with the chargé d'affaires of the United Arab Republic at a reception given by Chou.

14. On June 10, 1954, Chou visited Swiss President Rodolphe Rubattel, and French Premier Mendes-France two weeks later, while in Berne. *Chinese People's Republic Foreign Relations Documents*, Vol. III, p. 390.

15. Tachibana Yoshimori, *Invited to Visit Mainland China*, pp. 23–24.

16. Takagi Takeo, *The New World of Our Neighboring Country*, p. 52.

17. Doi Akio, *Facing Mao Tse-tung*, p. 125.

18. Hutheesing, *The Great Peace*, p. 41.

19. *The Sunday Times* (London, June 12, 1960), Magazine Section, p. 21.

20. Chou Ching-wen, *The Ten Stormy Years*, p. 518.

21. *Ibid.*, pp. 492, 509.

22. *The Selected Works of Mao Tse-tung*, Vol. 4, p. 1350. Chou Ching-wen, *The Ten Stormy Years*, p. 57. In December 1948, Mao and Chou wired a number of political leaders in Hong Kong, urging them to return to North China. These included Chairman of the Kuomintang Revolutionary Committee Li Chi-chen, Vice-Chairman of the Democratic League, Chairman of the Democratic Farmer-Worker Party Chang Po-chün, Chairman of the Association for the Promotion of Democracy, Chairman of the Chih-kung Party, and the unaffiliated Kuo Mo-jo, Shen Yen-ping (Mao Tun), and Chou Ching-wen.

23. On April 17, 1959, Vice-Chairman Li Wei-han reported to the Third Political Consultative Conference in Peking, on the expansion of the local committees. Between the Second and the Third Conference, 908 local committees had been set up, including 28 at the provincial level, 147 at the municipal level, 33 at the district level, 643 at the county level, and 67 at the subdistrict level.

24. The "removals" and "amnesties" occurred in September, November 1959, December 1961, and February–March 1963.

CHAPTER 12

1. *Imperialism and China*, pp. 187–88.

2. Chou En-lai, *Report on Government Work* (1959), p. 42. Chou En-lai, *The Current International Situation and Our Foreign Policy* (1958), p. 4.

3. *Important Documents of the Third People's Congress*, p. 38.

4. Ch'en Tu-hsiu, Chou En-lai, and others, *For What Are We Struggling Now*, p. 14.

5. Chou En-Lai, *The Shao-shan Report*, p. 9-A.

6. *The Common Program*, p. 1.

7. *The Organization Problem of the CCP at Present*, pp. 4–5. *The Shao-shan Report*, p. 8-A.

8. *The Shao-shan Report*, p. 9-A.

9. Chou En-lai, *The Ten Great Years*, p. 20.

10. *Important Documents of the Third People's Congress*, pp. 20–21.

11. *Ibid.*, p. 24.

12. *Ibid.*, p. 23.

13. *The Shao-shan Report*, p. 9-B.

14. *The Common Program*, pp. 11–12.

15. *Important Documents of the Third People's Congress*, pp. 5–6.

16. *The Shao-shan Report*, pp. 4-B and 5-B.

17. Chou En-lai, *The Ten Great Years*, pp. 20–21.

18. *Ibid.*, p. 21.

19. *Ibid.*, p. 22.

20. Chou En-lai, *Report on Government Work* (1959), p. 13.

21. *Important Documents of the Third People's Congress*, p. 23.

22. Chou En-lai, *The Organization Problem of the CCP at Present*, pp. 19–20.

23. *Important Documents of the Third People's Congress*, p. 29.

24. Liu Shao-ch'i and others, *Comrades Liu, Chou, and Chu, in the Midst of the Masses*, p. 23.

25. *Ibid.*, pp. 20–22.

26. On January 3 and 30, 1967, he pacified riots in the Peking area.

27. *The People's Daily* (January 22, 1967).

28. Mao said it to Montgomery. *The Sunday Times* (London, June 12, 1960), Magazine Section, p. 21.

29. Robert S. Allen, "Inside Washington," New York *Post* (December 31, 1958), Magazine Section, p. 1.

30. Informant No. 2.

31. Informant No. 4.

32. Informant No. 35.

33. Informant No. 42.

34. Informant No. 36.

35. Informant No. 5.

36. Interview in Taipei, summer of 1964.

37. Interview in Tokyo, August 22, 1964.

38. Liu Shao-ch'i and others, *Comrades Liu, Chou, and Chu in the Midst of the Masses*, passim. Lu Mu-lan, "We Happen to Meet Premier Chou En-lai by Chance," *China Youth*, No. 19 (October 1, 1958).

APPENDIX A

ORAL SOURCES

1. A teacher at the Nankai Middle School in the late 1910s. Jailed with Chou En-lai during the May 4 Movement, 1919.
2. Chou En-lai's classmate at Nankai. Shared a desk with Chou for four years and lived in the same house later in Kyoto, Japan, 1918.
3. Chou's schoolmate at Nankai. Worked with Chou in the May 4 student activities. Studied in France at the same time as Chou in the early 1920s.
4. Chou's schoolmate at Nankai. Studied in America later.
5. Co-organizer with Chou of the Chinese Communist Youth Corps in France, 1922. Leader of Chinese students in the Sun Yat-sen University, Moscow, mid-1920s. Active in the CCP in the late 1920s in Hunan Province.
6. Went to France on the same boat with Chou. Familiar with Chou's activities in France.
7. Jailed at Lyon, France, with Chou.
8. Studied in France in late 1910s-early 1920s. Familiar with most Chinese students in France in that period. Acquainted with Chou. Later a leader of "the third party." Observed Chou during the CCP-KMT negotiations during and after World War II.
9. Formerly CCP Central Committee member. Active during the Li Li-san period in the CCP. Participated in the intraparty power struggle.
10. Studied in Germany and Moscow. Worked as interpreter at the Sun Yat-sen University, Moscow, 1925–26.
11. Studied in France in the early 1920s. Active in the KMT branch in Paris during that period. Had frequent contact with Chou there.
12. Studied in France, 1920s. KMT member. Observed Chou's activities in Europe.

13. Member of the first class, Whampoa Academy. Key member in the Sun Yat-sen Society fighting against CCP influence in the KMT, 1924–27.

14. Member of the first class, Whampoa Academy, 1924–25. Acquainted with Chou in Canton.

15. Member of the fifth class, Whampoa. Knew Chou's work at that academy.

16. Member of the first class, Whampoa. Knew Chou there.

17. Member of the first class, Whampoa. Key member of the anti-Communist Sun Yat-sen Society.

18. Member of the first class, Whampoa. Later attended the Sun Yat-sen University, Moscow. Familiar with early Chinese Communist movement.

19. Member of the first class, Whampoa. Key member of the Sun Yat-sen Society. Specialized in the early history of the Republic of China.

20. Member of the fourth class, Whampoa. Acquainted with Chou's work in South China in the 1920s.

21. Studied in Japan and Germany. Active student leader. Member of the fourth class, Whampoa.

22. High official in the Navy Department during the Chung-shan Gunboat Incident, 1926.

23. Classmate of Teng Ying-ch'ao, Chou's wife. Shared room with her and was her sworn sister, late 1910s in Tientsin. Had contact with Teng in the late 1930s.

24. Active in women's groups in Canton, 1925. Acquainted with Chou and his wife.

25. KMT member, active in Canton, 1925. Acquainted with Teng Ying-ch'ao.

26. KMT branch chief in Shansi Province, 1930s. Acquainted with Chou.

27. Member of the Central Committee, KMT. Assigned by the Bureau of Investigation to take charge of the Ku Shun-chang case, 1930s.

28. Key member of the Bureau of Investigation. Assigned to work on the Ku Shun-chang case, 1930s.

29. Inspector, Hankow Bandit-Suppression Headquarters, 1930s. Arrested Ku Shun-chang.

30. On the staff of the Bandit-Suppression Headquarters, Sian, late 1930s.

31. KMT key member in the Shansi Provincial branch. Acquainted with Chou's dealings with warlord Yen Hsi-shan.

32. KMT general. In charge of Sian headquarters during the negotiation following the Sian Incident, 1936–37.
33. Veteran intelligence staff member in charge of investigating Communist activities.
34. Hunan Province KMT branch key member. Dealt with Communists in that area in the late 1930s.
35. KMT representative. Top negotiator facing Chou En-lai during and after World War II.
36. Studied in Japan in the early 1920s. Leading political theorist. Personally acquainted with Chou.
37. Studied in Germany in 1920s. Acquainted with Chou during the war.
38. Chou's close relative. A woman.
39. Political adviser to the Young Marshal. Key person in the Sian Incident, 1936.
40. Young Marshal's political adviser. Familiar with the CCP's activities in Manchuria in the 1930s and 1940s.
41. Senior scholar, civic leader. Participated in the CCP-KMT negotiations after World War II.
42. Studied in France in early 1920s. Opposed Chou's activities there. Frequent contact with Chou during the post-war negotiations.
43. Senior scholar, philosopher. Third party leader. Acquainted with Chou during the post-war negotiations.
44. Studied at the Sun Yat-sen University, Moscow. Active in the Whampoa Academy, Canton, in the 1920s.
45. Actively involved in KMT politics during the Northern Expedition, 1927, and the Hankow government.
46. A merchant accosted by the Communists during the Long March, who traveled with them for days.

PUBLISHED AND UNPUBLISHED WORKS USED

THE PUBLISHED AND UNPUBLISHED SOURCES used in the preparation of this book fall into five groups. Technical difficulty has prevented the inclusion of the original titles in Chinese or Japanese as had been planned at first.

(1) The documents, mostly unpublished, collected in the Resource Room, Bureau of Investigation, Department of Judiciary Administration, Executive Yüan, Government of the Republic of China in Taipei.

(2) Papers and reports collected by the late Vice-President of the Republic of China, General Ch'en Ch'eng, mainly during his command of the Nationalist campaigns against the Kiangsi Soviet in the 1930s.

(3) Information and source material collected by the Sixth Section of the Central Reform Committee, Kuomintang, which is in charge of political investigation.

(4) Documents and microfilms on Chinese communism in the Far Eastern collection of the Hoover Institution at Stanford.

(5) Other public and private collections of books, papers, and manuscripts in Hong Kong, Taipei, Tokyo, and the United States.

The Anti-Japanese National United Front Guide (Yenan, 1939).

Asahi News, East Asian Department, *The Chinese Communist Party* (Tokyo, October 1946).

Bolshevik, Vol. 4, No. 3 (May 10, 1931), No. 6 (November 10, 1931).

Brandt, Schwartz, and Fairbank, A *Documentary History of Chinese Communism* (London, George Allen and Unwin, 1952).

Chang Fa-k'uei, "Reminiscence of the CCP Canton Commune 30 Years Ago," *The United Review* (Hong Kong, December 26, 1958, through January 2, 1959).

Chang Han-ch'ing, *Personalities in This Great Era* (Shanghai, April 1938).

Chang Hao, "The CCP's Line of Strategy" (Lecture notes, War College, Yenan, 1938, Bureau of Investigation).

Chang Hsüeh-liang (Young Marshal), "Chang Hsüeh-liang and the CCP," *Prospect*, No. 69 (Hong Kong, September 1964. Original title: "A Confession About the Sian Incident" in the Taipei Magazine, *Hope*).

Chang Shu-shen, "Ch'en Tu-hsiu and the CCP," *Defense Against Communism* (December 1, 1936) (Hoover microfilm).

Chang Tzu-sheng, "The Resumption of Sino-Russian Diplomatic Relations," *The Eastern Magazine*, Vol. 21, No. 13 (July 7, 1924).

Chao Chün-hui, *Ten Years in the Red Army* (1938).

Chao Wen-hua, *The 25000-li Long March* (Shanghai, December 1937).

Chao Yü, *Armed Revolt* (June 1, 1929) (Camouflaged with a cover, "A Treatise on Art").

Ch'en Cheng-hsiang, "The Struggle to Prevent the Enemy (KMT) from Seizing the Strategic Points before the Cease-fire of 1946 Took Effect," *The People's Daily* (Peking, December 20, 1960).

Ch'en Shao-yü, Chou En-lai, and Ch'in Po-ku (Ch'in Pang-hsien), "Our Views on the Defense of Hankow and the Third Stage of the War of Resistance," *Liberation*, No. 45 (1938).

Ch'en Shao-yü, Chou En-lai, and Ch'in Po-ku (Ch'in Pang-hsien), "Reply to Mr. Tzu-chien," *The Masses*, No. 20 (1938).

Ch'en Tu-hsiu, *To All the CCP Comrades* (Hoover 4292.29/7942.28).

Ch'en Tu-hsiu, "On the National Government's Northern Expedition," *The Guide*, No. 161 (July 7, 1926).

Ch'en Tu-hsiu, Chou En-lai, and others, *For What Are We Struggling Now* (Canton, December 1926).

Ch'eng Ch'ing, "A Record of Friendship and Hatred Between Chiang Kai-shek and Mao Tse-tung," *The Spring and Autumn Annals*, No. 102 (Hong Kong, October 1, 1961).

Chia Chih-fang (trans.), *The Development of the People's Democracy* by Nishizawa Tomio (Shanghai, 1950).

Chiang Ch'in-feng, "Around Chairman Mao," *The Unfurling Red Flag* (Peking, 1957), pp. 332–61.

Chiang Kai-shek, *Russia in China* (Taipei, 1956).

Ch'iao Fu, "Lin Piao the Man," *Freedom Front*, No. 483 (Hong Kong, 1959).

Chih Chung, "A Study on the Canton Incident," *The Guide Weekly*, No. 148 (April 3, 1926), pp. 1379–81.

Ch'in Pang-hsien, "We Fight to Defend the Chinese Communist Party Under the Banner of Mao Tse-tung," *The Liberation Daily* (Yenan, July 12, 1933).

China Yearbook (1948).

China's Youth (Shanghai, 1923–27?) (CCP organ).

The Chinese Communist Party (Japan, International Investigation Bureau, 1956).

"The Chinese Communist Party during 1931–1933" (Bureau of Investigation).

The Chinese Communist Party in Perspective (Taipei, June 1962).

CCP, *Central Military Communique* (December 1929, and other issues, Hoover microfilm 4292.9/5640).

CCP, "The History and the Present Situation of the Chu-Mao Red Army," *Central Military Communique*, No. 1 (January 15, 1930, Hoover 4292.9/5640).

CCP, Central Committee, "A Brief History of the CCP" (Mimeographed, Bureau of Investigation).

CCP, Central Committee, *Background Information on Intraparty Matters* (mimeographed documents released by the CCP's Central Committee during the Fourth Plenum, Bureau of Investigation).

CCP, Central Committee, *Central Communique* (Bureau of Investigation).

CCP, Central Committee, "Directives from the Central Committee (Shanghai), and the Decisions by the Central Bureau (in Kiangsi), Relating to the Task of Expediting Victory in Kiangsi and Its Adjacent Provinces" (Mimeographed pamphlet, reproduced by the Third Red Army Corps, Ch'en Ch'eng collection).

CCP, Central Committee, "Resolution on the Reactionary Suppression Work in the Soviet Area," *The Struggle*, No. 47 (Juichin, Kiangsi, February 16, 1934).

CCP, Central Executive Committee, "To the Entire Membership of the CCP," dated April 15, 1937, in T'an Ts'en (ed.), *Documents on the KMT-CCP Cooperation against Japan* (Hankow, January 1938), pp. 95–101.

CCP, Central Revolutionary Military Affairs Committee, "Communique," *Red China* (May 18, 1934).

CCP, Central South China Committee, "An Outline of Discussion on Party Work in Villages" (June 10, 1937, mimeographed, Bureau of Investigation).

CCP, Northeast China Bureau, "The Situation and Our Mission in the Northeast," *Compendium of Chinese Communist Rebellious Mobilization Documents* (Chungking?, September 1946), p. 23.

CCP, Politburo, "Resolution on the Conduct of the CCP Delegation in Moscow in 1929–1930," *Building the Party*, No. 4 (March 8, 1931).

CCP, Wan-t'ai Committee, "The First Expanded Meeting of the Central Bureau in the Soviet Zone" (Mimeographed pamphlet, 1931, Ch'en Ch'eng Collection).

Chinese Communist Youth Corps, "Refuting the KMT Report on Hsiang Chung-fa's Defection" (July 4, 1931, Bureau of Investigation).

Chinese Communist Youth Vanguard, "Expand the Communist Youth Vanguard by 1,500,000 persons in all the Soviet Areas in the country," *Red China* (March 1, 1934).

Chinese People's Republic Foreign Relations Documents, Vol. 1: 1949–50 (Peking).

China Youth, Nos. 13–14 (Peking, 1961, not to be confused with *China's Youth*, CCP organ in the 1920s, Shanghai), and other issues of the same journal.

The Common Program and Other Documents of the First Plenary Session of the Chinese People's Political Consultative Conference (Peking, 1950).

Chou Ching-wen, *The Ten Stormy Years* (Hong Kong, January 1959).

Chou En-lai, *The Current International Situation and Our Foreign Policy* (Peking, 1959).

Chou En-lai, "For Land, for Freedom, and for the Political Regime of the Soviet, We Shall Fight to the End," *The Red Star Daily* (April 29, 1934).

Chou En-lai, "Imperialism and the Treaty of 1900," in *Imperialism and China*, edited by Kao Erh-sung (Shanghai, 1924?, Hoover 2489/0214).

Chou En-lai, "Learning Tactical Principles through Actual Combat," *The Red Battlefield Journal*.

Chou En-lai, "Letter to the Editor of the *Ta-kung-pao*," *The Masses* (June 10, 1941).

Chou En-lai, "The New Situation and the New Victory," *The Red Star Daily* (August 20, 1934).

Chou En-lai, "On the So-called 'The CCP's Line of Strategy,'" *The Masses*, No. 20 (1938).

Chou En-lai, *On the Present Situation of the War of Resistance* (Hankow, 1938).

Chou En-lai, "On the Wavering Opportunism Exemplified by Hsiao Ching-kuang," *The Red Star Daily* (January 14, 1934).

Chou En-lai, "Oppose the Lo Ming Line in the Red Army represented by Hsiao Ching-kuang," *The Struggle*, No. 38 (1933).

Chou En-lai, *The Organization Problem of the CCP at Present* (Camouflaged under cover, "Teachings on Prayer," Hoover 4292.1/7264).

Chou En-lai, *Report on Government Work* (Peking, 1959).

Chou En-lai, *The Shao-shan Report* (Mimeographed CCP document
distributed at the Fourth Plenum, Hoover 4292.23/7264).

Chou En-lai, *The Second Stage of the War of Resistance and the
Future* (1938).

Chou En-lai, "The Six Strategic Lines which will Cause the Enemy to
Disintegrate," *The Red Star Daily* (July 20, 1934).

Chou En-lai, "Support the Victory of All the Red Armies in the Country, and Resolutely Carry out the Policy of Positive Attack," *Honest
Talk*, No. 5 (Juichin, 1932).

Chou En-lai, *The Ten Great Years* (Peking, 1959).

Chou En-lai, "To Commemorate the August First (Nanchang Upris-
ing), We Must Wipe out the Enemy at the Threshold of the Soviet
Zone, and Disintegrate the Enemy in Their Own Rear Areas," *The
Red Star Daily* (May 5, 1965).

Chou En-lai, "The Worker-Peasant Red Army and the Masses of the
Entire Soviet Zone Rise to Fight in Defense of Kuang-ch'ang,"
The Red Star Daily (April 22, 1934).

Chou En-lai, and others, *Concerning National Unification and Con-
stitutional Rule* (May 1944).

Chou En-lai, and others, *On Nationalizing the Armed Forces* (no place,
no date, Hoover 4890.22/0634).

Chou En-lai and Teng Ying-ch'ao (Hankow, 1938).

Chou En-lai Grows Old as a Negotiator (July 1946).

Chou Fo-hai, "Flight from the Red Capital Wuhan," *A Compendium
of Historical Documents of the Communist Betrayal of the Nation*
(Taipei, 1964), Series I, Vol. 1.

Chou Fu-chen, "The Golden Era of the Kwangtung District Committee," *Contemporary Historical Data*, Vol. 2, pp. 312–15.

Ch'ü Ch'iu-pai, *The Chinese Revolution and the CP* (June 1, 1928,
Hoover 4292.22/6122).

Ch'ü Ch'iu-pai, "Ch'iu-pai's Explanation," *Building the Party*, No. 3
(February 15, 1931).

Ch'ü Ch'iu-pai, *Controversial Problems of the Chinese Revolution*
(April 1928, first edition).

Chu Li-fu, *The 25000-li Long March* (1937).

"Comment on the Open Letter of the Russian Communist Party,"
The People's Daily (Peking, September 6, 1963).

The Communist International (Moscow, December 21, 1936).

Compendium of Documentary Evidence of the Soviet Russian Plot, Vol. 5 (Bureau of Investigation).

Compendium of the Communist Bandit Rebellion Documents, Seven volumes (Nanchang, Generalissimo Chiang Kai-shek's Field Headquarters).

Contemporary Historical Data, Vols. 1–3 (Shanghai, March 1934, Hoover microfilm 2970/3122).

Current Event News (Shanghai, early twentieth century).

Dallin, David J., *Soviet Russia and the Far East* (Yale University, 1948).

Defense Against Communism (Hoover microfilm 4292.32/7471).

Doi, Akio, *Facing Mao Tse-tung* (Tokyo, 1957).

Draft History of the Central Military Academy (Nanking?, 1936).

The Eastern Magazine (Shanghai, 1903–?).

The Eighteen Years of the Chinese Communist Party (mimeographed, July 1, 1937; Bureau of Investigation).

Epstein, Israel, et al, *Mao Tse-tung in Chungking* (Shanghai, November 1945).

The Events of Modern China (Japan, Chugoku Kenkyujo, 1959).

"The Events of Nanchang," *Modern Historical Materials,* Vol. 4, Section 3 (August 1957), pp. 105–43 (Hoover microfilm 2748/3253).

Factual Records on the Elimination of Communism (Hoover 2982/3938).

Fan Ch'ang-chiang, *Journey Beyond the Great Wall* (Shanghai, 1937).

Fang Fang, "Establish a Strong National Defense Force to Guard the Southern Approach to our Homeland," *The Southern Daily* (Canton, August 1, 1951).

Farien, Antonio, "Background to the Purge in China," *World Outlook,* Vol. 4, No. 25 (August 12, 1966), pp. 4–15. (This is an interview with P'eng Shu-chih in Europe.)

Feng Wen-pin, "How to Carry out Party Work in the Villages" (A speech before the second session of the Youth National Salvation Association of Northwest China, dated November 21, 1938; Bureau of Investigation).

Forman, Harrison, *Report from Red China* (New York, Henry Holt, 1945).

The Guide (CCP organ, published irregularly at different places).

Hatano Kanichi, "A Biography of Chou En-lai," *Kaizo* (Japan, July 1937).

Hatano Kanichi, *A List of Hatano Kanichi Microfilm Collection* (Hoover microfilm J315.51/Jr42).

Hatano Kanichi, *A Study of Red China* (Tokyo, 1941).

Hatano Kanichi, *History of the Chinese Communist Party* (Tokyo, 1961).

Higuchi Masanori, *Biographies of Important Chinese in Recent Years* (Tokyo, Asahi News, February 1941).

Himori Torao, *History of the Twenty Years of the CCP* (Japan, January 1942).

Ho Ch'ang-kung, *Reminiscence of the Life of Work-and-Study in France* (Peking, 1958).

"Ho Meng-hsiung's Statements" (CCP document, Hoover 4292.23/2214).

Ho Sheng, "The Three Revolts in Shanghai," *Contemporary Historical Data*, Vol. 3, Section A., pp. 182–86.

Honest Talk (CCP organ, published in the Kiangsi Soviet 1932-35).

Hsia Chih-hsü, "Fragments of Reminiscence," *The Fluttering Red Flag*, Vol. 5 (December 15, 1957).

Hsiao Hsiang, "The Soviet Zone Today," *The Struggle*, No. 69 (Shanghai, April 15, 1934).

Hsiao Lang, *Chinese Communist Personalities* (Shanghai, 1949).

Hsiao San, "Comrade Mao Tse-tung Founds Communism," *China Youth*, No. 62 (1951).

Hsiao San, "The Greatest Sorrow and the Greatest Anger," *In Memory of the Martyrs of April 8* (Chungking, October 1946).

Hsiao Tso-liang, *Power Relations within the Chinese Communist Movement 1930–1934* (University of Washington, 1961).

Hsiao Ying-t'ang, "The Clever Crossing of the Gold Sand River," *The Unfurling Red Flag*, Vol. 3.

Hsin-k'e-lai (U. Sinclair) and others, *Profile of the Cadres of the Eighth Route Army*.

Hsü En-tseng, *My Memoirs* (Manuscript, Bureau of Investigation).

Hsu Kai-yu, *The Intellectual Biography of a Modern Chinese Poet: Wen I-to* (Unpublished doctoral dissertation, Stanford, 1959).

Hu Ch'iao-mu, *The Thirty Years of the Chinese Communist Party* (Peking, 1952).

Hu Hua, *History of the New Democratic Revolution in China* (Shanghai, 1950).

Hua Kang, "The CCP in the 1925–27 Great Revolution," *Bolshevik*, Vol. 4, No. 3 (May 10, 1931).

Huang Feng, *The Journal of the Eighth Route Army on the March* (Hankow, January 1938).

Hutheesing, Raja, *The Great Peace* (Harper, 1953).

I Chai, "Report on the Sino-French Education Commission in Paris and the Hunanese Students in the Work-and-Study Program," *Hunan Historical Data*, No. 4 (1959) (Hoover microfilm 3066/m3475).

Important Documents of the First Session of the Third People's Congress (Peking, 1965).

Important Documents on the KMT-CCP Talks during the Past Six Months (No date, no place, Hoover 2992.7/0724).

Ishikawa Masao, *A History of the Chinese Communist Party* (Tokyo, 1959).

The Izvestia (December 14, 1936).

Japanese Government, *The Present Situation of the Communist Movement in China* (Tokyo, October 1931).

Jung Tsu, "The Rise and Fall of Kao Yü-han," *She-hui News*, Vol. 2, No. 22 (Shanghai, March 6, 1933).

Kan Yu-lan, *Mao Tse-tung and His Group* (Hong Kong, 1954).

Kao Ch'ung-ming, *The Life-line* (Red propaganda pamphlet circulated in North China in 1936).

Kao Yin-tsu, *Chronology of the Republic of China* (Taipei, 1957).

Kawakami Hajimi (ed.), *Social Studies* (Journal published in Japan, 1910s).

Ku Kuan-chiao, *The Chinese Communist Party During the Past Thirty Years* (Hong Kong, August 1958).

Kuei Nien, "Chou En-lai during the Wuhan Days," *She-hui News*, Vol. 1 (Shanghai, November 18, 1932), No. 36.

Kung Ch'u, *The Red Army and I* (Hong Kong, 1955).

KMT, Central Committee, Editorial Committee for the Compilation of a History of the Party, *Documents on the Revolution* (Taipei, June 1955).

Kuo Wen-pin, *The Glorious New Warriors of China* (Shanghai, 1938).

Kuwashima Shukei and others, *Report on the Chinese Communist Movement* (Hoover microfilm J315.51/Jr42).

Leaders of Communist China, OIR Report No. 5126 (Department of State, Office of Libraries and Intelligence Acquisition, August 4, 1950).

Lee Tien-min, *A History of the Communist Betrayal of the Nation* (Taipei, 1956).

Li Ang, *The Red Stage* (Chungking, 1942).

Li Ch'ang-ch'uan, "Random Geographical Notes on the 25000-li Long March," *The Ta-kung Daily* (Peking, March 5, 1953).

Li Chih-kung, *A Brief History of the CCP* (Chungking, March 1942).

Li Chih-lung, "The Cause and Effect of the Forced Resignation of

Wang Ching-wei, Chairman of the National Government" (Hand-written, Hoover Library 2980/6482, Vol. 1).

Li Wei-han, "Lo Man's Explanation," *Building the Party*, No. 3 (February 15, 1931).

Liang Sou-ming, "Who Is Responsible for the Civil War in the Past?" *The Chinese World* (San Francisco, February 4–9, 1949).

Liberation (CCP organ published in Yenan, 1937–41).

The Liberation Daily (Yenan, 1930s–1940s).

Liu Ning, *The Autobiography of a Proletarian* (Chungking, April 1941).

Liu Ning, "A Comprehensive Report on the Current Situation of the CCP" (Handwritten manuscript, Bureau of Investigation, 1938).

Liu Nung-ch'ao, "Odds and Ends About the August First Uprising," *Progress Daily* (Peking, July 27, 1951).

Liu Shao-ch'i, "On Intraparty Struggle" (Bureau of Investigation).

Liu Shao-ch'i and others, *Comrades Liu, Chou, and Chu in the Midst of the Masses* (Peking, 1958).

Liu Tao-sheng, "The Red Army Academy in the Woods," *The Unfurling Red Flag* (Peking, August 1957).

Liu Ya-lou, "Crossing the Great Grassland with only a Handful of Ching-k'o Barley," *The People's Daily* (March 3, 1961).

Lo Fu (Chang Wen-t'ien), *The CCP during the Past Ten Years* (Yenan, January 1938).

Look (New York, January 1961).

Lu Chieh-shou, "Chou En-lai Flees to the Red Zone," *Contemporary Historical Data*, Vol. 3 (Shanghai, 1934).

Lu Mu-lan, "We Happen to Meet Premier Chou En-lai by Chance," *China Youth*, No. 19 (October 1, 1958).

Ma Ch'ao-chün and others, *A History of the Chinese Labor Movement* (Taipei, 1959).

Mao Ssu-ch'eng (ed.), *Chiang Kai-shek Before 1926* (1936) (Hoover, 2269/445.14).

Mao Tse-tung, "Resolution on Certain Historical Problems," *The Selected Works of Mao Tse-tung* (Peking, one-volume edition, 1964), pp. 995–1002.

Mao Tse-tung, *The Selected Works of Mao Tse-tung* (Peking, September 1960).

Mao Tse-tung, "We Struggle to Win Over Hundreds and Thousands of the Masses to Join the United Front Against Japan," *The Selected Works of Mao Tse-tung*, Vol. 1 (Peking, 1960), p. 278, Footnote 5.

Martyr Hsiang Ching-yü (Peking, December 1958).

The Masses (1930s–1947?, published by the CCP in Yenan and in Hong Kong).

Matsuno Tanio, *The Early Years of the Chinese Communist Leader Chou En-lai* (Tokyo, 1961).

Matsuno Tanio, *The True Face of Communist China* (Tokyo, 1960).

Mif, Pavel, *The Fifteen Years of the Chinese Communist Party's Heroic Struggle* (Bureau of Investigation).

Mo Lan, "An Interview with Teng Ying-ch'ao," *Recent Statements by Chou En-lai and Teng Ying-ch'ao* (Canton, 1938).

Montgomery, Viscount, "Monty in China," *The Sunday Times* (London, June 12, 1960), Magazine Section, p. 21.

Nakayasu Yosaku, *Most Recent History of the CCP*, rev. ed. (Tokyo, 1944).

The National Essence Journal (Published in the early years of the twentieth century).

National Salvation (Young China Party organ, France, 1924).

The Nationalist Fortnightly (KMT organ in France, 1920s).

New China Daily News (Published at various places).

North, Robert, *Moscow and Chinese Communists* (Stanford, 1953).

Okubo Hiroshi, *Red China* (Japan, 1938).

Osaka Taishi Economic Alliance, *The Communist Movement in China, Manchuria, and Russia* (Tokyo, September 1934).

Otsuka Reizo, *A History of the Chinese Communist Party* (Japan, July 1930).

"Outline of Report on Smashing the Anti-revolutionary Activities of Chang Kuo-tao" (Handcopied, Hoover 4292.3/1356).

P'eng Shu-chih, "After Reading the February 21 Speech by Chiang Kai-shek," *The Guide*, No. 192 (March 18, 1927).

P'eng Shu-chih, *Basic Problems of the Chinese Revolution* (May 15, 1928).

P'eng Shu-chih, "Statement Before the Enlarged Conference" (Mimeographed, Hoover 4292.29/4233).

"Peng Shu-tse (P'eng Shu-chih) on China," *The Militant* (February 13, 20, 1967).

Po Hsin, "Unofficial History of the Shanghai Labor Movement," *Contemporary Historical Data*, Vol. 1, pp. 299–300.

Red Archives (Hoover microfilm, 2984/2371).

Red China (Juichin, Kiangsi Soviet organ, a daily, Ch'en Ch'eng collection).

Red Documents (Yenan, February 1938).

The Red Flag (Shanghai, 1929–30?, CCP organ, a periodical appearing approximately once every three days).

The Red Light (Chinese Communist journal, early 1920s, France).

The Red Star Daily (Published by the CCP in Kiangsi, early 1930s).

"Remembering the Shanghai Revolts," *The Red Flag*, No. 86 (March 22, 1930).

"Report on the Investigation into the Visit to Chekiang by Chou En-lai, Member of the CCP's Central Committee" (Mimeographed, Bureau of Investigation).

Schwartz, Benjamin, *Chinese Communism and the Rise of Mao* (Harvard University Press, 1958).

Shao Li, "Chou En-lai and Teng Ying-ch'ao," *Contemporary Historical Data*, Vol. 3 (Shanghai, 1934, Hoover microfilm 2970/3122).

Shen Tzu-min, "The August First Uprising in Nanchang," *The Progress Daily* (August 1, 1952).

Shen Yün-lung, *The Origin of the Chinese Communist Party* (Taipei, January 1959).

Shih Chih, *Iron Curtain Personalities* (Hong Kong, April 1955).

Snow, Edgar, *The Other Side of the River* (New York, Random House, 1962).

Snow, Edgar, *Red Star Over China* (New York, Random House, 1938).

Society for the Study of Marxism, Peking University, "Announcing the Organization of a Society for the Study of Marxism," *Modern Historical Materials*, No. 5 (Peking, National Academy of Science, Historical Research Institute, 1955), pp. 161 ff.

"The Story of the Rift in the Chinese Communist Party During the Fourth Plenum of the Central Committee" (Handwritten confession of a defected CCP leader, Bureau of Investigation).

The Struggle (Juichin, Kiangsi, CCP organ, 1930s, Hoover 4292.01/7225).

Su, Chi-ch'ang, *Noted Persons of This Era* (Chungking, May 1947).

Suzue Genichi, *The History of China's Liberation Struggle* (Tokyo, 1953).

Symposium in Honor of the 80th Birthday of the Late President of Nankai University, Chang Po-ling (Taipei, April 5, 1956).

Tachibana Yoshimori, *Invited to Visit Mainland China* (Tokyo, Mainichi, 1956).

Takagi Takeo, *The New World of Our Neighboring Country* (Tokyo, Domei, 1955).

The Ta-kung-pao (Chungking, during WW II).

T'an Hsi-lin, "Spring Awakens over the Lower Yangtze River," *The People's Daily* (Peking, August 22, 1961).

T'ao Hsi-sheng, and others, *A Compendium of Historical Documents of the Communist Betrayal of the Nation* (Taipei, 1964, limited circulation).

Teng Chung-hsia, *History of Chinese Labor Movement* (Yenan, 1943).

T'ieh-chiang, "The Development of the Struggle against the Li Li-san Line," *Building the Party*, No. 3 (February 15, 1931).

T'ien Ch'i-i, "The Possibility for Liu Shao-ch'i to Succeed Mao Decreases," *Tsu-kuo Weekly*, No. 327 (Hong Kong, April 13, 1959).

Time (New York, May 10, 1954).

"The True Story of the New Fourth Army Incident" (Political Department of the New Fourth Army leaflet, January 29, 1941, Bureau of Investigaton).

Ts'ai Ch'ang, "In Memorium of Comrade Wang Jo-fei," *In Memory of the Martyrs of April 8* (Chungking, CCP delegation, October 1946).

Tseng Mu-han (Tseng Ch'i), *The Works of Tseng Mu-han* (Taipei, 1954).

Tso Lin, "Fragments of Reminiscence of the Hsin-an Tour," *Fighting Experience* (Peking, 1959), pp. 84–95.

Tsou Lu, *A Short History of the Chinese Nationalist Party* (Taipei, 1951).

Tsou Ts'ui-fen, "The Central Committee of the KMT during the Kwangtung Period," *Contemporary Historical Data*, Vol. 2, p. 105.

Tsou Ts'ui-fen, "Unofficial History of the Political Department, General Headquarters," *Contemporary Historical Data*, Vol. 2, pp. 135–42.

Union Research Service, *Index to Biographical Service*, No. 3 (Hong Kong, July 1, 1956–December 31, 1957).

United Front Guide, Vol. 6 (Yenan, 1939).

U. S. State Department, *United States Relations with China: with Special Reference to the Period 1944–49* (Department of State Publications 3573, August 1949).

Wales, Nym, *Inside Red China* (New York, Doubleday, 1939).

Wan Ya-kang, *A Short History of the CCP* (Hong Kong, January 1951).

Wang Chien-ming, *History of the Chinese Communist Party*, 3 volumes (Taipei, 1965).

Wang I-p'ing, *The Chinese Communist Party Before the War of Resistance* (Chungking, 1942).

Wang Min-chao, "All Depends on the Party and the Masses," *New China Daily News* (August 7, 1951).

Wang Ssu-ch'eng, *Mao Tse-tung and the Red Disaster* (Taipei, the 6th Section of the Central Committee, KMT, 1959).

Wang Wei-lien, "Ch'en Tu-hsiu and the CCP," *Contemporary Historical Data*, Vol. 1, p. 129.

Wang Wei-lien, "Wang Ching-wei Arrives in Wuhan From Marseilles," *Contemporary Historical Data*, Vol. 1.

Wei Hung-yüan, *The August 1 Uprising* (Hupeh, 1957).

Wen Shu, "Ch'en Kung-po and the CCP," *Contemporary Historical Data*, Vol. 1, p. 65.

Woodhead, H.G.W., *The China Year Book* (Tientsin, 1928).

The World (A general magazine published in Tokyo).

Wu Hao, "Kwangtung Province after Sun Yat-sen's Departure for the North," *The Guide*, No. 98 (January 7, 1925).

Wu Hao, "The Most Recent General Political Situation in Canton," *The Guide*, No. 92 (November 19, 1924).

Wu Yü-chang, "In Memorium of Comrade Po-ch'ü," *The People's Daily* (June 2, 1960).

Wu Yü-chang, "Remembering Martyr Chao Shih-yen," *The People's Daily* (July 19, 1962).

Yang Ch'eng-wu, "Chairman Mao Guides Me to Cross the Grassland," *A Spark Sets the Entire Plain Aflame* (Hong Kong, July 1960).

Yang Chia-lo, *The Main Diplomatic and Military Events between China and Japan* (Changsha, 1941).

Yang Shang-k'un, "The Grand Reunion of Main Red Forces," *Struggle*, No. 108 (August 15, 1936).

Yang Shang-k'un, "Oppose the Rightist-opportunist Policy of Fleeing and Escaping," *Red China* (February 19, 1933).

The Yearbook of New China (Japan, Kyokuto Shobo, 1963).

Yen Ch'ang-lin, "The Great Turning Point," *Reminiscence of the Liberation War* (Peking, 1961).

Yen Wu and others, "A Visit to the Revolutionary Army Museum of the Chinese People," *The People's Daily* (August 1, 1960).

Yoshioka Bunroku, *Personalities of Modern China* (Tokyo, Jishosha, October 1938).

The Youth (CCP organ in France 1922, later changed to *Ch'ih-kuang* or *The Red Light*).

Yu Chi-yü, *The August 1 Uprising in Nanchang* (Shanghai, 1958).

Yü Ming, "The Development of the Cheka System in the Communist Area," *Contemporary Historical Data*, Vol. 3-B.

Yün Nung, "The Beginning of the Chinese Communist Bandit Party," *The Democratic Tide*, Nos. 140 and 141 (Taipei, 1957).

Yün Tai-ying, "Since the May 4 Movement," *China's Youth*, No. 26 (April 12, 1924).

INDEX

Wuhan Military Political Academy,
  250 n. 1
Wu Hao, 35, 107
Wu P'ei-fu, 39
Wu Yü-chang, 155, 245 n. 35,
  248 n. 22

Yang Hsi-min, 240 n. 4
Yang Hu-ch'eng, General, 130, 131,
  134; orders arrest of Chiang Kai-
  shek, 135
Yangtze River delta region, 3
Yang Yin, 252 n. 23
Yang Ying-chih, 246 n. 38
Yang Yi-teh, police chief, 24
Yao-hsien, 136
Yeh Chien-ying, 131, 134, 154
Yeh (Yeh Ch'ing), 36
Yeh T'ing, General, 72, 73, 153
Yellow Gangs, 94

Yellow River, 155
Yenan, 125
Yen Chih-k'ai, 236 n. 5
Yenching University, 180
Yen Fan-sun, 26
Yen Hsi-shan, 150, 151, 156
Yi-ch'ien, 110
Yin K'uan, 35, 44
Young China Party, inaugurated, 41
Young Soldiers Association, 52
Yuan Shih-k'ai, 13; regime, 17
Yü Fei, 251 n. 10
Yü Han-mou, General, 248 n. 20
Yun-liang, 236 n. 1
Yün-men, Chou En-lai's grandfather,
  3
Yün Tai-ying, 242 n. 14, 246 n. 36,
  248 n. 15, n. 22
Yü Shu-te, 246 n. 40
Yü-tu, 110